CHENG & TSUI
"Bringing Asia to the World"™

25 West Street
Boston, MA 02111-1213 USA
p: 617-988-2400
f: 617-426-3669

chengtsui.co

We sincerely apologize for any inconvenience that this may cause.

A NOTE TO THE USERS OF THIS VOLUME:

Go Far with Chinese 3, Simplified Textbook
ISBN 978-1-62291-546-0
Second printing, 2023

We recently became aware of two pages out of order in this printing of *Go Far with Chinese 3*. While there is no content missing from the book, you will find the Unit 2 (page 85) and Unit 3 (page 169) openers immediately following page 140.

We sincerely apologize for any inconvenience that this may cause.

趣学中文

Go Far

WITH CHINESE

Simplified Characters

Textbook 3

CHENG & TSUI

"Bringing Asia to the World"™

趣学中文

Go Far

WITH CHINESE

Simplified Characters

Textbook 3

Senior Curriculum Adviser
Ying Jin 金瓔

Lead Instructional Contributors

Chunmei Guan 关春梅

Cilei Han 韩慈磊

Mairead Harris 何小蔓

Yi-Wen Liu 劉羿彣

Zoey Liu 刘喆医

Diane Neubauer 杜雁子

Erica Pollard 狄瑞和

CHENG & TSUI

"Bringing Asia to the World"™

First Edition 2023

27 26 25 24 23   2 3 4 5 6

ISBN 978-1-62291-546-0

Library of Congress Cataloging in Publication data applied for.

Printed in the United States of America

The *Go Far with Chinese* series encompasses textbooks, workbooks, teacher's resources, audio, video, a digital edition, and more. Visit cheng-tsui.com for more information on the other components of *Go Far with Chinese*.

Publisher
JILL CHENG

Curriculum Development Manager
MEGAN BURNETT

Senior Editor
LEI WANG

Curriculum Development Team
JIE BAI, AARON BALIVET, YINGCHUN GUAN, JINGGE LI, JINGJING LI, EMILY PETIT, MARIAN STACEY, TAMSIN TRUE-ALCALA

Managing Editor
KAESMENE HARRISON BANKS

Production Coordinator
TODD BROWN

Design
MARINA LI, KATE PAPADAKI, CHRISTIAN SABOGAL

Story Illustrator
MARGARET LOR

Photographs
© Cheng & Tsui
© NASA
© Shutterstock

Icons of the Sustainable Development Goals on page 81 used with permission from the United Nations. https://www.un.org/sustainabledevelopment/
The content of this publication has not been approved by the United Nations and does not reflect the views of the United Nations or its officials or Member States.

Additional photo credits are listed on p. 345

Cheng & Tsui Company, Inc.
25 West Street, Boston, MA 02111-1213 USA
P: 617.988.2400 / 800.554.1963
F: 617.426.3669
cheng-tsui.com

Series Contributors

Senior Curriculum Adviser

Ying Jin (金瓔) is a Chinese teacher in the Fremont Union High School District in California. She has more than 20 years of experience in Chinese instruction and is active in the teaching community through STARTALK, CLASS, California Language Teachers' Association, and more. In 2018, ACTFL named her the National Language Teacher of the Year, the first Chinese language teacher to receive this honor. She is passionate about promoting greater understanding of Chinese language and culture.

Lead Instructional Contributors

Chunmei Guan (关春梅) is a Chinese instructor at Logansport Community School Corporation, Logansport, Indiana. She is president of the Indiana Foreign Language Teachers Association, serves on the Advisory Council for Central States Conference on the Teaching of Foreign Languages, and is an active member of ACTFL, CLTA, CLASS, and ASSCE. She has received numerous awards for her teaching and leadership, such as Chinese Teacher of the Year and the Outstanding Contribution Award by the Indiana Chinese Language Teachers Association in 2016 and Indiana Network for Early Language Learning's Professional Development Award in 2019. As a professional educator and community service leader, she is dedicated to promoting foreign languages and cultures and global awareness.

Cilei Han (韩慈磊) is a teacher of Chinese language at Lake Oswego School District in Oregon as well as a Challenge Program instructor at Portland State University. She served as the Chair of the K-12 Committee of the Chinese Language Teachers Association, USA (CLTA-US), and founded the Selection of American K-12 Outstanding Chinese Works. She is the president of her regional CLTA association and was appointed editor-in-chief of the journal K-12 Chinese Language Teaching (K-12 CLT) by CLTA-US and works actively with regional association leaders. She is dedicated to assisting in the development of stronger K-12 Chinese Language programs nationwide.

Mairead Harris (何小蔓) is a lecturer in the Greenberg-Starr Department of Chinese Language and Literature at Middlebury College, as well as the associate director of the Middlebury Chinese School. Before moving into higher education, she taught Chinese, Spanish, and English in K-12 schools for over a decade. She has served as a board member for the Chinese Language Teachers Association (CLTA-US) and the New England Chinese Language Teachers Association (NECLTA). She is dedicated to promoting collaboration and professional learning between educators in K-12 and higher education, as well as global understanding among students.

Yi-Wen Liu (劉羿彣) teaches Mandarin Chinese at Ravenscroft School in Raleigh, North Carolina, and in the summers, she teaches at immersion programs, such as Middlebury Chinese School. She serves as the president of the Chinese Language Teachers Association of North Carolina and the 2nd Vice President of the Foreign Language Association of North Carolina. She often presents at language conferences such as ACTFL, the International Annual Conference of Teaching Chinese as a Second Language, the CLTA annual conference, and the FLANC fall conference. She devotes her time to organizing professional conferences, blogging about her teaching ideas, and developing online learning materials for Chinese language learners.

Zoey Liu (刘喆医) is a Chinese teacher at Monta Vista High School. She received a masters in education at Stanford and, as a lifelong learner, is currently proficient in four languages: Mandarin, English, Spanish, and Japanese. She also teaches at the Stanford World Language Project and the California Language Teacher Association Summer Seminar. With over a decade of teaching experience, Zoey is committed to instilling global competence in her students and promoting their social emotional learning by deepening their knowledge of Chinese language and culture.

Diane Neubauer (杜雁子) is a Mandarin Chinese instructor who has taught elementary, middle, and high school courses as well as elective and adult classes for over 15 years. Her doctoral research at the University of Iowa focused on classroom interaction in beginning Chinese language classes in online and hybrid formats. She served as an officer of ACTFL's Comprehension-based Communicative Language Teaching (CCLT) Special Interest Group from 2018–2022. Her book, *Comprehension-Based Chinese*, provides numerous strategies to help Chinese teachers who are interested in more comprehension-based instruction. Diane also runs an active blog and shares videos for language teachers and Chinese language learners.

Erica Pollard (狄瑞和) is the foreign language department director and an AP®[1] Chinese instructor at Hingham Public Schools in Massachusetts. She has extensive experience in curriculum design and has developed curricula for Chinese language courses from beginner to AP® levels. She also shares her teaching insights and knowledge through her work on the College Board's AP® Chinese Language and Culture Development Committee.

Publisher's Note

Over the last four decades, Cheng & Tsui has grown from a scrappy distribution operation into a leading publisher of Chinese, Japanese, Korean, and Arabic language and culture materials, introducing Asia not only to America, but also to the rest of the world. We want to thank all of you, the many dedicated authors, staff, educators, and learners, who have made this milestone anniversary possible.

While we look back on past achievements — like the 1997 publication of the first edition of the global bestseller *Integrated Chinese*, followed by *Adventures in Japanese* in 1998 — we also look forward to a bright future. Over the years, trusting in our commitment to innovative, effective, and high quality language pedagogy, many educators have asked us for a new beginning Chinese textbook series for secondary school students. On our 40th anniversary, we are excited to answer this call with *Go Far with Chinese!*

You told us that you want a new textbook series that

- is innovative and effective;
- is age-appropriate, thematically-organized, and proficiency-based;
- offers careful vocabulary and grammar control;
- is designed with appropriate pacing and thoughtful articulation;
- provides robust support for teachers and students with authentic materials;
- is informed by the most current research on best practices in second language acquisition;
- is based on real classroom experiences of teachers and students;
- will have both print and online editions for hybrid and remote learning; and
- promises to lead new generations on a lifelong path to Chinese language learning!

In planning for such an ambitious project, we sought the advice and participation of outstanding teachers, researchers, and learners throughout America. Collaborating closely with our many advisers, Cheng & Tsui's highly dedicated and thoughtful curriculum development staff have made your requests a reality in *Go Far with Chinese!*

We know that it is difficult for any single textbook to meet the needs of every different kind of student audience and classroom setting. But as you use this material, we hope you will find that *Go Far with Chinese* provides enough structure and flexibility to make teaching easier and students' learning more fun and effective.

We truly believe that your success is our success, so we ask that you continue to let us know what you need and what you have on your wishlist. Only with your input can we continue to develop materials that will help you achieve your goals. Please contact your Cheng & Tsui account representative or editor@cheng-tsui.com with your suggestions.

All of us at Cheng & Tsui are grateful for your support!

Acknowledgments

Go Far with Chinese was developed thanks to the advice and contributions of countless educators from all across the United States. We would like to express our gratitude and appreciation to all those who contributed, including those listed below.

何仲健
Carol Bi
Boulder Creek High School
Anthem, Arizona

常小林
Xiaolin Chang, M.A.
Consultant to College Board
AP®² Chinese, former Chair of the
Language Department
Lowell High School
San Francisco, California

赵哲莹
Che-Ying Joy Chao
Woodbridge High School
Irvine, California

姜文静
Wenching Chiang
Sunset Ridge Middle School
East Hartford, Connecticut

簡淑玲
Shwuling Jane
Jonas Clarke Middle School
Lexington, Massachusetts

景晓姝
Xiaoshu Jing, M.A.
Marlborough High School
Marlborough, Massachusetts

林玫
Mary Lane, M.A.
Tenafly Public Schools (retired)
Tenafly, New Jersey

李宜
Yi Lee
Henry J. Kaiser High School
Honolulu, Hawaii

李娜
Na Li, M.A.
Chinese Teacher and
World Language Curriculum
Coordinator
Columbus Academy
Gahanna, Ohio

林静容
Janet Lin
St. Mark's School of Texas
Dallas, Texas

刘兵
Bing Liu, M.A.
Hartford Magnet Trinity
College Academy
Hartford, Connecticut

刘伟
Wei Liu, PhD
The Hotchkiss School
Lakeville, Connecticut

卢文雅
Wenya Lu, M.A.
Teacher and Curriculum
Developer
Northside College
Preparatory High School
Chicago, Illinois

陳惠棻
Petra Lynch
Greenhill High School
Addison, Texas

秦莉杰
Lijie Qin, M.A.
Washington County School
District
St. Georges, Utah

芮尚勤
Dr. Reed Riggs
Brigham Young University–
Hawaii

史迪菲
Difei Shi
Tenakill Middle School
Closter, New Jersey

孙毅
Preston Sundin, M.A.
Emma Willard School
Troy, New York

吴萍
Ping Wu, M.Ed.
Columbus School for Girls
Columbus, Ohio

赖华睿
Reid Wyatt, M.A.T.
Brooks School
North Andover, Massachusetts

薛莉
Li Xue, M.A.
Wainwright Intermediate School
Fircrest, Washington

张世红
Shihong Zhang, M.A. & M.Ed.
Glen Ridge High School
Glen Ridge, New Jersey

*All Chinese names are listed in accordance with the way they were provided.

²AP® is a trademark registered by the College Board, which is not affiliated with, and does not endorse, this product.

Contents

Unit 1: Thinking About Our Environment

Chapter 1: Shanghai: A New Environment

Chapter 2: Learning About Environmental Problems

Chapter 3: An Environmental Protection Competition

Unit 2: Working Together

Chapter 4: Confidence Matters

Chapter 5: Coming to an Agreement

Chapter 6: Miko's Life in Taipei

Unit 3: Contemporary Society

Preface

The origins of *Go Far with Chinese* are firmly rooted in the experience of Chinese teachers and students at the secondary school level. The series covers three to four years of beginning Chinese language instruction in a traditional U.S. secondary school setting. Students who complete the three-level series will be ready to study the widely used *Integrated Chinese* series Volumes 3 and 4 either for AP®[3] preparation or at the college level. Upon completing *Go Far with Chinese* students will be able to confidently embark on their own language learning journeys.

Foundational Ideas

The curriculum of *Go Far with Chinese* was developed in accordance with the best practices defined by current research in second language acquisition. In particular, the curriculum is fully aligned to the World-Readiness Standards and Guiding Principles for Language Learning recommended by the American Council on the Teaching of Foreign Languages (ACTFL). Below are some of the foundational ideas that shaped the program.

Proficiency-Based Instruction

Go Far with Chinese places strong emphasis on real-world communication—that is, on what students can actually *do* with the language they have learned. Using a backward design process, the curriculum development team first identified language and cultural content learning goals, and then used those goals to write the illustrated stories at the end of each Chapter. The team also outlined Unit-level Integrated Performance Assessments and worked with expert Chinese language educators from across the United States to plan the task-based learning experiences and instructional materials that would help students reach those goals.

Vocabulary Control

Careful attention was paid to vocabulary control. High-frequency "function" words, such as 想, 喜欢, and 去, are introduced early in Level 1 to give students the ability to have authentic conversations about their likes, wants, and plans. Throughout the series, the program prioritizes vocabulary relevant to students' lives, such as words related to academics, sports, shopping, and online activities.

Grammar in Context

Current research indicates that the most effective method for teaching grammar is to present it in context, focusing on the communicative meaning of a form rather than on explaining the form itself. In the Textbook, students are encouraged to get the gist of the meaning of new language before focusing on the details of form. Complex grammatical structures, such as resultative, potential, and directional complements, are introduced gradually and explained in non-technical language. In this way, even as students progress to more difficult forms, the emphasis remains firmly on language acquisition rather than explicit grammar instruction. In addition, instruction is spiraled, and previously-learned grammar points are reviewed and expanded in Level 3, ensuring mastery of foundational elements of Chinese grammar.

[3]AP® is a trademark registered by the College Board, which is not affiliated with, and does not endorse, this product.

Emphasis on Meaning-Based Tasks & Activities

Go Far with Chinese emphasizes authentic communicative tasks that ask students to express ideas and opinions, rather than formulaic drills or rehearsed exercises. Practice sections in the Textbook move from brief exercises to independent tasks designed to elicit meaning-based communication.

Literacy & Character Learning

While literacy instruction should be an integral part of any beginning Chinese program, there is also a clear need to set realistic goals given the challenges of learning a new writing system. *Go Far with Chinese* is designed to support literacy instruction while giving teachers flexibility with regard to writing assignments. For example, students are expected to learn to read and write only the words in the vocabulary lists, though supplemental vocabulary is provided for specific activities. Pinyin is provided for new words and then phased out over the course of each Section to help students develop strong reading skills. Expanded reading passages in Level 2 provide necessary repetition and build comprehension skills with longer, interconnected ideas.

In Level 3, reading passages continue to grow in length and complexity and include open-ended comprehension questions. These questions assess the development of more advanced reading skills, including identifying the main idea of a passage and inferring meaning. In order to allow for differentiation, teachers may choose to have students answer in English or, for a more advanced class, in Chinese.

To accelerate students' word recognition, *Go Far with Chinese* explicitly teaches recurring components in the "What a Character!" feature. The stroke order for all characters is given in the Character Workbook. Students can answer open-ended questions in the Textbook and Workbook either by typing or hand writing their responses, as teachers direct.

Use of Target Language

To help achieve ACTFL's goal for teachers to conduct 90% of classroom learning in the target language, *Go Far with Chinese* teaches students useful classroom phrases early in the series. Additional comprehensible input strategies provided in the Teacher's Resources also help maximize students' exposure to Chinese during class time.

Personalization

In order to increase student interest and create opportunities for real-world communication, activities and exercises were designed to relate to students' lives and to encourage them to express their own ideas and opinions. Additionally, the Teacher's Resources suggest ways to tap into students' specific interests and adapt classroom content accordingly.

Stories as a Teaching Tool

The final Section of each Chapter combines the new language students have studied in an engaging illustrated story. Age- and level-appropriate plots foster student interest and engagement. In Level 2 and Level 3, these final stories are progressively longer and more complex, which reinforces previously-learned vocabulary and helps students build extensive reading skills.

Authentic Materials

The ACTFL Guiding Principles for Language Learning encourage the use of authentic materials even in the beginning stage of language learning. Tasks based on realia, photos, and videos of China help students build cultural literacy and develop the ability to analyze authentic materials.

References

Adair-Hauck, Bonnie, Eileen W. Glisan, and Francis J. Troyan. *Implementing Integrated Performance Assessment.* Alexandria, VA: American Council on the Teaching of Foreign Languages, 2013.

Clementi, Donna, and Laura Terrill. *The Keys to Planning for Learning, Second Edition.* Alexandria, VA: American Council on the Teaching of Foreign Languages, 2017.

"Guiding Principles for Language Learning." The American Council on the Teaching of Foreign Languages. Accessed August 6, 2019. https://www.actfl.org/guiding-principles

Hadley, Alice Omaggio. *Teaching Language in Context, Third Edition.* Boston: Heinle & Heinle, 2001.

Mart, Cagri. "Teaching Grammar in Context: Why and How?" *Theory and Practice in Language Studies* Vol. 3, No. 1 (2013): 124-129.

Rezende Lucarevschi, Claudio. "The Role of Storytelling on Language Learning: A Literature Review." *Working Papers of the Linguistic Circle of the University of Victoria* Vol. 26, No. 1 (2016): 23-44

VanPatten, Bill. *While We're On the Topic.* Alexandria, VA: American Council on the Teaching of Foreign Languages, 2017.

Wong, Wynn and Bill VanPatten. "The Evidence is IN: Drills are OUT." *Foreign Language Annals* Vol. 36, No. 3 (2003): 403-423.

Waltz, Terry. *TPRS with Chinese Characteristics.* Squid for Brains Educational Publishing, 2015.

Textbook Organization

Each Level in *Go Far with Chinese* includes a Textbook, Workbook, Character Workbook, audio, video, and Teacher's Resources.

Level 3 is divided into four thematic Units consisting of three Chapters each. In every Unit, a broad, thought-provoking Essential Question challenges students to reflect on how they view language, their own culture and other cultures, and the world at large. Unit Projects, in the form of Integrated Performance Assessments (IPAs), test students' ability to understand and use the language they have learned in a real-world scenario.

Each Chapter of *Go Far with Chinese* follows a tiered approach to instruction: students move from processing teacher-provided comprehensible input to brief, semi-guided exercises, and finally to independent tasks. To keep the pace manageable, the target vocabulary and grammar are divided and introduced over the first three Sections of each Chapter. The fourth and final Section, Put the Pieces Together!, combines the Chapter's new vocabulary and grammar into an illustrated story and provides additional projects to round out the Chapter.

Can-Do Goals · 能力目标

Each Chapter begins with Can-Do Goals to set clear expectations for what students will learn to do in the three modes of communication. The Can-Do Goals are restated at the end of each Chapter so students can check their own progress and take ownership of their learning.

Culture Connection · 文化联接

This feature opens a window into contemporary Chinese culture, highlighting cultural products and practices that are a part of the daily lives of people in China. Relatable and interesting content, full-color authentic photographs, topical words and expressions, and reflection questions all help students explore the Unit's Essential Question and build intercultural competence. For a challenge, encourage students to return to the Culture Connection at the end of each chapter to answer the comprehension questions in Chinese.

Language Model · 语言范例 [Target Language Input]

The images on the Language Model pages can be used in conjunction with PowerPoint presentations in the Teacher's Resources to introduce the target structures and vocabulary for the Section through interactive class discussion. This ensures that students' exposure to the new language comes in a meaningful context through comprehensible input.

New Words in Context · 语境中学新词 [Interpretive]

In New Words in Context, the Section's vocabulary and grammar are presented in a single, cohesive dialogue or passage. Students first listen to the audio and try to grasp the gist of the meaning based on the language input they received during the Language Model discussion. Then, with the aid of the pinyin text and vocabulary list, they read the dialogue or passage, deepening their comprehension and connecting the new language to its written form.

Puzzle It Out • 动动脑 [Progress Check]

Students complete these exercises to check their comprehension of the language points presented in Language Model and New Words in Context.

Language Reference • 语言注解

Clear explanations, presented alongside annotated example sentences, serve as a reference for students to consult to clarify and consolidate their understanding of new grammar and word usage. The language points are presented contextually as ways to convey meaning, rather than as rules to be memorized. In Level 3, the Language Reference also reviews more complex grammar points, clarifying and expanding on forms taught in earlier levels.

Using the Language • 语言应用 [Interpersonal/Presentational]

Interactive tasks elicit spontaneous, unscripted conversation between students by creating situations with a genuine communicative need. Some Using the Language activities are designed to be followed by a class discussion, giving students an opportunity to speak presentationally on the topic at hand. Others consist of games or puzzles that provide a clear communicative goal to encourage interaction.

Put the Pieces Together! • 融会贯通

In the final Section, students first read an extended dialogue or passage that combines the new language of the Chapter in a single, engaging story. Then, students complete additional exercises covering all three modes of communication to consolidate their grasp of Chapter content and to prepare for the Unit level IPA. Each Put the Pieces Together! Section features an interpretive exercise built on authentic materials as well as a final project that asks students to work collaboratively on a presentational performance or piece of writing. In addition, the following three floating features appear at least once in each Chapter.

Language Challenge

The Language Challenge gives motivated and more advanced students an additional opportunity to apply their new language skills and personalize their learning. This feature enriches instruction with language puzzles and introduces students to different culturally rich applications of Chinese language, such as Chinese idioms, poetry, and more! Teachers can use the Language Challenge as extra credit or as a way to differentiate instruction, providing an activity for advanced or heritage students who are moving more quickly than their peers.

5Cs

This feature expands on topics that emerge in the Chapter, integrating the 5Cs into the flow of language instruction and helping teachers effectively implement the ACTFL World-Readiness Standards for Language Learning.

What a Character!

Students are introduced to common radicals and character components that appear in some words in a Chapter, resulting in an integrated, context-driven foray into character analysis.

Scope & Sequence

Unit 1: Thinking About Our Environment

Essential Question: How do we connect to and protect an environment?

Chapter	Can-Do Goals	Language Points
Chapter 1: Shanghai: A New Environment Culture Connection: Shanghai Welcomes You! 上海欢迎你！	• Understand some of the ways Chinese people refer to members of their extended family • State how long you spent doing an activity • Explain that you spent a long time doing something • Understand when someone says there is or is not enough space to do something • Express having or not having done something enough	• Explaining how long you have done something • Using 一直 to express direction and time • Expressing that there is not enough space • Doing something enough or not enough • Kinship terms
Chapter 2: Learning About Environmental Problems Culture Connection: Trash Management and Recycling in China 垃圾处理与回收	• Describe efforts in China to encourage recycling and to discourage the use of plastic • Understand one way of expressing exaggeration • State an exact date, including the year • Discuss some environmental problems • Use percentages to support your argument • Talk about needing or wanting to do something	• Giving the date, including the year • Using 死了 to exaggerate • 要 and 需要 • Describing actions with certain results • Numbers from ten thousand to ten million
Chapter 3: An Environmental Protection Competition Culture Connection: Water Resources in the North and South of China 北方和南方的水资源情况	• Analyze how local climate affects environmental issues in a region • Talk about and understand when others discuss ongoing actions • Express "how is (something) so. . .?" • Talk about how long it's been since something has been done • Explain the goal of or motive for an action	• Talking about an ongoing action • Asking "How come (something) is so. . . ?" • Describing how long it's been since something has been done • Using 为了 to explain a goal or motive

Unit 2: Working Together

Essential Question: What affects the choices you make?

Chapter	Can-Do Goals	Language Points
Chapter 4: Confidence Matters Culture Connection: Expanding Choices for People Who are Hard of Hearing or have Visual Impairments 增加听力和视力障碍者的选择	• Describe characteristics of Chinese braille and Chinese Sign Language • Describe actions in which something moves toward or away from the speaker • Support a statement by providing additional examples • Understand when others describe something happening immediately after something else • Develop and respond to basic interview questions	• Moving toward and moving away • Not even one • Point out what two things have in common • Doing something right away
Chapter 5: Coming to an Agreement Culture Connection: China's International Appeal 中国的国际化魅力	• Describe some ways in which China has changed in the past several decades • Express that two different people or things share a certain characteristic • Say if something is easy or difficult to do • Give others suggestions after some consideration • Understand when someone talks about something that is currently happening	• Two different people or things with a similar situation • Describing something as easy to do or difficult to do • Suggesting an alternative option • Expressing an action in progress
Chapter 6: Miko's Life in Taipei Culture Connection: Taiwan 101 台湾概况	• Discuss how Taiwan's history has influenced its language and culture • Describe something's location as being inside, outside, or between other things • Indicate the direction of an action • Express ideas such as "whoever," "wherever," and "whenever" • Talk about how many times you have done something	• Describing something's location as "inside," "outside," or "in the middle" • Expressing the direction of an action • Talking about "whoever," "whatever," "wherever," etc. • Expressing how many times

Unit 3: Contemporary Society

Essential Question: How is technology both the problem and the solution?

Chapter	Can-Do Goals	Language Points
Chapter 7: Getting Things for Owen's New Place Culture Connection: Smart Technology and E-commerce 智能科技与电子商务	• Describe some of the ways technology affects how people buy and sell things in China • Understand complex numbers when used to represent prices • Estimate a quantity by providing an approximate number • Express whether someone can afford something or not • Describe certain quantities of different types of objects • Compare products and living spaces according to price and quantity	• Denominations of currency • Indicating an approximate number using 多 • Understanding different meanings of 不起 • Measure words
Chapter 8: Online LIfe Culture Connection: Going Online for Fun 网络娱乐生活	• Analyze how Chinese people do or do not benefit from spending time online • Discuss your thoughts about the internet • Express that something began and continued on • Understand when others indicate the motion and direction of an action • Briefly describe news related to a familiar topic	• Using 多 to ask questions about the amount or the degree • Indicating the beginning of an action or state with 起来 • Expressing placement and motion towards/away
Chapter 9: The Day of the Competition Culture Connection: Technology's Role in Protecting the Environment 科技在环保中的角色	• Talk about ways in which technology can impact the environment for the better • Describe how an action is performed • Give detailed information about the direction of an action • Understand and express that an action was done by someone or something • Identify formal transition words that indicate a sequence	• Describing an action • Using 来 and 去 to describe an action moving toward or away from someone • Expressing that an action was done (by someone)

Unit 4: Social Identity and Global Responsibility

Essential Question: What makes the identity of people and places unique and complex?

Chapter	Can-Do Goals	Language Points
Chapter 10: Advocating for Yourself and Others Culture Connection: Gender Equality in a Changing China 变化中的中国与性别平等	• Explain some ways in which gender equality has changed in China over the last century • Identify the basic structural elements of a letter or email • Express your opinion on a familiar subject • Summarize someone else's perspective on a familiar subject • Respond to other people's opinions with your own perspective • Discuss the effects of common stereotypes	• Using 是 to agree with a statement • Explaining a perspective • Expressing "no matter. . . "
Chapter 11: Touring Shanghai Culture Connection: Shanghai: An Influential City 上海：一个有影响力的城市	• Name some of Shanghai's attractions • Use 连 to introduce examples for added emphasis • Discuss certain societal issues • Understand basic information when others talk about cultural artifacts	• Giving an example with added emphasis • Expressing that something will continue into the future • Comparing 的, 得, and 地
Chapter 12: Looking Back, Looking Ahead Culture Connection: China Plans for the Future 中国的未来规划	• Talk about some plans for development that the Chinese government has initiated • Understand and talk about travel preparations • Express that an action has been completed successfully • Discuss challenges and responsibilities • Share your wishes for the new year and understand the wishes of others	• Using the word 成 (chéng) • Reviewing how to add detailed information to a verb • Review of 把 and 被 • Reviewing the uses of 了

Audio

This icon indicates that audio content is available. Audio can be downloaded at cheng-tsui.com.

Cast of Characters

Isabella and Martin Lopez moved to China two years ago, when their mother accepted an offer to work in her company's Beijing office. Now, Martin is going to high school at an international school in Beijing, and Isabella is attending college in Shanghai.

The Lopez Family

林静

(Lín Jìng)

Emma Lopez,
Isabella and Martin's mother,
working in Beijing

林春月

(Lín Chūnyuè)

Isabella Lopez,
college freshman in Shanghai

林马丁

(Lín Mǎdīng)

Martin Lopez,
high school junior in Beijing

Like Isabella, these characters have recently graduated from high school.

姜大文

(Jiāng Dàwén)

Owen Kang,
aspiring chef, looking for
work in Shanghai,
from the US

东方雪儿

(Dōngfāng Xuě'ér)

Xue'er Dongfang,
college freshman in
Shanghai, from China

张爱林

(Zhāng Àilín)

Ellen Jones,
college freshman in the
United Kingdom, from
the United Kingdom

二村美子

(Èrcūn Měizǐ)

Miko Futamura,
college freshman
in Taipei, from Japan

In Shanghai, Isabella gets to know some of Xue'er's family.

刘海生

(Liú Hǎishēng)

Liu Haisheng,
college freshman
in Shanghai, from China

雪儿的妈妈

Xue'er's mother,
from China

雪儿的爸爸

Xue'er's father,
from China

Here are some of Martin's friends and teachers at his high school in Beijing.

杨天浩

(Yáng Tiānhào)

Tianhao Yang,
high school junior in Beijing,
from China

杨梅雅

(Yáng Méiyǎ)

Maya Young,
high school junior
in Beijing, from the US

张可可

(Zhāng Kěkě)

Keke Zhang,
high school junior
in Beijing, from China

陈里奥

(Chén Lǐ'ào)

Leo Fischer,
high school junior
in Beijing,
from Germany

潘赛吉

(Pān Sàijí)

Sanjay Patel,
high school senior
in Beijing, from the US

王易

(Wáng Yì)

Yi Wang,
high school teacher
in Beijing, from China

赵健新

(Zhào Jiànxīn)

Jianxin Zhao,
high school teacher
in Beijing, from China

THINKING ABOUT OUR ENVIRONMENT

In Unit 1, you will learn to talk about some environmental issues. You will also learn how to discuss goals and motivations.

Essential Question
How do we connect to and protect an environment?

CHAPTER 1
Shanghai: A New Environment

Isabella and Owen join Xue'er's family for dinner.

CHAPTER 2
Learning About Environmental Problems

Martin meets up with some of his friends to catch up on what everyone did over the summer.

CHAPTER 3
An Environmental Protection Competition

Martin and some friends decide to take part in a competition but disagree on the topic of their presentation.

At the end of the unit, you will pick an imaginary organization to grant funding for. You will:

- Read proposals for different projects that are in need of funding

- Discuss which project you believe should receive the grant money

- Present your group's choice and explain why you decided to award the grant money to that particular project

Shanghai: A New Environment

两个星期以前，大文来到了上海找工作。春月今天早上也离开了北京，来到了上海。

大文：喂？春月，你到学校了吗？

春月：喂？大文，我刚到学校！你现在住在雪儿家，对吧？你住得习惯吗？

大文：挺习惯的！雪儿的爸爸每天都会给我们做很多好吃的上海菜。我找到工作，自己住以后，一定会很想她爸爸做的菜！

春月：是吗？雪儿这个周末要带我去她家跟你们吃饭，那我得多吃点儿！

Can-Do Goals · 能力目标

In this chapter, you will learn to:

- Understand some of the ways Chinese people refer to members of their extended family
- State how long you spent doing an activity
- Explain that you spent a long time doing something
- Understand when someone says there is or is not enough space to do something
- Express having or not having done something enough

Shànghǎi   huānyíng   nǐ

上海欢迎你!

Shanghai Welcomes You!

Skyscrapers crowd the banks of the Huangpu River in Shanghai. This area, called Pudong, was mainly rice fields up until the 1990s.

With a population (人口, rénkǒu) of over 20 million, Shanghai is one of the largest cities in the world. Like Beijing, it is considered a megacity (特大城市). However, while Beijing is the country's political capital and has been a major urban center for centuries, much of Shanghai's growth has occurred in recent decades. Shanghai is a modern economic (经济, jīngjì) powerhouse.

上海的人口多吗?
上海是中国的什么中心?

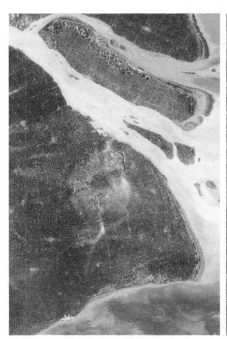

Satellite images taken by NASA in 1984 (left) and 2019 (right) show Shanghai's growth.

Shanghai's Geography

Shanghai is situated on China's coastline, at the mouth of the Yangtze River (长江, Cháng Jiāng). This location, close to the sea and along one of the most important rivers in China, makes the city an important port and has contributed to its growth. The city more than tripled in size between 1984 and 2014 despite being divided by the Huangpu River (黄埔江, Huángpǔ Jiāng) and hemmed in by the sea and the massive Yangtze.

在左边的照片里,你能找到长江和黄浦江在哪儿吗?

Food in Shanghai

Shanghainese food is characterized by frequent use of soy sauce and sugar, creating rich, dark sauces. In addition, many dishes are somewhat sweet: for example, Shanghai's version of red-cooked pork is famous for being sweeter than versions from other parts of China. Its location on the coast and in the heart of a major rice growing region also has an effect on local cuisine: dishes are often eaten with rice (米饭, mǐfàn), and many people from Shanghai like to eat a lot of fish and shellfish. Hairy crab (大闸蟹, dàzháxiè) is one example of a local favorite.

上海有很多吃起来甜甜的菜吗？

如果去上海玩儿，你想尝尝上海菜吗？为什么？

By the Numbers

Cities with high population densities can face many issues, such as congested traffic, heavy pollution, and a shortage of government services, like education. One way that the Chinese government (政府, zhèngfǔ) and the Shanghai city government (市政府) plan to deal with these challenges is to limit the city's population to 25 million people by 2035.

你觉得上海市政府的计划怎么样？

你现在住的地方有这样的问题吗？

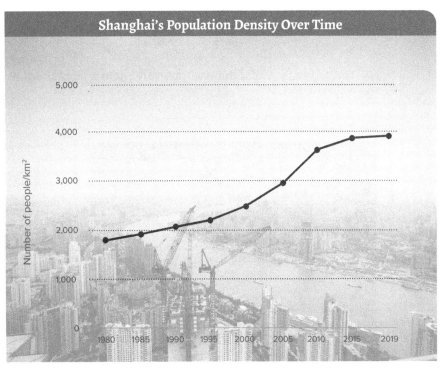

Shanghai's Population Density Over Time

Number of people/km²

Source: Shanghai Statistical Yearbook, 2020

REFLECT ON THE ESSENTIAL QUESTION

How do we connect to and protect an environment?

1 What is the geography like where you live? How has it affected the way your community has developed?

2 How does the size or distribution of the local population affect your community?

3 How would your community and its nearby ecology change if the local population grew dramatically every year? Is there anything that would be lost or need protecting?

Having done something for a while

1a Language Model · 语言范例 TARGET LANGUAGE INPUT

Your teacher will lead a discussion about the images below. Try to participate as much as you can. If there is anything you don't understand, let your teacher know.

Zuótiān　wǎnshàng　wǒ　yìzhí　zài　zuò　zuòyè.
昨天－晚上－我－一直－在－做－作业。

Last night, I spent the whole night doing homework.

Wǒ　zuò　le　wǔ　gè　xiǎoshí　de　zuòyè.　Nǐ　ne?
我－做－了－五－个－小时－的－作业。－你－呢?

I did homework for five hours. How about you?

1b New Words in Context · 语境中学新词 INTERPRETIVE

Audio

Listen to the audio and try to understand as much as you can. Then read the passage, using the pinyin text and vocabulary list to figure out unfamiliar words.

我今天早上到上海了！我一想到自己马上就要上
大一¹了，就很高兴！这个暑假过得很慢，所以
我一直想早点儿来上海，早点儿来学校。早上我
坐地铁到学校以后，先收拾了一个小时的东西，
然后去餐厅里吃饭了。我买了一份米饭，还有一
份家常豆腐和一份红烧肉。我觉得那两个菜都做
得马马虎虎，吃起来有点儿甜，得再多放点儿盐。
下午吃饭的时候，我再尝尝²别的菜吧！

Wǒ jīntiān zǎoshang dào Shànghǎi le! Wǒ yì xiǎng dào zìjǐ mǎshàng jiù yào shàng

dà yī le, jiù tèbié gāoxìng! Zhège shǔjià guò de hěn màn, suǒyǐ

wǒ yìzhí xiǎng zǎo diǎnr lái Shànghǎi, zǎo diǎnr lái xuéxiào. Zǎoshàng wǒ

zuò dìtiě dào xuéxiào yǐhòu, xiān shōushi le yí gè xiǎoshí de dōngxī,

ránhòu qù cāntīng lǐ chī fàn le. Wǒ mǎi le yí fèn mǐfàn, hái yǒu yí

fèn jiācháng dòufu hé yí fèn hóngshāo ròu. Wǒ juéde nà liǎng gè cài dōu zuò

de mǎmǎ-hūhū, chī qǐlái yǒu diǎnr tián, děi zài duō fàng diǎnr yán.

Xiàwǔ chī fàn de shíhou, wǒ zài cháng chang biéde cài ba!

Comprehension Check

T   F

1 Isabella thinks the summer has gone by too fast. ◯ ◯

2 Isabella took the subway to get to school. ◯ ◯

3 Isabella thought the food in the cafeteria was too salty. ◯ ◯

4 Describe how Isabella feels in this passage and why she feels this way.

Vocabulary · 生词

Audio

	Word	Pinyin	Meaning
1	慢	màn	slow
2	一直	yìzhí	always, continuously; straight
3	米饭	mǐfàn	cooked rice
4	家常	jiācháng	home-style
5	豆腐	dòufu	tofu, bean curd
6	马马虎虎	mǎmǎ-hūhū	not very good, just so-so
7	盐	yán	salt
8	尝	cháng	to try (a food), to taste

1c Puzzle It Out · 动动脑 PROGRESS CHECK

Complete the exercises below to check your understanding of what you learned in Section 1. If you have questions, consult the Language Reference section.

Exercise 1 Choose the best option to complete each sentence.

1 我姐姐很喜欢看书，……
   (a) 她每天都看两个小时的书。
   (b) 她每天都看四个小时的电影。

2 我弟弟昨天下午去公园里做运动了，……
   (a) 他打了两个半小时的篮球。
   (b) 他在家里休息了一下午。

3 我昨天约王明去我们小区附近的咖啡馆了，……
   (a) 我在那儿给王明打了两个小时的电话。
   (b) 我们还在那儿拍了一会儿照片。

Exercise 2 For each sentence, choose the correct location (1 or 2) in which to add the word 一直.

1 他 (1) 想 (2) 去陕西的茶园看看，可是太忙了，没时间去。

2 今天上午我 (1) 在 (2) 上课，没看到你的短信。

3 我想学 (1) 跳舞，但是 (2) 没有找到合适的老师教我。

4 (1) 别 (2) 在手机上看视频了，多看看书吧。

Language Reference · 语言注解

1 Explaining how long you have done something

In Chinese, time phrases that describe duration—that is, how long an action takes—come after the verb. However, as shown in the following examples, when there is an object in the sentence, the time phrase can come either before or after the object, changing the sentence structure slightly. (The object of each sentence is highlighted in gray.) It is similar to the sentences "I have studied Chinese for two years" and "I have studied two years of Chinese"; these sentences have the same meaning but different structures.

Option 1: V + O + V + time phrase   **Option 2: V + time phrase (的) + O**

1 你学中文学了多长时间了?   2 你学了多长时间 (的) 中文了?

How long have you been studying Chinese?

3 我学中文学了两年了。   4 我学了两年 (的) 中文了。

I have been studying Chinese for two years.

5 他每天跳舞跳半个小时。   6 他每天跳半个小时 (的) 舞。

He dances for half an hour every day.

2 Using 一直 to express direction and time

一直 (yìzhí) is often used to emphasize that something took a long time or has been going on for a long time. Used in this way, it means "continuously, always, keep (doing something)."

yìzhí
1 我们一直想去日本旅行，可是去那儿旅行太贵了!

We have always wanted to travel to Japan, but it's too expensive to go there!

yìzhí
2 这个题特别难，我早上一直在做这个题。

This homework problem is especially difficult. I was working on it all morning.

3 我希望我能一直做自己喜欢做的事。
yìzhí

I hope I can keep doing the things I like to do.

一直 (yìzhí) can also be used to describe moving in a straight direction.

4 你想去钟楼？那你一直往前走，到了第二个路口往
yìzhí
左拐……

You want to go to the Bell Tower? In that case, walk straight ahead and take a left when you get to the second intersection.

5 从这儿一直走，十分钟以后，你就会看到古城墙了。
yìzhí

From here, go straight, and in ten minutes you will see the Ancient City Wall.

1d Using the Language · 语言应用 INTERPERSONAL/PRESENTATIONAL

How was everyone's summer? Get into pairs and ask your partner some questions about his/her summer vacation. At the end of the activity, your teacher will collect the information from the class to see how students spent their summer and if they were able to do things they wanted to do.

Step 1: Ask your partner about different activities he/she did over the summer. If appropriate, ask how much time he/she spent doing those different activities.

Example:

暑假的时候，你练街舞了吗？你每个星期练多长时间的
街舞？

Step 2: Make a list of things that you have always wanted to do over summer vacation. Did you have the opportunity to do any of those things over the summer? Discuss with your partner.

Example:

A: 我一直想跟朋友暑假的时候去听演唱会。

B: 那你去了吗？

A: 没有，我的钱不够……

Step 3: Were you and your partner able to do some of the things you wanted to do this summer? Be prepared to tell the teacher about your and your partner's summers.

The word 马马虎虎 (mǎmǎ-hūhū) literally means "horse-horse-tiger-tiger." Part of the reason this word may seem distinctive is that it comes from Manchu, the language of the Manchu people (满族人, Mǎnzú rén), one of China's ethnic minorities. A Manchu army overthrew the last emperor of the Ming Dynasty in 1644 and established the Qing Dynasty, which lasted until 1911. During the Qing Dynasty, some signs and court documents were written in both Manchu and Chinese. Nowadays, very few people can speak or read Manchu, but some groups are trying to revive its use.

The plaque in the picture above is located at the entrance of Guanju Palace (关雎宫, Guānjū Gōng), which is on the grounds of Shenyang Imperial Palace, Liaoning Province. The left side is written in Manchu and the right side is written in traditional Chinese characters. Are there multilingual signs in your community? What languages do you see most often, and what kinds of signs tend to be multilingual?

Not enough room

2a Language Model · 语言范例 `TARGET LANGUAGE INPUT`

Your teacher will lead a discussion about the images below. Try to participate as much as you can. If there is anything you don't understand, let your teacher know.

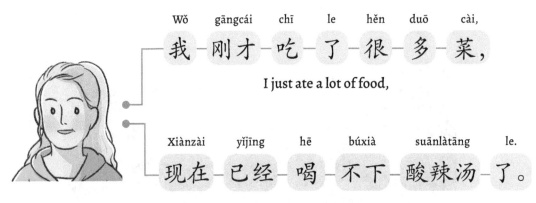

Wǒ gāngcái chī le hěn duō cài,
我 刚才 吃 了 很 多 菜，
I just ate a lot of food,

Xiànzài yǐjīng hē búxià suānlàtāng le.
现在 已经 喝 不下 酸辣汤 了。
and now I am too full to eat hot and sour soup.

suānlàtāng
酸辣汤
hot and sour soup

chǎo qīngcài
炒青菜
stir-fried vegetables

hóngshāo yú
红烧鱼
red-cooked fish

Owen is eating lunch with his new friend, Haisheng. Listen to their conversation and try to understand as much as you can. Then read the dialogue, using the pinyin text and vocabulary list to figure out unfamiliar words.

 刘海生，我们来¹个红烧鱼、家常豆腐、炒青菜，然后再要一个酸辣汤，怎么样？

Liú Hǎishēng, wǒmen lái gè hóngshāo yú, jiācháng dòufu, chǎo qīngcài, ránhòu zài yào yí gè suānlàtāng, zěnmeyàng?

 我们两个人吃得完这些菜吗？

Wǒmen liǎng gè rén chī de wán zhè xiē cài ma?

 吃得完，我很饿。而且中国人经常说，"午饭要吃饱²！"

Chī de wán, wǒ hěn è. Érqiě Zhōngguó rén jīngcháng shuō, "wǔfàn yào chī bǎo!"

 好吧！对了，你会用筷子吗？

Hǎo ba! Duìle, nǐ huì yòng kuàizi ma?

 会啊，我在家里有的时候也用筷子。那我找服务员点菜吧。……

Huì a, wǒ zài jiā lǐ yǒude shíhou yě yòng kuàizi. Nà wǒ zhǎo fúwùyuán diǎn cài ba. …

 这几个菜真好吃！

Zhè jǐ gè cài zhēn hǎo chī!

 是啊，而且还不贵！我们要不要再点一盘菜尝尝？

Shì a, érqiě hái bú guì! Wǒmen yào bú yào zài diǎn yì pán cài cháng chang?

 这儿的菜便宜是便宜，可是我已经吃不下了……

Zhèr de cài piányi shì piányi, kěshì wǒ yǐjīng chī búxià le…

Comprehension Check

T F

1 Owen and Haisheng ordered three dishes and a soup. ○ ○

2 Owen is confident that they will finish all of the food that they ordered. ○ ○

3 After Haisheng's last line, what do you think Owen will say?

NOTE

1   The verb 来 is often used for ordering food or small items at a store. 我们来个红烧鱼 is similar to saying "Let's have (one order of) red-cooked fish."

2   饱 is often added after the verb 吃 to indicate that a person has eaten enough and is now full.

Audio

Vocabulary · 生词

	Word	Pinyin	Meaning
9	鱼	yú	fish
10	青菜	qīngcài	bok choy, any leafy green vegetable
11	酸辣汤	suānlàtāng	hot and sour soup
12	午饭	wǔfàn	lunch
13	饱	bǎo	full, stuffed (after a meal)
14	筷子	kuàizi	chopsticks
15	盘	pán	(plate, dish, measure word for food)
16	不下	búxià	(added to a verb to indicate there is not enough space to hold something)
	刘海生	Liú Hǎishēng	Liu Haisheng (a person's name)

LANGUAGE CHALLENGE

There is a Chinese rhyme that means "For breakfast, you should eat well. For lunch, you should eat until you're full. For dinner, you should eat very little." Can you guess the missing characters to complete the original Chinese saying below?

早饭要吃1 _____ , 午饭要吃2 _____ , 晚饭要吃3 _____ 。

Complete the exercise below to check your understanding of what you learned in Section 2. If you have questions, consult the Language Reference section.

Choose the sentence that best matches each picture.

a 我吃不下这块蛋糕了。

b 我吃得下这块蛋糕。

c 我的包放得下这些书。

d 我的包放不下这些书。

Language Reference · 语言注解

3 **Expressing that there is not enough space**

When 不下 follows an action, it indicates that there is not enough physical space to complete the action. When 得下 follows an action, it indicates that there is enough physical space to complete the action.

1 这本书太大了，我的包放不下。
   This book is too big to fit in my bag.

2 我刚才吃了很多水果，现在吃不下这些零食了。
   I just ate a lot of fruit; I'm too full now to eat these snacks.

3 我们教室坐得下三十个学生。
   Our classroom can seat thirty students.

Play a guessing game with your partner.

Step 1: Think of a place or item that you know how to say in Chinese, such as 公园, 包, 笛子, 舞台, but don't tell your partner what it is. Your partner will also think of a place or item.

Step 2: Take turns asking each other yes/no questions about the item he or she has chosen. If you want to know how big the item is, remember to use 放得下.

Example: 这个东西是吃的吗？我们教室里放得下吗？

Step 3: When you think you have enough information about the item, instead of asking a question, you can guess what the item is. The first student to guess correctly wins.

The word 盘 (pán) contains the component 皿 (mǐn), which means "vessel, container." It is often used in words that relate to containers or things that are typically kept in containers.

Below are some words for different containers. In addition to the 皿 component, these words contain other components you have learned that hint at each word's pronunciation. Use this knowledge to match the pinyin words on the left with the correct characters.

1 lánzi

2 hézi

3 cházhōng

4 huāpén

a 盒子

b 花盆

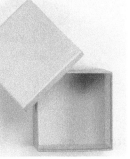

c 篮子

d 茶盅

Doing enough of something

Your teacher will lead a discussion about the image below. Try to participate as much as you can. If there is anything you don't understand, let your teacher know.

Zhège　qiūtiān　yào　chuān　de　yīfu　wǒ　yǐjīng
这个 - 秋天 - 要 - 穿 - 的 - 衣服 - 我 - 已经

I have already bought enough of the clothes I want for this fall.

mǎi　gòu　le.　Nǐ　ne?
买 - 够 - 了。 - 你 - 呢?

How about you?

People shopping at Qipu Lu Clothing Market in Shanghai

3b New Words in Context · 语境中学新词 INTERPRETIVE

Listen to the audio and try to understand as much as you can. Then read the dialogue, using the pinyin text and vocabulary list to figure out unfamiliar words.

 天浩，你买新耳机了？

Tiānhào, nǐ mǎi xīn ěrjī le?

 我最近在网上教我表妹[1]学英文，耳机是我姨妈送我的。

Wǒ zuìjìn zài wǎng shàng jiāo wǒ biǎomèi xué Yīngwén, ěrjī shì wǒ yímā sòng wǒ de.

 你表妹是你姨妈的女儿吗？

Nǐ biǎomèi shì nǐ yímā de nǚ'ér ma?

 对。我姨妈还有一个儿子，不过我表哥的英文不好，所以我姨妈让我教我表妹。但是这个周末我没空教她了。

Duì. Wǒ yímā hái yǒu yí gè érzi, búguò wǒ biǎogē de Yīngwén bù hǎo, suǒyǐ wǒ yímā ràng wǒ jiāo wǒ biǎomèi. Dànshì zhège zhōumò wǒ méi kòng jiāo tā le.

 你这个周末有事吗？

Nǐ zhège zhōumò yǒu shì ma?

 我叔叔带我奶奶来北京了，买一种在老家买不到的助听器。他们在北京玩儿了几天了，但是还没玩儿够，所以周末我们要一起再去几个地方。

Wǒ shūshu dài wǒ nǎinai lái Běijīng le, mǎi yì zhǒng zài lǎojiā mǎi bú dào de zhùtīngqì. Tāmen zài Běijīng wánr le jǐ tiān le, dànshì hái méi wánr gòu, suǒyǐ zhōumò wǒmen yào yìqǐ zài qù jǐ gè dìfang.

 从你老家到北京买助听器啊？

Cóng nǐ lǎojiā dào Běijīng mǎi zhùtīngqì a?

 是啊，我叔叔说父母的身体最重要，远一点儿没关系。对了，你周末有空教我表妹吗？

Shì a, wǒ shūshu shuō fùmǔ de shēntǐ zuì zhòngyào, yuǎn yìdiǎnr méi guānxi. Duì le, nǐ zhōumò yǒu kòng jiāo wǒ biǎomèi ma?

 有！那你给你姨妈说一下吧？

Yǒu! Nà nǐ gěi nǐ yímā shuō yíxià ba?

 我们给她打个电话吧？你可以叫她阿姨。她一定会喜欢你的[2]！

Wǒmen gěi tā dǎ gè diànhuà ba? Nǐ kěyǐ jiào tā āyí. Tā yídìng huì xǐhuan nǐ de!

Comprehension Check

		T	F
1	Tianhao is giving English lessons to his aunt online.	○	○
2	Tianhao's uncle brought Tianhao's grandmother to Beijing to buy a hearing aid.	○	○
3	What do you think Tianhao will say when he calls his aunt?		

NOTE

1　表妹 (biǎomèi) means "younger female cousin." 表哥 (biǎogē), 表姐 (biǎojiě), and 表弟 (biǎodì) mean "older male cousin," "older female cousin," and "younger male cousin," respectively. See the Language Reference section for additional information about kinship terms.

2　When using 会 to say that something will happen in the future, 的 is often added at the end of the sentence to emphasize certainty.

Vocabulary · 生词

Audio

	Word	Pinyin	Meaning
17	耳机	ěrjī	headphones, earbuds
18	表妹	biǎomèi	younger female cousin (on the mother's side or the daughter of the father's sister)
19	姨妈	yímā	aunt (mother's sister)
20	女儿	nǚ'ér	daughter
21	儿子	érzi	son
22	叔叔	shūshu	uncle (father's younger brother); respectful way to address a male adult
23	助听器	zhùtīngqì	hearing aid
24	父母	fùmǔ	parents, father and mother (formal)
25	阿姨	āyí	respectful way to address a female adult; aunt (rarely used)

Complete the exercises below to check your understanding of what you learned in Section 3. If you have questions, consult the Language Reference section.

Exercise 1 Choose the word from the list on the left that best completes each sentence. Use each word only once.

爷爷

叔叔

姨妈

1 我叔叔的爸爸是我的 _____。

2 我妈妈的姐姐是我的 _____。

3 我爸爸的弟弟是我的 _____。

Exercise 2 For each sentence, choose the correct location (1 or 2) in which to add the word 够.

1 我吃 (1) 家常豆腐了，因为这个星期我吃 (2) 了六次了。

2 我们四个人点 (1) 五个菜，应该 (2) 吧？

3 那个演唱会一点儿也不好看，我看 (1) 了十分钟就看 (2) 了。

Language Reference · 语言注解

4 Doing something enough or not enough

The word 够 can be paired with a verb to express that the action has been done enough. In negative examples, 没有 or 没 is used rather than 不 (see examples 3 and 4).

1 今天我写了一百个汉字了，已经写够了。
   I wrote a hundred Chinese characters today; that was enough.

2 他们不喜欢住旅馆，住了三天就住够了。
   They don't like staying in a hotel. They stayed for three days, and that was enough.

3 昨天我去买了这个学期要用的东西，可是还没买够。
   Yesterday, I went to buy things I need for this semester, but I did not finish buying what I need yet.

4 这本书太好看了，我每天都看，可是还没有看够。
   This book is so good. I have been reading it every day, but I still can't get enough of it.

5 Kinship terms

Words for family members and relatives are much more specific in Chinese than they are in English. Different terms are used depending on whether a relative is on the father's side or the mother's side and whether a relative is older or younger than his/her siblings. Some terms also depend on where in China the speaker is from. The chart below shows some kinship terms commonly used to refer to relatives. Use the chart to help you find kinship terms that are relevant to you. Ask your teacher if you want to know how to say words for family members that are not listed here.

Relatives on the father's side

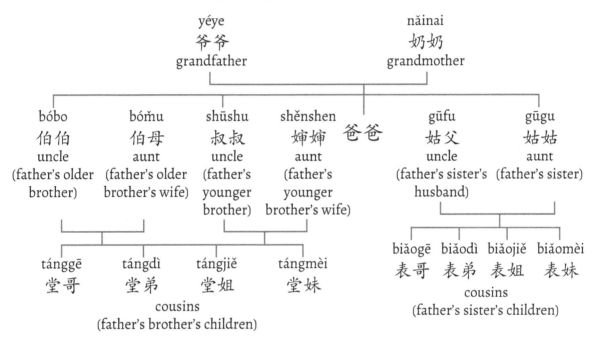

Relatives on the mother's side

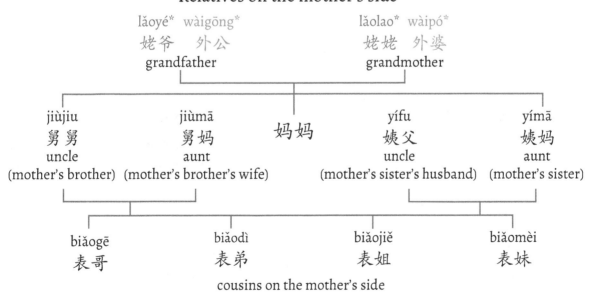

*Terms in blue are more common in northern China and terms in green are more common in southern China.

Activity 1 Imagine that a video streaming service has selected you and your classmates to brainstorm new ideas for a TV show. The streaming service wants to focus on family-related content, so the TV show you come up with should focus on a particular family, whether the family members are related by blood or closely connected in some other way.

Step 1: Brainstorm ideas with your partner. After you both agree on your favorite idea, create a presentation to explain the show's concept. Your presentation should:

- Describe the main characters and their relationships to each other
- Explain what makes the show interesting or entertaining
- Describe one or two problems the family has in the first season, and how they solve the problem(s)

Step 2: Present your idea to a small group of your classmates. Your teacher will only give you a certain amount of time to present, so make it exciting! Listen to the other students in your group present and take notes on what you like about their presentations.

Step 3: With your partner, discuss the other presentations you heard. Choose at least one thing you liked about each presentation and incorporate into your pitch the ones that might work in yours.

Activity 2

Step 1: Make a list of books and movies that you have been wanting to see, or music groups and songs that you have been wanting to listen to.

Step 2: Make a second list of books, movies, music groups, and songs. This list should include items that you have seen or heard enough and aren't interested in watching or listening to again.

Step 3: Compare both of your lists with your partner. Tell your partner how you feel about the items on his/her list. Are you interested in the same books, movies, and music as your partner, or have you seen or heard them enough?

Example:

A: 我一直想看这个电影，但是还没看。
B: 这个电影我已经看过了。我觉得挺好看的！

A: 他的歌我已经听够了，不想再听了。
B: 我也已经听够了。

5Cs

CULTURES

COMMUNITIES
COMMUNICATION
COMPARISONS
CONNECTIONS

The Analects (论语, Lúnyǔ) is an ancient text that records teachings attributed to Confucius. Confucius often spoke of a person's duty to his/her 父母 (fùmǔ)—the formal term for a person's father (父亲, fùqīn) and mother (母亲, mǔqīn). One famous saying is "父母在，不远游。游必 (bì) 有方。" It means "While a person's parents are alive, he/she should not travel far away. If that person does travel, he/she must have a fixed place to go." Nowadays, sometimes only the first part of this expression is quoted to emphasize the importance of staying close to one's parents to take care of them. The second sentence, however, suggests that people who have no choice and must travel far from their parents should settle in a "fixed place" so that their parents can get in touch if necessary.

Search online or in books on ancient China to find another expression that is attributed to Confucius. Do you agree with the expression you found? Use an example from your own life or the life of someone you know to explain whether you agree with Confucius or not.

Put the Pieces Together! • 融会贯通

Audio

A Reading and Listening • 阅读和听力 INTERPRETIVE

Passage 1 What's next for Isabella and her friends? Read on...

Ding dong~

 一定是雪儿回来了。

 姨妈,那我去看看。……雪儿,你回来了啊! 她一定就是你的好朋友吧?

 对! 我给你们介绍一下。她是我在北京认识的好朋友,林春月。他是我哥,叫刘海生。

 你好!

 雪儿, 你怎么没说过你还有一个哥哥啊?

 我爸爸妈妈只有我一个女儿。海生其实是我的表哥,是我二姨妈的儿子。

对，我跟你们一样，今年也上大一，所以我姨妈叫我今天过来跟你们一起吃饭，聊聊天儿。

 海生其实只比我大几天，不过没办法，我只能叫他哥哥……

 春月，欢迎你来我们家！来，坐吧，你们一边吃午饭，一边聊吧。大文做完菜就过来。

 好，谢谢阿姨！

 姨妈，还有菜啊？这么多菜桌子上放不下了吧？

 这是最后一个菜。今天家里人多，所以他们多做了几个菜。你们一会儿慢点儿吃啊。

 好！对了，海生，你的耳机真好看，你是在哪儿买的啊？

 这不是耳机，是我的助听器。这个颜色好看吧？

 好看，我也很喜欢这个颜色！

 最后一盘菜也做好了！

 雪儿的爸爸和大文做了一上午的菜了，你们快来尝尝。

 都是些家常菜。如果你们喜欢吃，就多吃点儿，跟在自己家一样啊。

  爸，妈，你们不知道，春月刚来上海，所以每天都跟我说，"上海菜太甜了！我想放点儿盐。"

 是吗？春月，你第一次来上海，可能还不太习惯。来，尝尝大文做的家常豆腐和酸辣汤，都不太甜。他说这个菜和这个汤你们以前都特别喜欢。

你们也尝尝叔叔做的红烧鱼和炒青菜吧，特别香！

 好！

 来，多吃点儿。春月，你筷子用得真好啊。

 谢谢阿姨！

 妈，春月已经在中国住了两年多了，她筷子当然用得好啊。

 雪儿，马丁也在中国住了两年多了，不过他筷子用得……马马虎虎啊。

 马丁是你们的朋友吗？

 不是，是我弟弟。他现在还在北京上高中。

 那你现在来上海上大学了，你弟弟一定很想你吧？来，再来点儿米饭吧！

 啊，好吧……谢谢叔叔。我弟弟在北京有很多朋友，不会想我的。

 来，你们多吃点儿鱼吧。春月，你第一次来我们家，得吃饱吃好啊。

 是啊，春月，不要客气，来，再吃点儿肉吧。

 好……谢谢叔叔阿姨。

 你太客气了，春月，不用一直说谢谢。你们觉得这些菜够吗？

 够了，够了，姨妈。我们都吃不下了……

是啊，我们都吃饱了。对吧，春月？

 对，对，对，其实我刚才就已经也吃饱了。

 叔叔做的菜好吃吧？

 好吃！你做的菜也很好吃！

 对了，雪儿，我记得你以前想去纽约上大学，后来怎么不去了？

 我刚去北京上学的时候，经常想家，有的时候会哭很长时间……我一个人在别的城市住够了，所以现在回上海上大学了。

 我知道了，这就叫："父母在，不远游"，对吗？

 对！

 大文，你最近跟叔叔阿姨学到了很多东西啊？

 是啊，叔叔阿姨每天都教我一个小时的中文。如果你和雪儿有空，一定要多回来看看！

Comprehension Check

		T	F
1	Haisheng and Xue'er are not related by blood.	○	○
2	Owen and Xue'er's father spent very little time making lunch.	○	○
3	Although Isabella has lived in China for two years, she is not very good at using chopsticks.	○	○
4	Isabella says that her brother doesn't miss her because he has a lot of friends in Beijing.	○	○
5	Owen says that Xue'er's parents have been teaching him how to cook for an hour each day.	○	○
6	Choose one character and describe what the character does in the story.		

Passage 2 The picture below is of a restaurant in Shanghai, but it doesn't specialize in 上海菜. Based on the signs, what kind of food do you think they serve here?

Passage 3 Listen as one student tells his friend about his family tree. Are the statements that follow true or false?

		T	F
1	The boy drew both his mother and father on the family tree.	○	○
2	The boy's aunt is his father's older sister.	○	○
3	The boy's cousin is only one month older than him.	○	○
4	The boy's cousin is wearing headphones.	○	○

Passage 4 Listen to the student describe a family get-together. Look at the pictures of dishes below and choose the ones described by the student in the recording. Then, list at least three things you learned about her family. Write in complete Chinese sentences on a separate sheet of paper.

B Speaking · 口语 INTERPERSONAL

You are going to draw a family tree and share it with a partner. For this activity, you may create a family tree for a celebrity or fictional character, or you can share your real family tree.

Step 1: Draw a family tree for the person you chose. Show as many family members as you can, and label each person with the correct Chinese kinship term. In addition to direct relatives, you may include other people important to the person, such as friends or even pets. You decide how these relationships connect to the family tree.

Step 2: Without showing the family tree to your partner, describe the people shown using the correct Chinese kinship terms. Your partner will try to draw and label the information as you describe it.

Example:

Student A: 除了我爸爸以外，我的爷爷奶奶还有一个儿子。
Student B: 那他比你爸爸大还是比你爸爸小呢？
Student A: 比我爸爸小，所以我叫他叔叔。

Step 3: Compare the drawing your partner made based on your description of the family tree you created. Are they similar?

C Final Project · 结课项目 PRESENTATIONAL

Funny Family Get-Together

For this project, you will work in a group to perform a skit about having dinner at a family get-together. You may choose a family tree from the Speaking exercise to guide you as you create characters for the skit. Imagine that the family in this skit has a funny or unique family habit—maybe everyone has to dance when someone enters the room, or everyone says thank you three times when someone gives them something. You will need to show this habit in the skit.

Step 1: Decide who will perform which character in the big family. Who will host the get-together? Who will be cooking the dishes? Who will help cook?

Step 2: Map out the plot of your skit. Prepare as much or as little as you feel you need. You can write a detailed script or just outline what each character will say. Your scene should include at least three of the following:

- Each family member's food preferences
- How much time the host spent preparing the meal
- Guests' reactions to the dishes
- The host(s) encouraging guests to eat more

Step 3: Perform your skit for the class. Watch other groups perform their skits. Pay attention to figure out the family habit being shown in each skit. Write your guess on a piece of scrap paper. Who can spot the most family habits?

Can-Do Goals · 能力目标

Talk with your teacher if you have questions or if you are not certain you can do the following tasks:

- Understand some of the ways Chinese people refer to members of their extended family

- State how long you spent doing an activity

- Explain that you spent a long time doing something

- Understand when someone says there is or is not enough space to do something

- Express having or not having done something enough

Cultural Knowledge · 文化知识

How has geography affected Shanghai's development?

Learning About Environmental Problems

天浩：马丁，你今天下课以后有时间吗？我们一起聊聊天儿吧？

马丁：好啊！不知道大家暑假都过得怎么样。

天浩：是啊……

马丁：那我们问问梅雅和可可想不想一起去吧？

天浩：好，我们在学校旁边的饮料店见吧！

马丁：好主意！那我们现在去找她们吧。

Can-Do Goals · 能力目标

In this chapter, you will learn to:

- Describe efforts in China to encourage recycling and to discourage the use of plastic
- Understand one way of expressing exaggeration
- State an exact date, including the year
- Discuss some environmental problems
- Use percentages to support your argument
- Talk about needing or wanting to do something

lājī chǔlǐ yǔ huíshōu
垃圾处理与回收
Trash Management and Recycling in China

The World Bank has estimated that, on average, a person produces .74 kilograms (1.6 pounds) of trash (垃圾, lājī) per day. Not all of this trash has to end up in a landfill, though: some of that .74 kilograms includes trash that people could recycle (回收, huíshōu). With a population of more than 1 billion people, China recognizes that reducing waste and encouraging recycling are important for the future of the country.

By the Numbers

In 2017, the United States and China produced (产生, chǎnshēng) more trash than any other country (国家, guójiā) in the world: the U.S. produced 243 million metric tons and China produced 215 million metric tons. Ten of China's cities, combined, produced a little over 25 percent of that trash, but many of these cities have since invested heavily in ways to more efficiently process and recycle trash.

哪些国家产生的垃圾最多？

在中国，哪几个城市产生的垃圾最多？

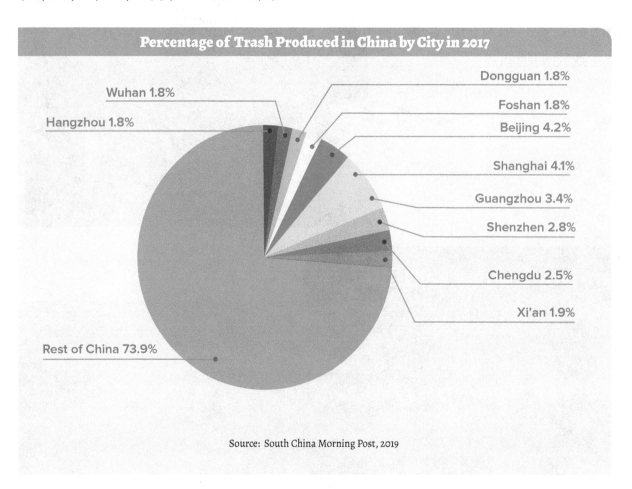

Percentage of Trash Produced in China by City in 2017

Dongguan 1.8%
Foshan 1.8%
Beijing 4.2%
Shanghai 4.1%
Guangzhou 3.4%
Shenzhen 2.8%
Chengdu 2.5%
Xi'an 1.9%
Wuhan 1.8%
Hangzhou 1.8%
Rest of China 73.9%

Source: South China Morning Post, 2019

Reducing Waste

In 2007, the government (政府, zhèngfǔ) of China issued a law to limit the use of plastic bags (塑料袋, sùliàodài). In 2020, further restrictions on the use of plastic (塑料, sùliào) were introduced, including a ban on non-degradable single-use plastic bags and utensils (餐具, cānjù). Today, city grocery stores are no longer allowed to give free plastic bags, and instead encourage buyers to use reusable bags. In addition, many apps and businesses that provide take-out food allow buyers to notify the restaurant about their needs and preferences for straws and utensils.

中国政府想让大家平常少用些什么东西？
你觉得在中国用塑料袋和塑料餐具的人会越来越多还是越来越少？

A man in the city of Shenzhen carrying take-out food in plastic bags. This photo was taken in 2018; with the recent plastic bag restrictions, this type of plastic bag will become less common.

A public trash can in Xi'an with bins for each of the four kinds of waste

Promoting Recycling

Beginning in 2019, several large cities in China have started using a new system for sorting and recycling trash. Under this new system, all waste would be sorted into four categories: general recyclables (可回收垃圾, kě huíshōu lājī), food waste (厨余垃圾, chúyú lājī), harmful waste (有害垃圾, yǒuhài lājī), and other (其他垃圾, qítā lājī). While some people welcome the change, others think it requires a lot of adjustment in how people go about their daily lives.

塑料饮料杯是哪种垃圾？

REFLECT ON THE ESSENTIAL QUESTION

How do we connect to and protect an environment?

1. What measures are in place in your community to encourage the recycling and reduction of waste?

2. What choices can you make to ensure that you are not creating unnecessary trash?

3. What methods could you use to remind yourself to recycle?

What influences you, and what you influence

1a Language Model · 语言范例 TARGET LANGUAGE INPUT

Your teacher will lead a discussion about the images below. Try to participate as much as you can. If there is anything you don't understand, let your teacher know.

Zhèr　de　lājī　duō　sǐ　le!

这儿 – 的 – 垃圾 – 多 – 死 – 了！

There's a ridiculous amount of trash here!

Shì　a,　zhè　xiē　lājī　yǒu　kěyǐ　huíshōu　de　ma?

是 – 啊，– 这 – 些 – 垃圾 – 有 – 可以 – 回收 – 的 – 吗？

There is; is any of the trash here recyclable?

Listen to the audio and try to understand as much as you can. Then read the dialogue, using the pinyin text and vocabulary list to figure out unfamiliar words.

 马丁，你最近怎么样？

Mǎdīng, nǐ zuìjìn zěnmeyàng?

 我们的作业多死了！我压力很大。

Wǒmen de zuòyè duō sǐ le! Wǒ yālì hěn dà.

 如果你觉得压力大，可以找我或者你朋友多聊聊呀。

Rúguǒ nǐ juéde yālì dà, kěyǐ zhǎo wǒ huòzhě nǐ péngyou duō liáo liáo ya.

 好吧……最近我有一个作业很难。老师问我们，住在北京的人越来越多了，这对北京有什么影响[1]？2050年的北京可能会有哪些变化？我们现在能做些什么？

Hǎo ba... Zuìjìn wǒ yǒu yí gè zuòyè hěn nán. Lǎoshī wèn wǒmen, zhù zài Běijīng de rén yuè lái yuè duō le, zhè duì Běijīng yǒu shénme yǐngxiǎng? Èrlíngwǔlíng nián de Běijīng kěnéng huì yǒu nǎxiē biànhuà? Wǒmen xiànzài néng zuò xiē shénme?

 这个作业听起来难，但是你可以把问题想得简单一点儿。比如，人越来越多了，大家扔的垃圾也越来越多了，对吧？

Zhège zuòyè tīng qǐlái nán, dànshì nǐ kěyǐ bǎ wèntí xiǎng de jiǎndān yidiǎnr. Bǐrú, rén yuè lái yuè duō le, dàjiā rēng de lājī yě yuè lái yuè duō le, duì ba?

 我知道了！如果大家不做好垃圾回收，那2050年的时候我们可能就看不到干净的北京了。我们现在扔垃圾的时候，应该看看哪些是可回收垃圾[2]，哪些是不可回收垃圾。

Wǒ zhīdào le! Rúguǒ dàjiā bú zuò hǎo lājī huíshōu, nà èrlíngwǔlíng nián de shíhou wǒmen kěnéng jiù kàn bú dào gānjìng de Běijīng le. Wǒmen xiànzài rēng lājī de shíhou, yīnggāi kàn kan nǎ xiē shì kě huíshōu lājī, nǎ xiē shì bù kě huíshōu lājī.

 你说得很对！好，那你快去做作业吧，我跟妈妈聊一会儿。

Nǐ shuō de hěn duì! Hǎo, nà nǐ kuài qù zuò zuòyè ba, wǒ gēn māma liáo yíhuìr.

Comprehension Check

		T	F
1	Martin says that he has a huge amount of homework and is under a lot of pressure.	○	○
2	Isabella recommends that Martin talk to his teachers if he needs help.	○	○
3	Isabella gives the example that with more people living in Beijing, there will be more trash getting thrown out.	○	○
4	What response does Martin come up with for his homework assignment?		

> **NOTE**
>
> 1 Just as "A 对 B 有兴趣" means "A is interested in B," the expression "A 对 B 有影响" means "A has an influence on B."
>
> 2 可回收垃圾 (kě huíshōu lājī) is a shortened way of saying 可以回收的垃圾. It means "recyclable trash." 不可回收垃圾 (bù kě huíshōu lājī), therefore, means "non-recyclable trash."

Vocabulary · 生词

Audio

	Word	Pinyin	Meaning
1	死	sǐ	to die; (word sometimes used in an exaggeration)
2	压力	yālì	pressure
3	呀	ya	(word added at the end of a sentence to add emphasis, excitement, or surprise)
4	影响	yǐngxiǎng	influence, effect; to influence, to affect, to have an impact
5	变化	biànhuà	change; to change
6	扔	rēng	to throw
7	垃圾	lājī	trash, garbage
8	回收	huíshōu	to recycle
9	干净	gānjìng	clean

Complete the exercises below to check your understanding of what you learned in Section 1. If you have questions, consult the Language Reference section.

Exercise 1 Use the words in the list on the left to complete each sentence. You will use each word more than once.

年
月
号

1 我们是在 2020 ____ 9 ____ 1 ____ 刚上高中的时候认识的。

2 我奶奶的生日是 10 ____ 30 ____。下个星期一是她六十五岁的生日。

3 你还记得 2022 ____ 8 ____ 15 ____ 那天你在哪儿吗？

4 2008 ____ 的夏天，北京举办了一场很成功的比赛活动。

Exercise 2 Revise each sentence below to exaggerate its meaning using the expression 死了. Write your answers on a separate piece of paper.

1 纽约的冬天很冷。

3 他觉得他的姐姐太吵了。

2 这个苹果特别酸。

4 我太高兴了。

Language Reference · 语言注解

1 Giving the date, including the year

Dates in Chinese are given with the largest unit of time listed first. If the year is included in the date, state that first, followed by the month, and then the day. The year's number should be followed by the word 年.

1 1962 年 10 月 27 号对他很重要，因为那一天是他十八岁的生日。

October 27, 1962 was a very important date to him because it was his 18th birthday.

In previous lessons, 号 has been used to give the exact date of an event. Another way to give the date is to use 日, as shown below. 日 is more commonly used when giving the date in writing and more formal settings.

2 1775 年 4 月 19 日是美国历史上非常重要的一天。

April 19, 1775 is a very important day in U.S. history.

3 2134 年 6 月 3 号是星期几？

On what day of the week will June 3, 2134 fall?

When talking about a particular year in Chinese, it is more common to pronounce each digit in the year than to read it out as a single number. So when talking about something that happened in 1923, you would read that date as 一九二三年, not as 一千九百二十三年. For years that include a zero, the zero (written as either 〇 or 零) should be read as líng; for example, 2008 is 二〇〇八年 (said: èrlínglíngbā nián).

2 Using 死了 to exaggerate

死了 (sǐ le) comes after a descriptive word to add extreme emphasis. A somewhat literal translation of the phrase would be "to (the point of) death," but 死了 (sǐ le) is typically used for exaggeration and not to reflect actual danger. 死了 (sǐ le) should be used by itself to add emphasis; additional methods of adding emphasis, such as 特别, 太, and 很, should not be used together with 死了 (sǐ le).

1 那只小狗可爱死了！
That little dog is so cute!

2 今天我累死了，我走路走了三个小时！
I'm exhausted today; I walked for three hours!

3 我们去吃饭吧，我饿死了！
Let's go eat — I'm starving!

What were some important years or dates in your classmates' lives?

Step 1: By yourself, think of some specific dates or years that have had a big influence on your life. Choose three that you feel comfortable sharing with the class.

Step 2: Get into pairs and discuss with your partner. Ask follow-up questions to learn more about how they were influenced by those times or what changes they made afterwards. Take notes to help remember your partner's answers.

Example: 你为什么觉得那一年／那一天对你的影响很大？

Step 3: When the teacher calls on you, be prepared to report your partner's most influential dates/years to the class. Pay attention as other students report on their partner's most influential dates/years. What kind of important life events did your classmates share? Were they more likely to share something about a momentous year, or did some important events take place on specific days?

Example: 很多人觉得刚上高中的那一年对他们的影响很大，因为在生活和学习上都有很多变化，很多人觉得自己得快点儿长大了……

COMMUNITIES

CULTURES
COMMUNICATION
COMPARISONS
CONNECTIONS

In China, some people collect recyclable trash to make a living or to earn extra money. They might gather items that others have littered, or they might gather recyclables at their offices or apartments. Then they sell what they have collected to recycling centers, which in turn resell those materials. For example, a recycling center might resell used newspapers to a company that makes paper goods.

Can recycling be used as a way to make money in your community?

A man in Beijing gathering recyclables

Protecting the environment

2a Language Model · 语言范例 TARGET LANGUAGE INPUT

Your teacher will lead a discussion about the image below. Try to participate as much as you can. If there is anything you don't understand, let your teacher know.

Wǒmen xiàwǔ yào zài gōngyuán jǔbàn huódòng,
我们－下午－要－在－公园－举办－活动，

This afternoon, we're holding an event at the park.

xūyào de dōngxi dōu zhǔnbèi hǎo le ma?
需要－的－东西－都－准备－好－了－吗？

Have we prepared everything we need?

Audio

Listen to the audio and try to understand as much as you can. Then read the passage, using the pinyin text and vocabulary list to figure out unfamiliar words.

你想过吗？我们的生活习惯会影响环境，环境也会影响我们的生活。最近几十年，气候变化、资源污染的问题越来越多。你知道吗？现在差不多有百分之二十九[1] 的人喝不到干净的水。如果我们不保护水资源，就会有越来越多的人喝不到干净的水。所以我们一定要保护好环境，保护好水资源。我觉得防止资源污染是我们每个人都应该做的事，环保[2] 也需要每一个人的努力。

Nǐ xiǎng guò ma? Wǒmen de shēnghuó xíguàn huì yǐngxiǎng huánjìng, huánjìng yě huì yǐngxiǎng wǒmen de shēnghuó. Zuìjìn jǐshí nián, qìhòu biànhuà, zīyuán wūrǎn de wèntí yuè lái yuè duō. Nǐ zhīdào ma? Xiànzài chàbùduō yǒu bǎi fēn zhī èrshíjiǔ de rén hē bú dào gānjìng de shuǐ. Rúguǒ wǒmen bù bǎohù shuǐ zīyuán, jiù huì yǒu yuè lái yuè duō de rén hē bú dào gānjìng de shuǐ. Suǒyǐ wǒmen yídìng yào bǎohù hǎo huánjìng, bǎohù hǎo shuǐ zīyuán. Wǒ juéde fángzhǐ zīyuán wūrǎn shì wǒmen měi gè rén dōu yīnggāi zuò de shì, huánbǎo yě xūyào měi yí gè rén de nǔlì.

Comprehension Check

                                                                     T   F

1 According to Martin, our life habits can influence the environment. ○ ○

2 In the final phrase, Martin states that people who help protect the environment are all hard workers. ○ ○

3 What specific problem does Martin mention? Is that a problem where you live?

NOTE

1 百分之 (bǎi fēn zhī) literally means "100 divided into ___" or "___ out of 100." So when giving a percentage in Chinese, the number comes after 百分之 . For example, 40% would be expressed as 百分之四十 .

2 环保 (huán bǎo) is an abbreviation for 环境保护 (huánjìng bǎohù), meaning protecting the environment or environmental protection.

Audio

	Word	Pinyin	Meaning
10	环境	huánjìng	environment, surroundings
11	气候	qìhòu	climate
12	资源	zīyuán	natural resource
13	污染	wūrǎn	pollution, contamination; to pollute, to contaminate
14	百分之	bǎi fēn zhī	percent
15	保护	bǎohù	to protect, to safeguard
16	防止	fángzhǐ	to prevent, to guard against
17	需要	xūyào	to need, to require; requirement, needs

2c Puzzle It Out · 动动脑 PROGRESS CHECK

Complete the exercise below to check your understanding of what you learned in Section 2. If you have questions, consult the Language Reference section.

Complete the sentences by adding 要 or 需要 . Write your answers on a separate piece of paper.

我下午 1.＿＿＿ 跟朋友去打篮球，可是我找不到我的篮球了。我问妈妈："我现在很 2.＿＿＿ 一个新的篮球，你能帮我买一个吗？"妈妈说："我今天比较忙。你有什么 3.＿＿＿，去找你爸爸吧。"可是爸爸说："你最好再找找。你不能一找不到东西就要新的。"这个时候，我朋友打电话给我，他说："你的篮球怎么在我的包里？下午见面的时候我带给你。"太好了，现在我不 4.＿＿＿ 买新篮球了。

Language Reference • 语言注解

3 要 and 需要

Two common ways to express needing something in Chinese are 需要 (xūyào) and 要. Generally speaking, 要 is less formal than 需要 (xūyào). Using 需要 (xūyào) puts the focus on what is needed or required. By contrast, using 要 focuses on the person and what he or she needs to do. In addition, due to the multiple meanings of 要, sentences with 要 can often be interpreted in a few different but related ways, as the following examples show. Despite the differences between 需要 (xūyào) and 要, there are many cases in which either word can be used with only a slight change in the meaning.

1a 你需要休息一下吗？
Do you need to rest?/
Is it necessary for you to rest for a bit?

1b 你要休息一下吗？
Do you want to rest?/
Do you need to rest?

2a 你需要去看医生吗？
Do you need to go see the doctor?/
Is seeing the doctor a need that you have?

2b 你要去看医生吗？
Do you need to go see the doctor?/
Are you going to go see the doctor?/
Do you want to go see the doctor?

3a 你需要的是这本书还是那本书？
Is the book you need this one, or is it that one?

3b 你要的是这本书还是那本书？
Do you need/want this book or that book?

Although these words are sometimes interchangeable, there are also situations in which only 要 or only 需要 (xūyào) can be used: Only 要 can be used in sentences expressing "to want (something, or to do something)," or "to be going to (do something);" only 需要 (xūyào) can be used after descriptive words like 很, 特别 and 非常; and only 需要 (xūyào) can be used as a noun.

4 我们俱乐部现在非常需要一个懂音乐的学生。
Our club really needs someone now who understands music.

5 每个人都有自己的需要。
Everyone has his/her own needs.

Additionally, when expressing that something does not need to be done, only 不需要 (xūyào) can be used. 不要 means "to not want (something)" and is also used as a command when telling someone not to do something.

6 我们的钱已经够了，不^{xūyào}需要赚更多的钱了。

We already have enough money; we don't need to earn more.

7 你不要吃我的饺子！

Don't eat my dumplings!

What a Character!

fù 阝

1 阝   2 阝

The word 防止 (fángzhǐ) contains the component 阝 (fù). When 阝 appears on the left side of a character, this component comes from the character 阜 (fù), meaning "mound, hill." Words with the 阝 (fù) component on the left often relate to hills, barriers, raised platforms, or stairs.

Each of the Chinese characters below contains the 阝 (fù) component on the left and has a definition provided. Can you think of a connection between the meaning of the 阝 (fù) component and the meaning of the character?

1 防 (fáng)
  to protect, to defend, to prevent

2 际 (jì)
  border, edge, boundary

3 院 (yuàn)
  courtyard

2d Using the Language · 语言应用 INTERPERSONAL

What does the class think about environmental protection?

Step 1: Your teacher will divide the class into small groups. Work with your group to decide on one statement relating to environmental protection that you want to hear your classmates' opinions on.

Example: 保护环境需要每一个人的努力。

Step 2: Your teacher will label three corners of the classroom with 同意, 不同意, and 不确定. Within your group, try to predict what percentage of the class will choose each option in response to your statement.

Example: 我觉得可能有百分之八十的人同意……，有百分之十的人不同意……，有百分之十的人不确定……

Step 3: One person from your group will read your statement aloud to the entire class and ask if everyone agrees with it or not. After hearing your statement, all of the students will go to the corners that correspond to their answers. Pay close attention to how everyone responds: Did you successfully predict the percentage of students who agreed, disagreed, or were uncertain?

Step 4: Discuss the reasons for your choice with your classmates in the same corner. One person from each corner will give a summary explaining the reasons for that choice to the rest of the class.

Consider the summaries from each corner in response to your statement. If the percentages you guessed in Step 2 were very wrong, did listening to the summaries help you understand why your classmates' responses were different from what you expected?

A young woman in Zhongshan City doing an activity to test her understanding of how to correctly sort garbage

Discussing data

3a Language Model · 语言范例   TARGET LANGUAGE INPUT

Your teacher will lead a discussion about the image below. Try to participate as much as you can. If there is anything you don't understand, let your teacher know.

Zhège   tí   de   dá'àn   shì   liù   wàn   ma?
这个 — 题 — 的 — 答案 — 是 — 六 — 万 — 吗？

Is the answer to this question sixty thousand?

Bú   duì.   Nǐ   zuìhǎo   zài   kàn   yíxià   nǎr
不 — 对。 — 你 — 最好 — 再 — 看 — 一下 — 哪儿

zuò   cuò   le.
做 — 错 — 了。

No; you had better look again to see where you made a mistake.

Listen to the audio and try to understand as much as you can. Then read the dialogue, using the pinyin text and vocabulary list to figure out unfamiliar words.

里奥，已经四点一刻了，篮球比赛马上就要开始了，我怎么没看见你呀？

Lǐ'ào, yǐjīng sì diǎn yí kè le, lánqiú bǐsài mǎshàng jiù yào kāishǐ le, wǒ zěnme méi kàn jiàn nǐ ya?

我不能去看比赛了。我数学课的数据分析作业还没做完。要是我今天分析不完，明天上课的时候就不能参加讨论了。可是，三十万条数据，多死了……我怎么分析啊？

Wǒ bù néng qù kàn bǐsài le. Wǒ shùxué kè de shùjù fēnxī zuòyè hái méi zuò wán. Yàoshi wǒ jīntiān fēnxī bù wán, míngtiān shàng kè de shíhou jiù bù néng cānjiā tǎolùn le. Kěshì, sānshí wàn tiáo shùjù, duō sǐ le... Wǒ zěnme fēnxī a?

里奥，你看错了！老师让我们分析三万条数据，不是三十万条。而且，网上有一些关于数据分析的课，你可以看看。

Lǐ'ào, nǐ kàn cuò le! Lǎoshī ràng wǒmen fēnxī sān wàn tiáo shùjù, bú shì sānshí wàn tiáo. Érqiě, wǎng shàng yǒu yì xiē guānyú shùjù fēnxī de kè, nǐ kěyǐ kàn kan.

哈哈，太好了！只有三万条数据啊！那你等我一下，我现在去篮球馆，晚上再做作业。

Hāha, tài hǎo le! Zhǐ yǒu sān wàn tiáo shùjù a! Nà nǐ děng wǒ yíxià, wǒ xiànzài qù lánqiú guǎn, wǎnshàng zài zuò zuòyè.

Comprehension Check

T   F

1 At first, Maya wondered why she didn't see Leo at the competition. ○ ○

2 Leo needs to analyze data so he can participate in a class discussion tomorrow. ○ ○

3 Maya told Leo that the math teacher asked them to analyze 350,000,000 pieces of data. ○ ○

4 What was Maya's suggestion to Leo?

	Word	Pinyin	Meaning
18	一刻	yí kè	fifteen minutes, a quarter of an hour
19	数据	shùjù	data
20	分析	fēnxī	to analyze; analysis
21	参加	cānjiā	to participate in, to take part in, to join
22	讨论	tǎolùn	to discuss
23	万	wàn	ten thousand
24	关于	guānyú	about, in regard to
25	哈哈	hāha	ha ha

5Cs CONNECTIONS

COMMUNITIES
COMMUNICATION
COMPARISONS
CULTURES

Chinese words for units of time have evolved throughout history, reflecting both ancient Chinese methods of measuring time and cultural exchange with Western countries. Thousands of years ago, Chinese people used water clocks to tell the time. A common type of water clock consisted of a series of basins with draining spouts, and a measuring rod in the final basin to track the water level over time. Each measurement line on the rod was one 刻. One full day and night was 100 刻 or 12 时辰 (shíchen).

Late in the Ming dynasty (1368–1664 CE), Western clocks were introduced to China. Since the Western method of calculating time measured a full day and night in 24 hours, Chinese people referred to these smaller units of time as 小时. The Chinese word for "hour" still includes the word "small" even though the larger 时辰 are no longer used in daily speech.

Around the same time, the measurement of a 刻 was changed so that one full day and night was 96 刻, making 1 刻 equal 15 minutes. This is why today, 15 minutes can also be referred to as 一刻 when telling the time.

Ancient Chinese people also used sundials like the one below. The 12 时辰 are in the middle ring. Why might they have used water clocks in addition to sundials to tell time?

3c Puzzle It Out · 动动脑 PROGRESS CHECK

Complete the exercises below to check your understanding of what you learned in Section 3. If you have questions, consult the Language Reference section.

Exercise 1 Choose the option from the list on the left that best completes each sentence. You may use some options more than once.

听见
看见
听错
看错

1 A: 你刚才 _____ 服务员说我的凉皮做好了吗?

 B: 没有啊, 我没 _____。你可能 _____ 了。刚才服务员说, 有一碗炒凉皮做好了。

2 A: 我没 _____ 吧? 那个在舞台上跳街舞的人是我们的中文老师!

 B: 你没 _____, 他就是我们的中文老师。我昨天还 _____ 他在教室里练习跳街舞了。

Exercise 2 On a separate piece of paper, use Chinese characters to write the underlined numbers.

1 那本书今年卖了 10,000 本!

2 有 25,000 人去看了她们的演唱会。

3 在 2020 年的时候, 西安差不多有 13,000,000 人。

Language Reference · 语言注解

4 Describing actions with certain results

In *Go Far with Chinese* 2, examples were given of how 完, 到, 懂, 好, 清楚, and 会 can be paired with verbs to describe the result of an action. Other words that can be used this way include 见, 对, and 错. In the example sentences that follow, the verbs that these words are paired with are highlighted in gray.

When showing the result of an action, 见 is most often paired with 看 or 听, indicating that the information from seeing or listening has been successfully received. 听见 and 看见 can usually be replaced with 听到 and 看到 without changing the meaning.

1 昨天我在电视上看见了一个又帅又特别有个性的人。

Yesterday, I saw on TV a person who was both handsome and had a lot of personality.

2 老师说的话我没听见。

I didn't hear what the teacher said.

对 and 错 are paired with a verb to indicate whether the result of an action is correct or incorrect.

3 这个字我写对了吗？

Did I write this character correctly?

4 你刚才说的话我听错了！

I misheard what you just said!

5 这些题他都做错了。

He did all of these (homework) problems incorrectly.

5 Numbers from ten thousand to ten million

In English, we count things in tens, hundreds, thousands, and millions. Chinese is a bit different: like English, it also counts in tens (十), hundreds (百), and thousands (千), but the next level of counting for Chinese is tens of thousands (万, wàn). This means that for quantities ten thousand and up, the numbers will look different in Chinese and English. Below is a table to help get a sense of this. The "Representation of Chinese Numeral" column indicates how the digits might be divided up in the mind of a Chinese-speaker, not how the number would actually appear in writing.

Chinese	Representation of Chinese Numeral	Numeral	English
一万 (wàn)	1 | 0000	10,000	ten thousand
十万 (wàn)	10 | 0000	100,000	one hundred thousand
一百万 (wàn)	100 | 0000	1,000,000	one million
一千万 (wàn)	1000 | 0000	10,000,000	ten million
三万五千 (wàn)	3 | 5000	35,000	thirty-five thousand
八千六百万 (wàn)	8600 | 0000	86,000,000	eighty-six million

3d · Using the Language · 语言应用 INTERPERSONAL

How might a change in the population size of a place influence other things?

Step 1: As a class, look up data on how many people there are in your city or town this year and how many people there were fifty years ago. (Town = 镇 zhèn)

Example: 我们城市现在有多少人，五十年以前有多少人？

Step 2: Analyze the data to see how many more or fewer people there are this year than there were fifty years ago. What is the percent change in the number of people?

现在比五十年以前多 / 少了多少人？多 / 少了百分之多少？

Step 3: Do you think the change in the number of people has influenced any aspects of life in your town? If so, what kinds of changes have occurred? If the number of people continues to increase or decrease, what else do you think that might affect? In groups, discuss these questions.

讨论一下，这些变化有什么影响？

LANGUAGE CHALLENGE

Numbers are often used in ways that are not literal. Below are a few sentences that include expressions with 千 and 万 in them. Based on the context and other characters you may know, can you guess what these expressions mean?

1 走过千山万水，我最爱我的老家。

2 他们的表演千变万化，太好看了！

3 我父母千辛万苦把我送到这儿上学，所以我一定要努力学习。

Bonus: Can you create your own sentence that includes one of the expressions shown here?

Put the Pieces Together! • 融会贯通

Audio

A **Listening and Reading • 阅读和听力** INTERPRETIVE

Passage 1 What's next for Martin and his friends? Read on...

 你们暑假过得怎么样啊？

 还不错！我看了几本书，还预习了一下高三要学的东西。

 你暑假的时候还跟我一起学跳舞了。

 是啊，哈哈！你们呢？

 北京的夏天热死了，所以我去附近的山里玩儿了几天。

 我也在老家的山里住了很多天。我还帮爷爷奶奶采了很多茶叶。

 我暑假一直在城市里，还参加了一个大学举办的活动。

 什么活动啊？

 是关于环境保护的。我们讨论了很多问题，比如气候变化、环境污染、资源保护等等。

 你是在哪个城市参加那个活动的呀？

 就在北京。

那有大学里的老师给你们上课吗？

 有。除了上课以外，我们还需要自己选一个关于环境保护的问题，然后去分析一下。

 那你选的是什么问题？

 我选的是关于水资源的问题。我在网上找了一些数据，分析了一下。你们知道吗？2040 年的时候，中国的水资源压力会很大。

 这个问题的影响很大！我爷爷以前经常告诉我，茶树每个星期都要"喝"一两次水。我有一个姨妈，她家有一个苹果园。我记得有一年好几个星期没有下雨，我爷爷和我姨妈那个时候的压力都特别大。

 是吗？那防止水资源污染对他们也很重要。

 你们说的这些问题，我好像从来没有想过……对了，梅雅，你还会分析数据啊？太厉害了！

 其实开始的时候，在参加活动的学生里，有 90% 的人都不会分析数据。后来我们都觉得，数据分析听起来难，其实学起来不太难。

 那参加这个活动真的能学到很多东西。

 是啊。要是你们都对这个活动有兴趣，明年暑假可以一起参加。

 我也有兴趣！

 我其实没有太大兴趣。环境问题那么大，我们学生能做些什么呢？

 一个人只能做一点儿保护环境的小事，但是一百个人、一千个人、一万个人能做的会很多。

 如果大家一起努力，环境问题就一定会越来越少。

 你们说得对！梅雅，这个饮料杯是可回收垃圾吗？

 干净的饮料杯可以回收。

 好，那我先不扔了。

 对了，不知道春月、大文和雪儿现在在上海怎么样？

 他们在上海的生活一定很丰富吧？

 你说对了，特别丰富！春月每天都非常忙，只找我聊过一次天儿……她上个周末去雪儿家跟大文他们吃饭了，还认识了雪儿的哥哥。

 雪儿还有哥哥啊？

 我说错了，是表哥。

 对了，我听说上海挺好玩儿的。你们想去上海找他们玩儿吗？

 想是想，可是去上海玩儿太贵了，我们没有那么多钱啊。

 那我们再举办一场才艺秀吧？

 这个主意不错，但是我们今年春天刚举办过才艺秀……如果再举办一场，大家应该都没有兴趣了吧？

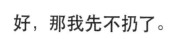 是啊……那我们应该怎么办呢？

Comprehension Check

		T	F
1	Summer is too hot in Beijing, so Keke spent the summer in Shanghai instead.	◯	◯
2	Over the summer, Maya studied and analyzed an environmental problem.	◯	◯
3	Tianhao's aunt, who has an apple orchard, felt a lot of pressure one year because it rained too much.	◯	◯
4	Although everyone thinks environmental protection is important, no one wants to spend next summer learning more about it.	◯	◯
5	Isabella seems to be enjoying her life in Shanghai.	◯	◯

6 At first, Keke wasn't very interested in participating in environmental protection activities. Why? What did Martin and Tianhao say that convinced her otherwise?

Passage 2 This image shows a sign that was placed near the shoreline of Lake Poyang, which can be seen in the distance. The water has receded in recent years due to drought. If 微笑 (wēixiào) means "smile," can you figure out the meaning of the sentence in white?

Passage 3 Listen to a school announcement. Answer the questions on a separate piece of paper.

1 What is the subject of the announcement?

   (a) a talent show at the school to raise money for environmental issues

   (b) a environmental protection campaign in the school

   (c) a dance at the school with the theme of environmental protection

2 What topics are mentioned in the announcement?

   (a) talent show performances, including singing, dancing, and playing an instrument

   (b) environmental problems, such as climate change, environmental pollution, trash, and recycling

   (c) when the dance will be held

3 If you want to participate in the activity, what do you need to do?

   (a) find a partner for the project

   (b) register with the club

   (c) buy tickets

Passage 4 Listen to the conversation and answer the questions that follow.

1 If the girl plans to make a poster for her project, which image would work the best?

2 Summarize the conversation in Chinese. Do you think the problem being discussed is a big problem? Why or why not?

B Speaking · 口语 INTERPERSONAL

Are students at your school good about recycling?

Step 1: The teacher will assign each student or a pair of students to a classroom or other location in the school. During lunchtime or after class, go to the place you were assigned and look at the waste bins there. Take notes on your findings, considering the following:

- Does the space have a place for both recyclables and non-recyclables?
- Roughly what percentages of the trash in that space are recyclable and non-recyclable?
- Did you notice any trash that was thrown away incorrectly? (That is, non-recyclable trash in the place for recyclable trash, or vice versa.)
- Did you notice any other problems with the trash/recyclables in that space?

Step 2: In class, ask your classmates the following questions and gather their answers.

- 你们去的那个地方的垃圾多吗?
- 那儿的垃圾有百分之多少是可回收的?
- 你在那儿看到了哪些问题? (比如:把垃圾扔错地方了,把不可回收垃圾扔在了放可回收垃圾的地方,或者把可回收垃圾扔在了放不可回收垃圾的地方;有很多东西其实还可以用,可是有人把它扔了,等等。)

Step 3: In groups, choose one of the problems that came up in the survey. This will be the focus of your group's poster. With your group mates, brainstorm what could be done differently to try to solve this problem.

C Final Project · 结课项目 PRESENTATIONAL

Improving Waste Management

Work in a group to create a poster to report your findings from the school waste research you did in the previous activity.

Step 1: As a group, choose one of the problems that came up in several spaces. On the poster, create a simple graph or chart to show what percentage of the spaces had that problem, as well as any other data from the survey that you think is important to include.

Step 2: On the poster, write a short paragraph describing the problem your group has chosen to focus on. Write one or two sentences about what students could do or what the school could do differently to fix this problem.

Step 3: As a group, come up with a slogan to encourage students to recycle more and dispose of their trash properly. Use this as the title of your poster.

Step 4: Present your poster in the class. Then, as a class, complete your posters with English translations and put up your posters around campus to generate more awareness about waste management at school.

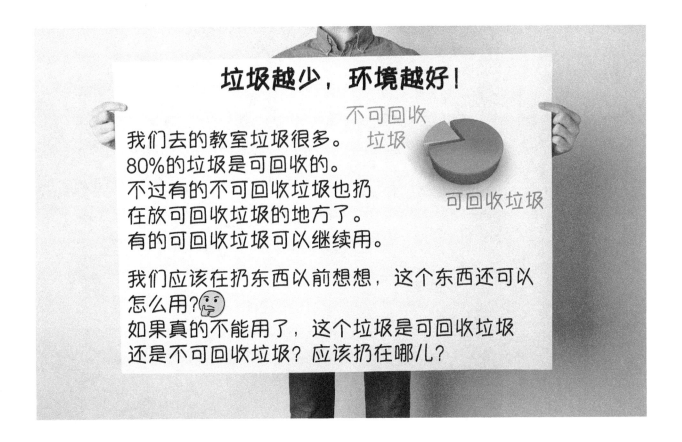

Can-Do Goals · 能力目标

Talk with your teacher if you have questions or if you are not certain you can do the following tasks:

- Understand one way of expressing exaggeration

- State an exact date, including the year

- Discuss some environmental problems

- Use percentages to support your argument

- Talk about needing or wanting to do something

- Describe efforts in China to encourage recycling and to discourage the use of plastic

Cultural Knowledge · 文化知识

What are some things that Chinese people are doing to keep their environment clean?

Bins for different types of trash in Beijing, China

An Environmental Protection Competition

大家参加完中文俱乐部这个学期
的第一次聚会以后……

马丁：对了，王老师刚才说，最近
　　　学校在宣传一个关于环境
　　　保护的比赛。

可可：是啊，那我们快去找一下
　　　那个宣传吧！

天浩：你们都想参加那个比赛吗？

梅雅：对，我也想参加！天浩，
　　　你不想参加吗？

天浩：我也觉得环境保护很重要，
　　　可是不一定要参加比赛吧？

梅雅：走吧，走吧，先去看看再说。

天浩：好吧……

Can-Do Goals · 能力目标

In this chapter, you will learn to:

- Analyze how local climate affects environmental issues in a region
- Talk about and understand when others discuss ongoing actions
- Express "how is (something) so...?"
- Talk about how long it's been since something has been done
- Explain the goal of or motive for an action

běifāng   hé   nánfāng   de   shuǐ   zīyuán   qíngkuàng

北方和南方的水资源情况

Water Resources in the North and South of China

Like many large countries, China has distinct climate issues in different regions. Water is a prime example of this: it is more plentiful in the country's south (南方, nánfāng) than its north (北方, běifāng). As a result, the two regions face different environmental issues related to water management.

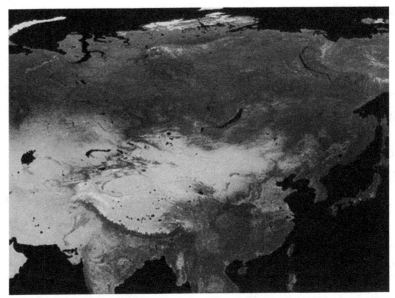

This satellite image taken by NASA in June 2021 shows vast expanses of dry area in the north of China.

在中国，北方的水资源更丰富还是南方的水资源更丰富？

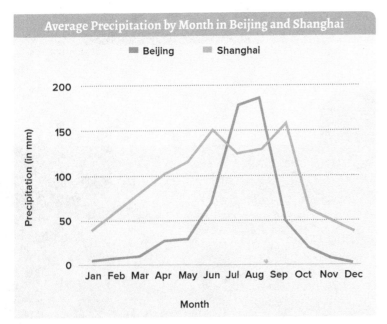

Average Precipitation by Month in Beijing and Shanghai

■ Beijing   ■ Shanghai

Precipitation (in mm)

Month

Source: World Meteorological Organization, 2021

By the Numbers

Different cities in China receive different amounts of precipitation. Northern cities typically get less rain than southern cities, as seen in the case of Beijing and Shanghai.

在上海，哪几个月下雨下得最多？哪几个月下得最少？北京呢？

Desertification in the North

Broad areas of northwest and northeast China have been experiencing desertification (沙漠化, shāmò huà), the process by which a desert expands. Decades of reduced rainfall coupled with the overuse of water resources through increased grazing, agriculture, and urban development have resulted in the expansion of desert areas. The resulting sandstorms affect even distant parts of the country.

什么是沙漠化？

A sandstorm in Beijing, one effect of desertification

Flooding in the South

Floods (洪水, hóngshuǐ) along both the Yellow River (黄河, Huáng Hé) in the north and the Yangtze River (长江, Cháng Jiāng) in the south have been part of China's legends and history for thousands of years. Today, however, flooding along the Yangtze and its tributaries is posing the more destructive problem. During extended periods of heavy rain, the dams built for flood control can be overwhelmed, resulting in catastrophic damage.

最近这些年，黄河附近的洪水更多还是长江附近的洪水更多？

Flooding in Jiujiang, a city in the southern province of Jiangxi

Trees to the Rescue

To combat both flooding in the south and desertification in the north, the Chinese government has planted (种, zhòng) billions of trees in key areas. The Green Great Wall (绿色长城, Lùsè Chángchéng) is a part of this effort. This tree planting project, which started in 1978 and is planned to continue until 2050, has already helped stabilize and rehabilitate many arid regions at risk of desertification.

什么是绿色长城？

REFLECT ON THE ESSENTIAL QUESTION

How do we connect to and protect an environment?

1. What role does water play in your community and environment?

2. Are any resources overly abundant or scarce in your region? What does your community do to manage these resources?

3. Is your region prone to certain kinds of weather events or natural disasters? How does your community prepare?

How are you so... ?

1a Language Model · 语言范例 TARGET LANGUAGE INPUT

Your teacher will lead a discussion about the image below. Try to participate as much as you can. If there is anything you don't understand, let your teacher know.

Kàn, xiànzài wǒ mèimei tāmen zhèngzài zuò hǎibào.
看，-现在-我-妹妹-她们-正在-做-海报。

Look, my younger sister and the others are making a poster right now.

Tāmen zěnme zhème nǔlì?
她们-怎么-这么-努力？

How are they so hardworking?

Audio

Listen to the audio and try to understand as much as you can. Then read the dialogue, using the pinyin text and vocabulary list to figure out unfamiliar words.

喂！马丁，我和梅雅正在练吉他。你想跟我们一起练吗？

Wéi! Mǎdīng, wǒ hé Méiyǎ zhèngzài liàn jíta. Nǐ xiǎng gēn wǒmen yìqǐ liàn ma?

天浩，你们练吧。我现在不太方便跟你讲话……

Tiānhào, nǐmen liàn ba. Wǒ xiànzài bú tài fāngbiàn gēn nǐ jiǎng huà....

怎么了？你这句话是什么意思啊？

Zěnme le? Nǐ zhè jù huà shì shénme yìsi a?

我先不跟你说了。我等一会儿再给你打电话。再见！

Wǒ xiān bù gēn nǐ shuō le. Wǒ děng yíhuìr zài gěi nǐ dǎ diànhuà. Zàijiàn!

梅雅，马丁把电话挂了……他最近对我怎么这么奇怪？

Méiyǎ, Mǎdīng bǎ diànhuà guà le... Tā zuìjìn duì wǒ zěnme zhème qíguài?

怎么了？你跟我讲讲吧，我比较了解他。

Zěnme le? Nǐ gēn wǒ jiǎng jiǎng ba, wǒ bǐjiào liǎojiě tā.

他最近好像不太愿意跟我讲话。我刚才给他打电话，他说他不能跟我讲话，不知道他是什么意思。

Tā zuìjìn hǎoxiàng bú tài yuànyì gēn wǒ jiǎng huà. Wǒ gāngcái gěi tā dǎ diànhuà, tā shuō tā bù néng gēn wǒ jiǎng huà, bù zhīdào tā shì shénme yìsi.

对了，他现在应该在图书馆里做海报！他说下个星期三以前得把海报做完。我怎么忘了……

Duì le, tā xiànzài yīnggāi zài túshūguǎn lǐ zuò hǎibào! Tā shuō xià gè xīngqīsān yǐqián děi bǎ hǎibào zuò wán. Wǒ zěnme wàng le...

这样啊！我知道了。那我等他给我打电话吧。

Zhèyàng a! Wǒ zhīdào le. Nà wǒ děng tā gěi wǒ dǎ diànhuà ba.

Comprehension Check

T   F

1 Martin and Tianhao had a long phone conversation. ⭘ ⭘

2 Maya says Tianhao knows Martin better than she does. ⭘ ⭘

3 What is Martin probably doing right now?

Audio

Vocabulary · 生词

	Word	Pinyin	Meaning
1	正在	zhèngzài	(word that shows an action is ongoing or in process)
2	讲	jiǎng	to speak, to say, to tell; to explain
3	句	jù	sentence; (measure word for speech)
4	意思	yìsi	meaning
5	这么	zhème	so, such, like this
6	了解	liǎojiě	to understand, to know someone well, to find out; understanding
7	愿意	yuànyì	to be willing, to want, to wish
8	图书馆	túshūguǎn	library
9	海报	hǎibào	poster

COMMUNITIES

CULTURES
COMMUNICATION
COMPARISONS
CONNECTIONS

Did you know that many libraries have Chinese language books or bilingual English-Chinese books? Ask your local or school librarians if they provide any Chinese language books. If they don't, put in a request. Libraries often purchase books based on the interests of the community. Ask your teacher for book suggestions!

A library in Nanchang, Jiangxi Province

Complete the exercises below to check your understanding of what you learned in Section 1. If you have questions, consult the Language Reference section.

Exercise 1 Read the Chinese sentences, then choose the best English translation.

1 今天的天气怎么这么热？

(a) Is it hot today?

(b) How is it so hot today?

2 图书馆里的书怎么那么丰富？

(a) How does the library have so many books?

(b) How does the library have so many big books?

3 你的海报怎么做得这么好？

(a) How did you make this poster?

(b) How is your poster so good?

Exercise 2 Rearrange the Chinese words and phrases in each row to translate the English sentences.

1 她们 ｜ 正在 ｜ 海报。｜ 做 ｜ 中文

They are making Chinese posters right now.

2 你们 ｜ 什么？｜ 做 ｜ 正在

What are you doing right now?

3 正在 ｜ 老师 ｜ 的意思。｜ 讲 ｜ 这句话

The teacher is explaining the meaning of this sentence right now.

Language Reference · 语言注解

1 Talking about an ongoing action

The word 正在 (zhèngzài) can be used before a verb to express that an action is ongoing, or that it was ongoing at the time something else happened. It is similar to 在 but more strongly emphasizes that the action is taking place right at this moment. In addition, 正在 (zhèngzài) can be more formal. 正在 (zhèngzài) is used with actions that last for some time, such as 举办 or 讲话, and not with actions that take very little time, such as 起床, 开始, or 进去.

túshūguǎn   zhèngzài

1 图书馆正在举办一个活动，我们不能进去。

The library is hosting an event right now; we can't go in.

2

zhèngzài jiǎng

老师正在讲话。我们先听他说完，一会儿再问问题。

The teacher is talking right now. Let's listen to him finish speaking first, then ask questions.

2 Asking "How come (something) is so...?

In both Chinese and English, it is common to ask questions as a way to emphasize feelings or opinions — that is, the speaker is not asking the question to gather information. An example might be, "How can your cat be so cute?" or "How cute is your cat?!" The phrase 怎么这么 (zhème)/ 那么 can be used to express this meaning in Chinese: 你的猫怎么那么可爱？This phrase is used after the subject in the sentence and before the descriptive word.

zhème

1 这儿的天气怎么这么冷?

Why is the weather so cold here?

túshūguǎn

2 你们学校的图书馆怎么那么大啊?

How is your school's library so big?

When the phrase 怎么这么 (zhème)/ 那么 is used to describe an action, the verb + 得 comes between 怎么 and 这么 (zhème) / 那么.

zhème

3 你今天怎么来得这么早?

How did you get here so early today?

1d Using the Language · 语言应用 INTERPERSONAL/PRESENTATIONAL

Activity 1 Play a game of charades with your classmates! For this game, your teacher will divide your class into teams.

Step 1: On a small piece of paper, write a sentence using 正在 that you think you could act out. Your teacher will collect the piece of paper and put it in a hat, bowl, or other container. Your teacher will also add a few of his or her own pieces of paper!

Example:

我正在拍视频。

Step 2: One team at a time will send a representative to be the actor. The actor will draw a piece of paper from the hat and act out what it says. Students from either team can guess, but if a student from the actor's same team guesses correctly, that team earns double points!

Activity 2 In this game, you will try to give the best response to a classmate's statement.

Step 1: Your teacher will put you into groups and give each group two sets of cards: statements and responses.

Step 2: Each person in your group will draw four response cards. Read them to yourself, and don't let your groupmates see them.

Step 3: Take turns pulling one statement card at a time from the pile. When it is your turn, pull a statement card and read it aloud, then put it face up on the table. Your groupmates will each choose a response card from their hands, read the card, and then lay it face up on the table. You must choose the response you think is best. The student who offered that response earns one point. Then mix the response cards back into the pile.

Step 4: All the students who played a response card must take a new response card from the pile and add it to their hand. (That way, students always have four response cards in their hands.) The student whose turn is next will draw a statement card to begin another round. Keep playing until all the statement cards have been used, or until your teacher calls time. The student who earns the most points wins the game.

LANGUAGE CHALLENGE

The word 意思 (yìsi) means "meaning," and we know that 有意思 means "interesting, fun." Based on the context in the dialogue below, can you guess the meaning of other commonly used words and phrases containing 意思? Try to match each word or phrase listed on the left to its meaning listed on the right!

A: 不好意思，我来晚了。祝你生日快乐！这是我的一点儿小意思。

B: 这个礼物太棒了！我很喜欢！你真够意思！

1. 小意思

2. 不好意思

3. 够意思

a kind, generous, great

b sorry, excuse me; to feel embarrassed, shy

c small gift, small token; nothing important

Saving water and electricity

2a Language Model · 语言范例 TARGET LANGUAGE INPUT

Your teacher will lead a discussion about the images below. Try to participate as much as you can. If there is anything you don't understand, let your teacher know.

Wǒ	hǎojǐ	gè	xīngqī	méi	guān	diànnǎo	le.	Nǐ	ne?
我	好几	个	星期	没	关	电脑	了。	你	呢?

I haven't turned my computer off for several weeks. How about you?

Nǐ	duō	cháng	shíjiān	méi	guān	diànnǎo	le?
你	多	长	时间	没	关	电脑	了?

How long has it been since you turned off your computer?

diànnǎo
电脑
computer

dēng
灯
light, lamp

水
water

2b New Words in Context · 语境中学新词 INTERPRETIVE

Listen to the audio and try to understand as much as you can. Then read the passage, using the pinyin text and vocabulary list to figure out unfamiliar words.

 很多人平常会有一些不太环保的生活习惯。比如：有的人一直不关电脑，有的人不用灯的时候还开着灯。我的邻居已经好几天没回家了，可是他家的灯一直没关……我觉得这样做很不环保。我们每个人都应该节约用水和节约用电[1]。比如：不用水的时候把水关了，不用灯的时候把灯关了，不用电脑的时候把电脑关了。我以前也经常会好几个星期不关电脑，这样对电脑也不太好。后来我换了新电脑，会在用完以后赶快把它关了。这样我的电脑会比较"健康"，还可以节约用电！

Hěn duō rén píngcháng huì yǒu yìxiē bú tài huánbǎo de shēnghuó xíguàn. Bǐrú: yǒude rén yìzhí bù guān diànnǎo, yǒude rén zài bú yòng dēng de shíhòu hái kāi zhe dēng. Wǒ de línjū yǐjīng hǎojǐ tiān méi huí jiā le, kěshì tā jiā de dēng yìzhí méi guān . . . Wǒ juéde zhèyàng zuò hěn bù huánbǎo. Wǒmen měi gè rén dōu yīnggāi jiéyuē yòng shuǐ hé jiéyuē yòng diàn. Bǐrú: bú yòng shuǐ de shíhou bǎ shuǐ guān le, bú yòng dēng de shíhou bǎ dēng guān le, bú yòng diànnǎo de shíhou bǎ diànnǎo guān le. Wǒ yǐqián yě jīngcháng huì hǎojǐ gè xīngqī bù guān diànnǎo, zhèyàng duì diànnǎo yě bú tài hǎo. Hòulái wǒ huàn le xīn diànnǎo, huì zài yòng wán yǐhòu gǎnkuài bǎ tā guān le. Zhèyàng wǒ de diànnǎo huì bǐjiào "jiànkāng," hái kěyǐ jiéyuē yòng diàn!

Comprehension Check

T   F

1   Owen's neighbor hasn't turned his lights off in days.   ○   ○

2   Owen thinks we should conserve water and electricity in everyday life.   ○   ○

3   One of the things Owen says to do is turn off the water when you're not using it.   ○   ○

4   According to Owen, what are the benefits of turning off your computer as soon as you are done using it? Do you agree with him?

NOTE

1 节约 (jiéyuē) 用水 / 用电 (diàn) means to save water or electricity or to cut down on water or electricity usage.

Audio

Vocabulary · 生词

	Word	Pinyin	Meaning
10	关	guān	to close, to turn off
11	电脑	diànnǎo	computer
12	灯	dēng	light, lamp
13	开	kāi	to open, to turn on
14	邻居	línjū	neighbor(s)
15	节约	jiéyuē	to save (money, electricity, water), to cut down (one's use of something)
16	电	diàn	electricity, battery power
17	换	huàn	to change (one thing for another), to exchange
18	赶快	gǎnkuài	at once, immediately, hurriedly

2c Puzzle It Out · 动动脑 PROGRESS CHECK

Complete the exercise below to check your understanding of what you learned in Section 2. If you have questions, consult the Language Reference section.

Rearrange the Chinese words and phrases in each row to translate the English sentences.

1 你 | 没 | 电脑了? | 关 | 多长时间

How long has it been since you turned off your computer?

2 好几天 | 没 | 我的邻居 | 关 | 她家的灯了。

My neighbor hasn't turned off the lights in her house for several days.

3 回老家了。 | 好几年 | 我哥哥 | 没有

It's been quite a few years since my older brother has come back to our hometown!

Go Far with Chinese 3

70

Language Reference · 语言注解

3 **Describing how long it's been since something has been done**

The time phrase that describes the duration since an action was last done comes before the verb. Note in the examples below that 了 is added at the end of the sentence if the speaker is still not doing the activity.

	Time Phrase	没（有）	Verb Phrase	了	
1	你 多长时间	没有	跑步	了？	How long has it been since you went running?
2	我 两个星期	没	跑步	了！	I haven't been running for two weeks.
3	你 多长时间	没有	见她	了？	How long has it been since you've seen her?

了 is not added if the speaker is describing a period of time in the past and has since done the action, as in the examples below.

4 我暑假的时候两个月没有说中文。

Over summer vacation, I didn't speak Chinese for two months.

5 他高中的时候三年没吃肉。

In high school, he didn't eat meat for three years (but now he does).

2d Using the Language · 语言应用 INTERPERSONAL

Step 1: Write two true sentences describing things you do (or have done) that have an impact on the environment. Then write a third sentence that is not true.

Step 2: Your teacher will put you in groups. Share your three sentences in random order with your groupmates and listen to theirs. Try to guess which of each of your groupmates' sentences isn't true!

Example:

Student 1: 第一句，我每次用完电脑都会赶快把电脑关了。第二句，有一次，我三天没关我房间的灯。第三句，我经常告诉邻居要节约用水。

Student 2: 第二句不是真的！

Student 1: 不对！应该是第一句。

What a Character!

yuè 月

1	2	3	4
月	月	月	月

The component 月 has two meanings. One meaning refers to the moon and often appears on the right side of characters whose meaning is related to the moon, periods of time, or light. The 月 in 明 and 期 has this meaning. The other meaning refers to flesh or meat, and often appears on the left side of characters that refer to parts of the body — for example, 脑 (nǎo). When this meaning is intended, the component 月 is read "ròu."

Each of the Chinese words below contains the 月 component and refers to a different part of the human body. With help from the picture and the pinyin, can you match each character to the correct body part?

Body parts: 心脏， 大肠， 手肘， 大脑， 肝

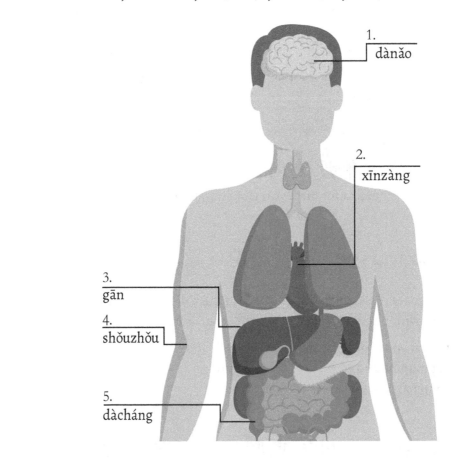

1. dànǎo

2. xīnzàng

3. gān

4. shǒuzhǒu

5. dàcháng

Giving goals and motives

3a Language Model · 语言范例 TARGET LANGUAGE INPUT

Your teacher will lead a discussion about the images below. Try to participate as much as you can. If there is anything you don't understand, let your teacher know.

Wèile　shēntǐ　jiànkāng,　wǒ　huì　jīngcháng　qù　pǎobù.
为了－身体－健康，我－会－经常－去－跑步。
For the sake of my health, I often go for a run.

Wèile　shēntǐ　jiànkāng,　nǐ　huì　zuò　shénme?
为了－身体－健康，你－会－做－什么？
What do you do for your health?

跑步
go running

吃早饭
eat breakfast

用健康app
use a health app

3b New Words in Context · 语境中学新词 INTERPRETIVE

Audio

Listen to the audio and try to understand as much as you can. Then read the passage, using the pinyin text and vocabulary list to figure out unfamiliar words.

为了提高大家对水资源问题的认识¹，最近我们在科学课上讨论了这个问题。上课以前，我们都先做了一些功课。上课的时候，我们先在小组里讨论，然后每个小组再给大家做报告。我们在报告里分析了一些数据，然后说："虽然现在我们还不能解决这个问题，也不能实现很大的目标，但是我们可以实现一些小目标。比如：节约用水。"最后，老师让大家投票选出哪个小组讨论的问题对大家的影响最大。大家把票投给²了我们小组。我们都很高兴！

Wèile tígāo dàjiā duì shuǐ zīyuán wèntí de rènshi, zuìjìn wǒmen zài

kēxué kè shàng tǎolùn le zhège wèntí. Shàng kè yǐqián, wǒmen dōu xiān zuò

le yìxiē gōngkè. Shàng kè de shíhou, wǒmen xiān zài xiǎo zǔ lǐ tǎolùn,

ránhòu měi gè xiǎo zǔ zài gěi dàjiā zuò bàogào. Wǒmen zài bàogào lǐ fēnxī

le yìxiē shùjù, ránhòu shuō: "suīrán xiànzài wǒmen hái bù néng jiějué

zhège wèntí, yě bù néng shíxiàn hěn dà de mùbiāo, dànshì wǒmen kěyǐ

shíxiàn yìxiē xiǎo mùbiāo. Bǐrú: jiéyuē yòng shuǐ." Zuìhòu, lǎoshī

ràng dàjiā tóu piào xuǎn chū nǎ gè xiǎo zǔ tǎolùn de wèntí duì dàjiā de yǐngxiǎng

zuì dà. Dàjiā bǎ piào tóu gěi le wǒmen xiǎo zǔ. Wǒmen dōu hěn gāoxìng!

Comprehension Check

		T	F
1	Maya thinks most people are very aware of issues related to water resources.	○	○
2	In Maya's science class, students first did some homework before class and then discussed water resource issues in small groups.	○	○
3	The rest of the class voted that the topic that Maya's group reported on is the most influential on people's lives.	○	○

4 What does Maya think highschoolers can do about water resource issues?

Go Far with Chinese 3

74

NOTE

1   In the phrase 提高对 . . . 的认识 (tígāo duì . . . de rènshi), the word 认识 means "awareness." So 提高对 . . . 的认识 means "to raise awareness (about something)."

2   把票投给 . . . (bǎ piào tóu gěi . . .) means to cast a vote for someone or something. Another way to express this is 投（给）. . . 一票 (tóu [gěi] . . . yí piào).

Vocabulary · 生词

Audio

	Word	Pinyin	Meaning
19	为了	wèile	for, for the sake of, in order to
20	提高	tígāo	to raise, to improve, to increase
21	功课	gōngkè	assignment, homework, classwork
22	小组	xiǎo zǔ	small group
23	报告	bàogào	to report; report, speech, presentation
24	解决	jiějué	to resolve, to solve
25	实现	shíxiàn	to achieve (a goal), to realize (an objective), to carry out (a plan)
26	目标	mùbiāo	goal, objective, target
27	投票	tóu piào	to vote, to take a vote

5Cs
COMMUNICATION
COMMUNITIES
CONNECTIONS
CULTURES
COMPARISONS

The words 功课 (gōngkè) and 作业 can both be translated as "homework" in English, but they have slightly different meanings. 作业 most frequently refers to assignments that students do outside of class time. 功课 can refer to a wide range of tasks, including homework, assignments done in class, and even research or study done to understand something better. Read the sentences below. What does 功课 mean in these sentences?

这门课的功课多吗？

买电脑以前，做做功课，才能买到又好又便宜的电脑。

他学习很努力，所以功课非常好。

Complete the exercise below to check your understanding of what you learned in Section 3. If you have questions, consult the Language Reference section.

Match the goal or motive in the first part of each sentence on the left with the action on the right that best completes the thought.

1 为了节约用水，　　　　　a 我做了一个很好的学习计划。

2 为了说好中文，　　　　　b 他用完水以后马上就把水关了。

3 为了他的家人，　　　　　c 我一有空就练习说中文。

4 为了实现我的学习目标，　d 他打算毕业以后就去工作赚钱。

Language Reference · 语言注解

4 Using 为了 to explain a goal or motive

The word 为了 (wèile) can be used to introduce the goal or motive for doing something. In Chinese, the goal or motive is usually given first, followed by the action.

　　　wèile　　tígāo　　línjū
1 为了提高邻居对环保的认识，我在小区里挂了一些关于环保的海报。

In order to raise my neighbors' awareness about environmental protection, I hung posters around the neighborhood.

　　　wèile
2 为了能有一个好成绩，我们小组用了很长时间才把
　　xiǎo zǔ
　bàogào
报告写好。

In order to get a good score, our team spent a long time writing the report properly.

　　　wèile　shíxiàn　　mùbiāo　　　　　　　diànnǎo
3 为了实现我的目标，我已经四天没在家玩儿电脑了。

In order to achieve my goal, I have not played computer games at home for four days already.

In addition, 为了 (wèile) can indicate that something is done for someone else.

　　　wèile
4 为了我们家的小猫，我妹妹真的什么都愿意做！

My younger sister really is willing to do anything for our cat!

Step 1: With your classmates, brainstorm a list of environmental problems that students can have an impact on. These could be problems that you see at your school, in your community, or even in the world at large. Use a dictionary or ask your teacher for help if you don't know how to talk about a problem in Chinese.

Step 2: Your teacher will put you in groups. Discuss the problems you have brainstormed with your groupmates and vote on which problem your group wants to try to solve.

Step 3: Write down the solution you decide on as a group. When your teacher calls on you, share the problem you chose and the solution you propose with the class.

Step 4: Listen as your classmates share their problems and solutions. After you have listened to all your classmates, vote for the following three "top" solutions: 1) the solution that will affect the most people; 2) the solution that is easiest to achieve; 3) the solution that most people will agree to.

CULTURES

COMMUNITIES
COMMUNICATION
COMPARISONS
CONNECTIONS

It is customary in Chinese communities to use the character 正 to tally votes. It is used similarly to the four lines plus a slash system you may be familiar with: ||||

Since one of the meanings of this character is "justice," it expresses the hope for a fair vote. If each of the five strokes in 正 represents one vote, how many votes did the two candidates below receive?

Audio

A **Listening and Reading** · 语境中学新词 `INTERPRETIVE`

Passage 1 What's next for Martin and his friends? Read on . . .

学生们找到了关于"环保比赛"的海报，正在一边看一边讨论……

 你们看，这个比赛是上海环境科学大学举办的。比赛要求参加的小组要选一个关于环保的问题，然后做一个报告。每个小组要在报告里讲一下，他们计划怎么提高学生对这个问题的认识，和怎么解决这个问题。

 那参加比赛的小组只需要做一个计划吗？还是也要把那个关于环保的计划实现了呢？

 参加比赛的时候，只需要做一个计划。如果能赢，那上海环境科学大学会请老师帮赢的那个小组实现这个计划。

 这个比赛听起来很有意思！不过，环保问题有很多。我们选哪个呢？

 水资源问题我们上个星期刚讨论过，大家好像都挺有兴趣的。那我们选这个吧？

好！我们可以在报告里讨论一下我找到的数据，然后建议大家节约用水。

我同意！

天浩，你的意思是，你也要跟我们一起参加这个比赛呀？

对，我想好了。 我想多了解一些关于水资源的问题，也让大家提高认识，希望以后可以帮到我爷爷、我姨妈他们。

太好了，那我们有四个人了。不过节约用水大家好像都知道吧？以前我常常看到我们小区里有关于节约用水和节约用电的宣传活动。比如，让大家不用水的时候记得把水关了，不在房间里的时候把灯关了，等等。我觉得我的邻居应该都知道要怎么做了，所以我已经很长时间没有看到这种宣传了。

你说得好像也对，那你想换一个问题讨论吗？

我对水污染问题也挺有兴趣的。

等一下，你们看！每个小组要先在学校里比赛，赢的那一组可以去上海跟别的学校的学生比赛。

上海！那要是我们赢了，就可以去找春月他们玩儿了！那我们讨论节约用水吧？我们有这么丰富的数据，应该很容易赢！我们赶快开始做准备吧！

我也很想去上海，但是我觉得我们不能为了更容易赢，去宣传一件同学们都已经知道的事。

所以你想讨论水污染问题？

对。

可可，天浩，你们觉得呢？或者，我们来投票吧！

我不知道学生能对解决水污染问题做些什么，那我选节约用水吧。

我……我投给马丁一票。

这个时候，里奥过来了……

 你们在讨论什么啊？怎么看起来这么不高兴？

 里奥，你听说我们学校要举办环保比赛的事了吗？如果你得选一个问题去参加环保比赛，你会选节约用水吗？

 还是更愿意选水污染问题？

 环保比赛啊，我听说了！我想想……节约用水吧。水污染我不太懂。

 马丁，现在有三个人选了节约用水问题。

 你们人多，但是不一定对啊。

 你这句话是什么意思？你的意思是我们没有你聪明吗？

 不知道……

 梅雅，马丁不是这个意思。

 是啊，大家都别生气了。

 我们已经说了半天了，现在已经四点一刻了……我的电脑下午没电了，我先去图书馆用那儿的电脑做一会儿功课。

 马丁，那你不参加环保比赛了吗？那我参加了啊？

Comprehension Check

1 To participate in the environmental protection contest, groups must come up with a plan to both raise awareness about and help solve an environmental problem.   ○ ○

2 Tianhao decides to participate in the contest because he already knows a lot about water resource issues.   ○ ○

3 Maya hopes to win the contest so they can go visit Isabella in Shanghai.   ○ ○

4 Martin thinks everybody already knows about saving water, so he doesn't want to use that as a topic for the contest.   ○ ○

5 The friends decide to take a vote on who should be the team leader for the contest.   ○ ○

6 Why does Leo cast his vote for Maya?

Passage 2 Take a look at the icons created by the United Nations to represent sustainable development goals. Based on the images and the Chinese words you recognize, which do you think are related to the topic of environmental protection?

Passage 3 Listen to the conversation. Are the statements that follow true or false?

T F

1 The boy is calling the girl to discuss a poster he made. ○ ○

2 The girl is working on her history assignment at the library. ○ ○

3 The boy forgot about the history assignment, and he just wanted to watch a movie. ○ ○

4 The girl and the boy will watch a history movie together, then write their reports. ○ ○

Passage 4 Listen to a school announcement about what students can do in their daily lives to protect the environment and conserve resources. Which of the suggestions do you agree with and feel you could carry out in your daily life? Make a brief recording or write a statement in Chinese about your environmental action goal.

B Speaking · 口语 INTERPERSONAL

Your school has decided to take measures to become more environmentally friendly. The school administration wants the student body's input on how best to achieve this goal.

Step 1: Brainstorm at least three ways that the school could save energy, save water, or create less trash. Use a dictionary or ask your teacher for help if you do not know how to express your ideas in Chinese.

Step 2: Your teacher will assign you to a group. Discuss your ideas with the students in your group and choose one or two ideas that you think are the strongest. Be prepared to explain your choices to the class.

Step 3: Your class will discuss each group's suggestions. Take notes when students from other groups share their ideas. Take a class vote to choose two or three ideas you think best suit your school.

C Final Project · 结课项目 PRESENTATIONAL

Environmental Editorials

The school newspaper would like to publish student opinions about environmental initiatives at school. Write an editorial in Chinese to submit to the school newspaper. You can write an editorial that supports the school taking certain actions, or you can write an editorial that explains why the school should not take specific measures. Whichever option you choose, be sure to give evidence to support your points and keep your tone polite and positive.

Can-Do Goals · 能力目标

Talk with your teacher if you have questions or if you are not certain you can do the following tasks:

- Analyze how local climate affects environmental issues in a region
- Talk about and understand when others discuss ongoing actions
- Express "how is (something) so . . . ?"
- Talk about how long it's been since something has been done
- Explain the goal of or motive for an action

Cultural Knowledge · 文化知识

What is the purpose of the Green Great Wall?

Groves of trees planted in the drylands of Zhangjiakou in northern China

Confidence Matters

春月：马丁，环保比赛你
们准备得怎么样了？

马丁：环保比赛？还……
还可以吧……

春月：你得加油呀！

马丁：知道了……

春月：怎么了？你听起来
好像不太高兴？

马丁：我没事。

春月：好，我先不跟你说
了。明天我有一件
很重要的事，我得
去准备准备。

Can-Do Goals · 能力目标

In this chapter, you will learn to:

- Describe characteristics of Chinese braille and Chinese Sign Language
- Describe actions in which something moves toward or away from the speaker
- Support a statement by providing additional examples
- Understand when others describe something happening immediately after something else
- Develop and respond to basic interview questions

zēngjiā   tīnglì   hé   shìlì   zhàng'àizhě
增加听力和视力障碍者
de   xuǎnzé
的选择

Expanding Choices for People Who are Hard of Hearing or have Visual Impairments

Societies are typically built to serve those who fit a certain definition of "normal," and individuals who fall outside of this definition face many barriers to accessing resources and education. In recent years, activists and advocacy groups for people with disabilities have made great strides in pushing for greater inclusion of people with disabilities within societies around the world, and China is no exception.

In Chinese braille, every initial consonant sound, final sound, and tone can be represented with raised dots. The sentence above reads "你的中文很棒！"

Alternate Forms of Communication

People who are blind (盲人, mángrén) or visually impaired (有视力障碍的人, yǒu shìlì zhàng'ài de rén) in China can use Chinese braille (盲文, mángwén) to read and write. The language represented by this system is the same as the language represented by Chinese characters.

By contrast, many Deaf people (聋人, lóngrén) and people who are hard of hearing (有听力障碍的人, yǒu tīnglì zhàng'ài de rén) in Mainland China communicate using Chinese Sign Language (中国手语, Zhōngguó shǒuyǔ), which has its own distinct vocabulary and grammar.

你认识会手语的人吗？你认识懂盲文的人吗？

Piano tuning is a common occupation for people who are blind in China.

Opportunities for Education and Employment

Historically, higher education was not easily accessible to students with disabilities in China. As a result, students with disabilities would often train for employment in fields in which their disabilities were perceived as advantages. For example, students who were blind often trained to work with instruments or to perform massage (按摩, ànmó). However, many students with disabilities have pushed for the opportunity to pursue a wider range of education and employment opportunities. This has led to new accommodations, such as the 2014 introduction of a braille version of the national college entrance exam (高考, gāokǎo). While many people with disabilities in China still attend specialized training schools, an increasing number are able to attend traditional higher education institutions.

在中国，学校可能会给有视力障碍的学生教哪些东西？
有视力障碍的学生能用盲文参加中国的高考吗？

REFLECT ON THE ESSENTIAL QUESTION

What affects the choices you make?

1 Can you think of one situation in which being in the majority could affect choices you might make? Can you think of a situation in which being in the minority could affect choices you might make?

2 What opportunities are available to people with disabilities in your community?

3 Have people in your community advocated for changes that support people with disabilities? How have people's lives changed as a result of advocacy?

Bringing toward and taking away

1a Language Model · 语言范例 TARGET LANGUAGE INPUT

Your teacher will lead a discussion about the image below. Try to participate as much as you can. If there is anything you don't understand, let your teacher know.

Qù   péngyou   jiā   wánr   de   shíhou,
去 — 朋友 — 家 — 玩儿 — 的 — 时候，

When going to a friend's house to hang out,

Wǒ   huì   dài   yìxiē   dōngxi   qù.   Nǐ   ne?
我 — 会 — 带 — 一些 — 东西 — 去。你 — 呢？

I usually bring some things with me. How about you?

1b New Words in Context · 语境中学新词 INTERPRETIVE

🔊 Audio

Listen to the audio and try to understand as much as you can. Then read the dialogue, using the pinyin text and vocabulary list to figure out unfamiliar words.

 赛吉，听说你明天就要开始去饭馆打工了？

Sàijí, tīng shuō nǐ míngtiān jiù yào kāishǐ qù fànguǎn dǎgōng le?

 是啊，虽然我上次面试得很好，可是这是我第一份¹工作，所以我现在很紧张。

Shì a, suīrán wǒ shàng cì miànshì de hěn hǎo, kěshì zhè shì wǒ dì yí fèn gōngzuò, suǒyǐ wǒ xiànzài hěn jǐnzhāng.

 那我和天浩可以当你的客人，帮你练习一下吧？

Nà wǒ hé Tiānhào kěyǐ dāng nǐ de kèrén, bāng nǐ liànxí yíxià ba?

 好主意，谢谢！那我开始了。先生，女士，你们好。请问你们今天想吃点儿什么？

Hǎo zhǔyì, xièxie! Nà wǒ kāishǐ le. Xiānsheng, nǚshì, nǐmen hǎo. Qǐngwèn nǐmen jīntiān xiǎng chī diǎnr shénme?

 请先给我们拿两杯水来吧。

Qǐng xiān gěi wǒmen ná liǎng bēi shuǐ lái ba.

 好，先生……这是两位的水。

Hǎo, xiānsheng...... Zhè shì liǎng wèi de shuǐ.

 这杯水太凉了……

Zhè bēi shuǐ tài liáng le...

 对不起，我马上给您换一杯。

Duìbuqǐ, wǒ mǎshàng gěi nín huàn yì bēi.

 你听，那边那位客人的孩子太吵了……

Nǐ tīng, nà biān nà wèi kèrén de háizi tài chǎo le...

 那两位换个地方坐吧？

Nà liǎng wèi huàn gè dìfang zuò ba?

 可是我们就想坐在这儿。

Kěshì wǒmen jiù xiǎng zuò zài zhèr.

 你们真的是在帮我练习吗？

Nǐmen zhēn de shì zài bāng wǒ liànxí ma?

Chapter 4 · Confidence Matters · Section 1

91

对啊，而且我们看你这么紧张，想给你带来²一些"快乐"。

Duì a! Érqiě wǒmen kàn nǐ zhème jǐnzhāng, xiǎng gěi nǐ dài lái yì xiē "kuàilè".

 哈哈，你们好像也给我带来了一些压力。

Hāha, nǐmen hǎoxiàng yě gěi wǒ dài lái le yì xiē yālì.

Comprehension Check

		T	F
1	Keke and Tianhao pretend to be customers at a restaurant to help Sanjay practice waiting tables.	○	○
2	A child interrupts Sanjay's practice interview, and he can't continue.	○	○
3	Do you think Sanjay will be ready for his new job? Why or why not?		

NOTE

1 份 is the measure word for 工作 and other types of work, such as internships.

2 Although 来 and 去 often indicate the physical movement of people, places, and things, they can also be used to describe the "movement" of abstract ideas. When Keke says 给你带来一些 " 快乐," she means "bring you a little happiness" or "cheer you up a little."

Vocabulary · 生词

Audio

	Word	Pinyin	Meaning
1	打工	dǎgōng	to work at a temporary or part time job
2	面试	miànshì	to interview (for a position); interview
3	当	dāng	to be, to work as, to serve as
4	客人	kèrén	guest, customer
5	先生	xiānsheng	Mr., sir, gentleman
6	女士	nǚshì	Miss, lady
7	位	wèi	(polite measure word for people)
8	孩子	háizi	child

What a Character!

zǐ 子 子 子 子

The character 孩 (hái) contains the component 子 (zǐ), which means "child, son, offspring." It is used in many words that relate to children.

Each of the Chinese words below is missing a character that contains the 子 component. Based on the English meanings shown and Chinese words you already know, try to complete the words under the pictures using characters from the word bank below.

Word bank: 学, 教, 孙 (sūn)

____ 练

coach, trainer

____ 子

grandson

留 ____

to study abroad

1c Puzzle It Out · 动动脑 PROGRESS CHECK

Complete the exercise below to check your understanding of what you learned in Section 1. If you have questions, consult the Language Reference section.

Choose the word from the list on the left that best completes each sentence. You may use the words more than once.

来

去

1 我这个周末要回老家 ____ 看我的爷爷奶奶。

2 我朋友给我送了一本书 ____ ，我正在看。

3 他刚才到邻居家 ____ 了，半个小时以后回来。

4 她给我拿了一些零食 ____ 。那些零食很好吃。

Language Reference • 语言注解

1 Moving toward and moving away

来 and 去 are added to verbs to indicate the direction of an action. 来 indicates a motion toward the speaker or the person being spoken to, and 去 indicates that the movement is going away from the speaker or the person being spoken to. If the action involves an object or a place (highlighted in gray below), the object or place is usually added between the verb and 来 or 去.

1 他送了一杯饮料来。   He brought (me) a drink.

2 她带了一些东西去朋友家。   She took some things to her friend's house.
                                        (the speaker is not at her friend's house)

3 他回北京去了。   He went back to Beijing.
                              (the speaker is not in Beijing)

4 你先进教室来吧。   How about you come into the classroom first.
                              (the speaker is in the classroom)

If the action has been completed and the object is not a location, the object can also come after 来 or 去.

5 他买了一些东西来。
       or   He bought some things.
他买来了一些东西。   (and brought them to where the speaker is)

1d Using the Language • 语言应用 INTERPERSONAL

Imagine that a group of exchange students from China are coming to visit your school. Your class has been asked to prepare a small welcome party for them.

Step 1: Discuss with your group what kind of a welcome party you would like to prepare for your guests. Do you think they will want to try food from your country, or do you think they will be more comfortable eating Chinese food? Will you have any activities or performances at the party? Do you want to take them to a particular place in your school or community?

Example: 我们可以带他们去看看学校的篮球馆！

Step 2: As a group, decide what you will bring and what you will need to buy for the party. Keep in mind that you have a limited budget, so you need to agree on the four most important things to have at the party.

Example: 你可不可以买一些喝的来？

Not a single one

2a Language Model · 语言范例 TARGET LANGUAGE INPUT

Your teacher will lead a discussion about the images below. Try to participate as much as you can. If there is anything you don't understand, let your teacher know.

Wǒ　jīntiān　děi　zuò　hǎojǐ　mén　kè　de　zuòyè!

我 - 今天 - 得 - 做 - 好几 - 门 - 课 - 的 - 作业!

Today, I have to do homework for quite a few classes!

Kěshì　xiànzài　wǒ　yì　mén　kè　de　zuòyè　dōu　méi　zuò　wán.

可是 - 现在 - 我 - 一 - 门 - 课 - 的 - 作业 - 都 - 没 - 做 - 完。

But I haven't finished my homework for even one class.

①

做作业

②

看足球比赛

③

写汉字

④

看书

Audio

Listen to the audio and try to understand as much as you can. Then read the dialogue, using the pinyin text and vocabulary list to figure out unfamiliar words.

 喂？春月，你在做什么呢？

Wéi? Chūnyuè, nǐ zài zuò shénme ne?

 喂？大文，我刚上车¹，现在在公交车上。我打算去明天要面试的公司看看。你呢？

Wéi? Dàwén, wǒ gāng shàng chē, xiànzài zài gōngjiāo chē shàng. Wǒ dǎsuàn qù míngtiān yào miànshì de gōngsī kànkàn. Nǐ ne?

 刚才我为了明天的面试去买衣服了，可是我一件衣服都没买到。我不知道明天应该穿哪件衣服去面试……

Gāngcái wǒ wèile míngtiān de miànshì qù mǎi yīfu le, kěshì wǒ yí jiàn yīfu dōu méi mǎi dào. Wǒ bù zhīdào míngtiān yīnggāi chuān nǎ jiàn yīfu qù miànshì . . .

 上次我们见面的时候你穿的那件衣服就很合适啊。

Shàng cì wǒmen jiànmiàn de shíhou nǐ chuān de nà jiàn yīfu jiù hěn héshì a.

 好吧！对了，听说那个餐厅对在那儿工作的人要求²挺高的，要是他们问我的问题我不会回答，怎么办啊？我有点儿担心。

Hǎo ba! Duì le, tīngshuō nàge cāntīng duì zài nàr gōngzuò de rén yāoqiú tǐng gāo de, yàoshi tāmen wèn wǒ de wèntí wǒ bú huì huídá, zěnme bàn a? Wǒ yǒudiǎnr dānxīn.

 别担心。你做的饭很好吃，他们一定会喜欢你的。

Bié dānxīn. Nǐ zuò de fàn hěn hǎo chī, tāmen yídìng huì xǐhuān nǐ de.

 谢谢！

Xièxie!

 你太客气了！我们找到工作以后，一起庆祝一下吧？哎！大文，我不能跟你说了……师傅，我要下车！

Nǐ tài kèqi le! Wǒmen zhǎo dào gōngzuò yǐhòu, yìqǐ qìngzhù yíxià ba? Āi! Dàwén, wǒ bùnéng gēn nǐ shuōle . . . Shīfu, wǒ yào xià chē!

Comprehension Check

		T	F
1	Isabella is on a bus when Owen calls her.	○	○
2	Owen just bought some clothes that he will wear to a job interview.	○	○
3	Owen is not worried at all about his job interview.	○	○
4	Why does Isabella end her conversation with Owen?		

NOTE

1 上车 means "to get on (a car, bus, train, etc.)" and 下车 means "to get off (a car, bus, train, etc.)."

2 The phrase "A 对 B 的要求" means "A's demands/requirements of B." 老师对我们的要求很高 means "The teacher's requirements for us are very high," or, in other words, "The teacher expects a lot from us."

Vocabulary • 生词

Audio

	Word	Pinyin	Meaning
9	上车	shàng chē	to get on (a car, bus, train, etc.)
10	公交车	gōngjiāo chē	bus
11	公司	gōngsī	company, corporation
12	要求	yāoqiú	requirements; to require
14	回答	huídá	to answer; answers to a question
15	庆祝	qìngzhù	to celebrate
16	哎	āi	(a word used to express surprise or dissatisfaction)
17	师傅	shīfu	master, master worker; term of address for a skilled worker

Complete the exercise below to check your understanding of what you learned in Section 2. If you have questions, consult the Language Reference section.

Match the first part of each sentence with the option that completes the thought.

1 我刚来我们学校的时候，   a 可是一个问题都没解决。

2 我不喜欢吃辣的，   b 一个人都不认识。

3 我们讨论了很久，   c 我一张门票都没买到。

4 门票都卖完了，   d 所以一碗酸辣汤都不想喝。

Language Reference · 语言注解

2 Not even one

The pattern "一 ... 都不 / 没 ..." means "not even one..." Note that 也 can be used in place of 都 without changing the meaning.

1 我对樱桃过敏，一个都不能吃。

I am allergic to cherries. I can't eat even one.

2 我很喜欢看书，可是暑假的时候没时间，所以一本都没看。

I really like to read, but I didn't have time during summer break, so I didn't read even one book.

3 那家商店的衣服很难看！我一件衣服都不喜欢。

The clothes in that store are ugly. I don't like any of them.

Uncountable nouns take 一点儿 in place of a measure word. This is similar to saying "not any" or "not even a little..." in English.

4 他吃素，一点儿肉都不吃。

He is a vegetarian. He doesn't eat any meat.

5 昨天我太忙了，一点儿时间都没有。

Yesterday I was too busy and didn't have any time.

2d Using the Language • 语言应用 〔INTERPERSONAL〕

Play a card game with your group. The rules of the game are similar to "Go Fish," but each card represents a food or drink, and the object is to obtain cards to make the most delicious meal possible.

Step 1: Brainstorm a list of five foods and drinks. Your list should include at least one food that uses the measure word 碗, at least one food that uses the measure word 盘, and at least one drink that uses the measure word 杯.

Step 2: Make two cards for each food on your list. Each card should say "一碗 [food]," "一盘 [food]," or "一杯 [drink]."

Step 3: Combine the cards from each student in your group to make a deck. Shuffle the deck. Each student draws three cards. Do not let other students in your group see your cards.

Step 4: Take turns asking each other for food items. If the student you ask has a card of the food item you asked for, he/she must give you the card. If the student doesn't have the card, he/she says "我一 … 都没有," and the student who asked the question draws a card from the deck.

> **Q:** 你有绿茶吗？
>
> **A:** 我一杯绿茶都没有。

Step 5: If you get a pair of the same food items, put the pair on the table in front of you. This represents your "meal." Once all of the food items have been put on the table, the game is over.

Step 6: Look at the foods in each player's "meal." Who has the most delicious meal?

5Cs

COMMUNICATION
COMMUNITIES
CULTURES
COMPARISONS
CONNECTIONS

The word 师傅 (shīfu) means "master" and is used to address a skilled worker or a person trained in a particular skill. Students who study in traditional Chinese arts and sciences, such as calligraphy, Chinese opera, Chinese medicine, and martial arts, often refer to their teacher as 师傅. 师傅 can also be used as a respectful way to address a middle-aged person that the speaker doesn't know, particularly skilled service workers, such as bus drivers, chefs, and mechanics.

In your day-to-day life, whom might you address as 师傅 if you were to speak to them in Chinese?

Providing additional examples

3a Language Model · 语言范例 TARGET LANGUAGE INPUT

Your teacher will lead a discussion about the images below. Try to participate as much as you can. If there is anything you don't understand, let your teacher know.

Zài	wǒmen	xiǎo	zǔ	lǐ,	chúle	tā	yǐwài,
在	我们	小组	里，	除了	他	以外，

In our group, not only he knows sign language,

tā	yě	huì	shǒuyǔ.
她	也	会	手语。

but she does as well.

1

rènzhēn
学习很认真
to study hard

2

jīngyàn
有一些工作经验
to have some work experience

3

zìxìn
很自信
to be confident

3b New Words in Context · 语境中学新词 INTERPRETIVE

Listen to the audio and try to understand as much as you can. Then read the passage, using the pinyin text and vocabulary list to figure out unfamiliar words.

今天我特别开心，因为我找到了一份在药店¹ 的
实习。我是这个星期四去面试的。可是星期三下午
我发高烧² 去医院了，所以面试的时候我觉得很累，
而且还有点儿紧张。不过，回答了几个问题以后，
我就越来越自信了。面试我的人说他们计划只选一
个大三或者大四的学生，问我为什么应该选我。我
告诉他们，虽然我刚开始学我现在的专业，水平还
不太高，经验也比较少，但是我做事非常认真，学
东西也很快。而且我了解很多种药，也喜欢帮别的
人，我还会手语。后来我了解到，除了一个大四的
学生以外，我也拿到了这份实习，因为申请实习的
人，只有我一个人会手语。以前，因为有的时候我
听不清楚别人说什么，所以会有点儿难过。不过，
现在我觉得会手语能帮我找到实习，我特别高兴！

Jīntiān wǒ tèbié kāixīn, yīnwèi wǒ zhǎo dào le yífèn zài yàodiàn de
shíxí. Wǒ shì zhège xīngqīsì qù miànshì de. Kěshì xīngqīsān xiàwǔ
wǒ fā gāo shāo qù yīyuàn le, suǒyǐ miànshì de shíhou wǒ juéde hěn lèi,
érqiě hái yǒudiǎnr jǐnzhāng. Búguò, huídá le jǐ gè wèntí yǐhòu,
wǒ jiù yuè lái yuè zìxìn le. Miànshì wǒ de rén shuō tāmen jìhuà zhǐ xuǎn yí
gè dà sān huòzhě dà sì de xuéshēng, wèn wǒ wèishéme yīnggāi xuǎn wǒ. Wǒ
gàosù tāmen, suīrán wǒ gāng kāishǐ xué wǒ xiànzài de zhuānyè, shuǐpíng hái
bú tài gāo, jīngyàn yě bǐjiào shǎo, dànshì wǒ zuò shì fēicháng rènzhēn, xué
dōngxi yě hěn kuài. Érqiě wǒ liǎojiě hěn duō zhǒng yào, yě xǐhuān bāng biéde
rén, wǒ hái huì shǒuyǔ. Hòulái wǒ liǎojiě dào, chúle yígè dà sì de
xuéshēng yǐwài, wǒ yě ná dào le zhè fèn shíxí, yīnwèi shēnqǐng shíxí de
rén, zhǐyǒu wǒ yí gè rén huì shǒuyǔ. Yǐqián, yīnwèi yǒude shíhou wǒ
tīng bù qīngchǔ biérén shuō shénme, suǒyǐ huì yǒu diǎnr nánguò. Búguò,
xiànzài wǒ juéde huì shǒuyǔ néng bāng wǒ zhǎodào shíxí, wǒ tèbié gāoxìng!

Comprehension Check

		T	F
1	Haisheng had been very sick the day before the interview.	○	○
2	Haisheng became more and more nervous during his interview.	○	○
3	The interviewer said that the pharmacy planned to hire a third-year or fourth-year college student.	○	○
4	Haisheng was the only person hired for the internship.	○	○
5	Do you think Haisheng will be good at his job? Why or why not?		

> **NOTE**
> 1 药店 means "drugstore," "pharmacy."
> 2 发高烧 means "to have a high fever."

Vocabulary · 生词

	Word	Pinyin	Meaning
17	实习	shíxí	an internship; to do an internship
18	医院	yīyuàn	hospital
19	自信	zìxìn	confident
20	专业	zhuānyè	major (in college), speciality
21	水平	shuǐpíng	skill level, level, standard
22	经验	jīngyàn	experience; to go through, to experience
23	认真	rènzhēn	conscientiously, earnest; to take seriously
24	手语	shǒuyǔ	sign language
25	申请	shēnqǐng	to apply; application

Below are signs used in China to indicate places that may be difficult to access because there are obstacles, or 障碍 (zhàng'ài), that may impede certain actions. Based on characters you already know, try to select the sign that best matches the description listed on the left.

1 听力障碍
2 行走障碍
3 视力障碍

a

b

c

3c Puzzle It Out · 动动脑 PROGRESS CHECK

Complete the exercise below to check your understanding of what you learned in Section 3. If you have questions, consult the Language Reference section.

Exercise 1 Choose the word from the list on the left that best completes each sentence of the passage. You may use some words more than once.

不但

而且

除了

以外

我们家 _____ 我奶奶 _____ ，我爷爷也很会做饭。我奶奶 _____ 会做上海菜， _____ 会做北京菜。我爷爷只会做北京菜。 _____ 我奶奶会做上海菜 _____ ，我妈妈也会做上海菜。但是我小时候，不太喜欢吃上海菜，因为有的上海菜有点甜。 _____ 我 _____ ，我爸爸小时候也不太喜欢吃上海菜。现在，我和爸爸 _____ 喜欢吃北京菜， _____ 喜欢吃上海菜。

我平常很忙。我早上六点半起床……

1 下课以后，我就去学校的篮球馆打篮球。
2 起床以后就去吃早饭。
3 吃完早饭以后我就去学校上课。

Language Reference · 语言注解

3 Point out what two things have in common

除了 … 以外,… 也 … means "in addition to …,… also…" or "besides…,…." In *Go Far with Chinese 2*, this pattern was used in sentences with one subject, but it can also be used in sentences with two subjects (in the examples below, the subjects are highlighted in gray). Note that when this pattern has only one subject, the subject either comes before 除了 or after 以外, and both 也 or 还 can be used without changing the meaning. When this pattern has two subjects, the first subject comes after 除了, the second subject comes after 以外, and only 也 can be used.

1 我们家除了我爸爸以外，我妈妈也会英文。
In our family, in addition to my father, my mother can also speak English.

2 除了节约用水以外，节约用电也可以保护环境。
In addition to saving water, saving electricity can also protect the environment.

3 除了中文以外，她还会手语^{shǒuyǔ}，所以一定能找到工作。

3 除了中文以外，她还会手语，所以一定能找到工作。
In addition to Chinese, she also knows sign language, so she will definitely be able to find a job.

4 Doing something right away

就 is often used to emphasize that something happens right away or immediately after something else. When 就 has this meaning, it often follows 以后.

1 我昨天晚上很累，做完作业以后就睡觉了。
I was very tired last night, so I went to bed right after I finished my homework.

2 我每天早上起床以后就洗澡。
I take a shower every morning right after I get up.

3 等老师到了，我们就开始上课。
We will start the class right after the teacher arrives.

3d Using the Language · 语言应用

Imagine that you and your group members are on a hiring committee to find a new English teacher for next year. You will help decide which two candidates will be asked to the school to interview.

Step 1: Read the profiles below. For each candidate, take notes on why you think he/she is (or is not) a good fit for your school.

Step 2: With your group, decide which two candidates you will pick to interview. Be prepared to explain your choices to the class.

Example:

除了刘祝以外，王大山的专业也是文学，不过我更喜欢
刘祝，因为……

	名字：王大山 专业：文学		名字：李明音 专业：英文、数学
工作经验：在高中教过四年 关于我：我很喜欢教课！大学毕业以后就开始当老师了。 兴趣：唱歌、看书、乒乓球		工作经验：在大学教过两年 关于我：我非常希望能到你们的学校去，希望每天都能看到学生新的变化。 兴趣：跳舞、篮球、做饭	
	名字：刘祝 专业：文学、音乐		名字：张万于 专业：英文
工作经验：在高中教过两年 关于我：我非常喜欢当老师。我希望能帮每个学生实现自己的目标。 兴趣：跳舞、唱歌、足球		工作经验：在大学教过两年，在高中教过一年 关于我：我特别喜欢和学生在一起，我愿意帮每个学生了解和提高自己。 兴趣：网球、武术、看电影	

Audio

A Listening and Reading · 语境中学新词 INTERPRETIVE

Passage 1 What's next for Isabella and her friends? Read on. . .

在大学生活动中心……

 春月，我表哥找到实习了。

 太好了！他要在哪儿实习啊？

 在药店。下午我们请他和大文来我们学校吃饭吧？一起庆祝一下？

 今天下午我和大文可能没时间……我们明天都有面试，所以今天下午得准备准备。

 你要面试的是那份教英文的工作吗？

 对。大文要去一个餐厅面试。

 加油！那等你们都找到工作以后，我们再一起庆祝吧？

 不用等了！我和大文都很厉害，我们明天一定会成功。我们明天下午一起吃饭吧！

 你那么自信啊。好，那明天吧。我一会儿去跟我表哥说一下。

第二天，海生来到了雪儿和春月的大学，还买了一些饮料来。

 大文还没到吗？

 还没有。我给他发短信说我面试成功了。他没回我，可能还在面试。

 春月，你面试成功了啊，太棒了！

 谢谢海生！今天我要请餐厅的师傅做两个我最喜欢吃的菜。

 哈哈。雪儿，你不想去打工吗？

 我是学表演的，还没有太多经验。所以我想先认真学习。我先跟你们了解一下，面试的时候，他们都会问些什么问题吧！

 一些比较简单的问题，比如，"你学什么专业，会做些什么，等等。"

 那你们是怎么回答的呢？

 我介绍了一下我自己，然后说我以后想当医生，而且对很多种药都有一些了解。我平常虽然用助听器，但是其实也会手语。如果有人来药店买药的时候用手语，我能明白他们的意思。

 你回答得真好！他们问我的问题跟问你的差不多，但是我回答得很简单。我说我是中文专业的，中文水平还可以，做事很认真，而且我特别喜欢孩子！公司的人说，虽然我一点儿教英文的经验都没有，但是我的英文很好，对自己的要求挺高的，也很自信，所以想让我试试。

 自信真的很重要！那你毕业以后想当老师吗，春月？

 我还不知道……对了，海生，你为什么想当医生啊？

 我十岁以前听得见，但是十岁的时候生过一次病，发了很高的高烧，后来就常常听不清楚了。在医院的时候，有一位医生帮了我很多。我希望自己能跟他一样，毕业以后当医生，多帮帮别的人。

 海生，你人真好！

这个时候，大家看大文还没来，所以让春月给他打了个电话。

喂，大文？你看到我给你发的短信了吗？现在除了海生以外，我也找到工作了！

你们真棒。

你面试得也不错吧？

哎，不太好。我今天第一次面试，有一点儿紧张，所以上车以后，我就在公交车上听音乐。然后我忘了看时间，下车的时候下错站了。

啊？那你迟到了吗？

迟到了……

那你回答问题回答得怎么样？

哎，也不太好……我走进餐厅以后，更紧张了。面试的时候，他们让我试着帮两位客人点菜，但是开始的时候，我忘了说"先生，您好！女士，您好！请问今天就你们两位吗？"这样的话。

那你不但迟到了，还忘了说这些应该对客人说的话啊……我还以为你跟我一样，第一次去面试，就会成功。没关系，多面试几次，就不会紧张了！现在你快来我们学校跟我们一起吃饭吧？

算了吧，我今天有点儿累。下次吧。

Comprehension Check

		T	F
1	Isabella is applying for a job as an English teacher.	○	○
2	Isabella is nervous that she won't get the job.	○	○
3	Xu'er doesn't want to get a part-time job because she wants to focus on her studies.	○	○
4	Owen calls Isabella because he can't figure out where Isabella, Xue'er, and Haisheng are.	○	○
5	Owen's job interview went very well.	○	○

6 Imagine that you are applying for the same job as Isabella. Introduce yourself in Chinese as if you are at the job interview, and tell the intevrviewer a few things about yourself.

Passage 2 The poster below is an advertisement for a job opening. What kind of job is the advertisement for and what are the job requirements?

Passage 3 Listen to a student reflect on his experience looking for a part-time job in college. Answer the questions on a separate piece of paper.

1 What are the requirements for the teaching position?

  (a) experience teaching sign language and enjoying being around children

  (b) knowing sign language and experience teaching children

  (c) knowing sign language and enjoying being around children

2 Why did the boy feel very nervous at the beginning of the interview?

  (a) because he was affected by an incident that happened on the bus

  (b) because he was late for the interview

  (c) because the interviewer asked very difficult questions

3 Why does the boy think he didn't do well at the interview?

  (a) because he was not qualified for the job

  (b) because he didn't have any relevant work experience

  (c) because he didn't do very well answering some of the questions

Passage 4 Listen to the discussion between two interviewers about the job candidates they spoke to today. Number the pictures in the order in which the interviewers discuss the candidates. Which candidate(s) do you think they should hire? Which candidate(s) do you think they shouldn't hire? Explain your reasoning in complete Chinese sentences on a separate sheet of paper.

B Speaking · 口语 INTERPERSONAL

Look back at Using the Language on page 105. Imagine that the committee that is hiring a new English teacher has decided to ask two of the candidates to come to the school to interview.

Step 1: Make a list of five qualities that you think are important for teachers. Share your list with your partner. With your partner, decide what you think the three most important qualities are for teachers.

Step 2: With your partner, make a list of three questions your committee can ask the candidate during the interview. When thinking of your questions, consider the list of important qualities you made in Step 1. What questions can you ask to determine whether or not the candidate has these qualities?

Final Project · 结课项目

Interview Workshop

Imagine that your school is collecting advice to help students and recent graduates interview for jobs, internships, and college admissions. You and your classmates have been asked to brainstorm advice for other students who are preparing for interviews.

Step 1: As a class, make a list of three commonly asked interview questions. Since you don't know what other students will be applying to, try to pick questions that could be used in interviews for different kinds of positions, rather than questions that are specific to only one kind of job or school. Consider using some of the questions you wrote when doing the Speaking exercise on page 110.

Step 2: Take turns asking and answering the questions with your group. Try to answer each question twice: once as if you are the best candidate for the job, and once as if you are the worst candidate for the job.

Step 3: With a group, make a poster of the "do's" and "don'ts" of interviewing. Consider some of the answers your group gave in Step 2 (good answers and bad answers). Remember to consider other aspects of the interview as well, such as what to wear and how to behave.

Can-Do Goals · 能力目标

Talk with your teacher if you have questions or if you are not certain you can do the following tasks:

- Describe characteristics of Chinese braille and Chinese Sign Language
- Describe actions in which something moves toward or away from the speaker
- Support a statement by providing additional examples
- Understand when others describe something happening immediately after something else
- Develop and respond to basic interview questions

Cultural Knowledge · 文化知识

What are some of the ways people in China communicate without spoken language?

Coming to an Agreement

春月正在给梅雅发短信……

春月：梅雅，你最近怎么样呀？

梅雅：挺好的。春月，你呢？

春月：我最近找到了一份工作，
所以特别高兴！

梅雅：你太棒了！

春月：谢谢！对了，我上次跟
马丁打电话的时候，问
他你们环保比赛准备得
怎么样，他听起来好像
不太高兴……但是也不
愿意告诉我为什么。

梅雅：春月，是这样的……

Can-Do Goals · 能力目标

In this chapter, you will learn to:

- Describe some ways in which China has changed in the past several decades

- Express that two different people or things share a certain characteristic

- Say if something is easy or difficult to do

- Give others suggestions after some consideration

- Understand when someone talks about something that is currently happening

Zhōngguó de guójì huà mèilì

中国的国际化魅力
China's International Appeal

According to the 2020 Chinese census, more than 845,000 foreigners (外国人, wàiguó rén) live in China. The number of people from abroad choosing to live in China has risen in recent decades, likely due in part to a series of policies initiated by the Chinese government in 1978 called "Reform and Opening Up" (改革开放, gǎigé kāifàng).

Both Chinese and international companies occupy the buildings that line Shenzhen's skyline.

China Decides to Open Up to the World

Starting in the 1950s and extending through the late 1970s, China had limited trade relationships with other countries. A part of the Reform and Opening Up process, some cities, including Shenzhen (深圳, Shēnzhèn), were designated as special economic zones (经济特区, jīngjì tèqū) — areas where the Chinese government encouraged trade and foreign investment. As a result, Shenzhen is now a major export hub. There's a good chance that an electronic product that you own (a TV, cell phone, or drone, for example) was built in Shenzhen!

中国的改革开放对外国人的影响大吗？为什么？

The ten cities deemed the most attractive to foreign residents

Beijing	Guangzhou
Shanghai	Nanjing
Shenzhen	Chengdu
Hefei	Qingdao
Hangzhou	Suzhou

Choosing a Place to Live

Before Reform and Opening Up, relatively few foreigners visited or lived in China. In recent decades, the expat population has grown, though it is not evenly distributed throughout the country. A 2019 survey conducted by China's Ministry of Science and Technology ranked Mainland Chinese cities that foreign professionals found most appealing to live in, considering criteria such as living and working environments and whether there is potential for scientific innovation (科学创新, kēxué chuàngxīn), a factor that attracts some foreign workers to China. Not surprisingly, Shenzhen appears in the top ten. Many other top choices are near Shanghai, allowing people access to the city without the stress of living in the megacity. And Chengdu (成都, Chéngdū) is attractive to some foreign residents in part because it is considered a relaxing place to live.

外国人最喜欢住在中国的哪些城市？
为什么这些城市特别受欢迎？

Going to China

Most foreigners spending time in China need a passport (护照, hùzhào) and visa (签证, qiānzhèng). Typically, even tourists need a visa to visit! People who want to study or work in China will need the help of a school or employer to arrange the documents necessary to get a visa.

如果你想去中国学习或者工作，你需要有哪些东西？

跟老师和同学讨论一下，怎么申请去中国的签证？

By the Numbers

In 2018, more than 492,000 students from around the world studied abroad (留学, liúxué) in China. Of those students, 16 percent studied in Beijing, 12 percent studied in Shanghai, and the remaining 72 percent studied elsewhere in China. The chart below shows which continents these study abroad students came from.

哪些国家的学生最喜欢去中国留学？

2018年在中国留学的学生中有百分之多少的人生活在北京和上海？

Top 10 Countries (国家, guójiā) of Origin for Students Studying in China

South Korea

Thailand

Pakistan

India

United States

Russia

Indonesia

Laos

Japan

Kazakhstan

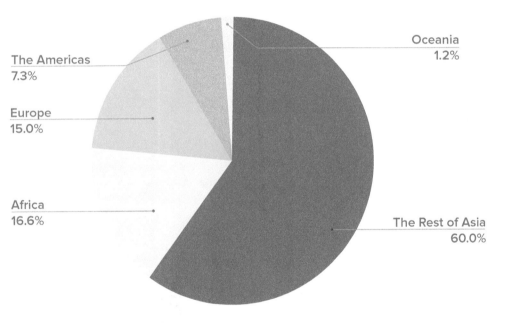

Oceania
1.2%

The Americas
7.3%

Europe
15.0%

Africa
16.6%

The Rest of Asia
60.0%

REFLECT ON THE ESSENTIAL QUESTION

What affects the choices you make?

1. What factors would make you want to live in a community in another region or country, as opposed to visiting a place as a tourist?

2. What are some of the reasons people choose to move to your community?

3. If you could choose to move to a city in China, which city would you choose? Why?

Life in the city

1a Language Model · 语言范例 TARGET LANGUAGE INPUT

Your teacher will lead a discussion about the image below. Try to participate as much as you can. If there is anything you don't understand, let your teacher know.

Xiànzài búdàn wǒ biǎogē zhǎo dào le gōngzuò,
现在 - 不但 - 我 - 表哥 - 找 - 到 - 了 - 工作,

Now, not only has my cousin found a job,

érqiě Chūnyuè yě zhǎo dào le gōngzuò.
而且 - 春月 - 也 - 找 - 到 - 了 - 工作。

Isabella has also found one.

Zài nǐ shēnghuó de dìfang, gōngzuò hǎo zhǎo ma?
在 - 你 - 生活 - 的 - 地方,- 工作 - 好 - 找 - 吗?

Are jobs easy to find where you live?

Listen to the audio and try to understand as much as you can. Then read the passage, using the pinyin text and vocabulary list to figure out unfamiliar words.

上海是一个国际化的大城市，有很多外国的公司在
上海有办公室。你看，前边那些高楼，里边差不多
都是外国公司的办公室。很多外国公司会跟中国
公司合作，他们不但需要外国人，也需要中国人。
如果你有经验或者英文比较好，工作会比较好找。
所以不但有很多外国人喜欢来上海找工作，而且
中国别的城市的人也愿意来上海找工作。不过来
上海的人越来越多，也带来了一些问题。比如，
我觉得上海没有我小时候那么安静了。对了，来
上海学习的外国人也挺多的。你们看，我们右边的
这个国际学校，校园¹ 很漂亮吧。上海还有不少这样
的国际学校，而且很多高中还有国际部²。

Shànghǎi shì yí gè guójì huà de dà chéngshì, yǒu hěn duō wàiguó de gōngsī zài
Shànghǎi yǒu bàngōngshì. Nǐ kàn, qiánbian nà xiē gāo lóu, lǐbian chàbuduō
dōu shì wàiguó gōngsī de bàngōngshì. Hěn duō wàiguó gōngsī huì gēn Zhōngguó
gōngsī hézuò, tāmen búdàn xūyào wàiguó rén, yě xūyào Zhōngguó rén.
Rúguǒ nǐ yǒu jīngyàn huòzhě Yīngwén bǐjiào hǎo, gōngzuò huì bǐjiào hǎo zhǎo.
Suǒyǐ búdàn yǒu hěn duō wàiguó rén xǐhuan lái Shànghǎi zhǎo gōngzuò, érqiě
Zhōngguó biéde chéngshì de rén yě yuànyì lái Shànghǎi zhǎo gōngzuò. Búguò lái
Shànghǎi de rén yuèláiyuè duō, yě dài lái le yìxiē wèntí. Bǐrú,
wǒ juéde Shànghǎi méiyǒu wǒ xiǎo shíhou nàme ānjìng le. Duì le, lái
Shànghǎi xuéxí de wàiguó rén yě tǐng duō de. Nǐmen kàn, wǒmen yòubian de
zhège guójì xuéxiào, xiàoyuán hěn piàoliang ba. Shànghǎi hái yǒu bù shǎo zhèyàng
de guójì xuéxiào, érqiě hěn duō gāozhōng hái yǒu guójì bù.

NOTE

1 校园 (xiàoyuán) means "school campus."

2 国际部 (guójì bù) means "International Department." At some Chinese schools, this is the department that manages the international students enrolled at the school; at other schools, this department might serve students who are planning to pursue higher education abroad.

Comprehension Check

		T	F
1	Shanghai is a very international city.	◯	◯
2	The skyscraper Haisheng points out has an even mix of offices for foreign and Chinese companies.	◯	◯
3	Shanghai is less quiet now than when Haisheng was young.	◯	◯

4 According to Haisheng, what could make it easy to find a job in Shanghai? Why?

Vocabulary · 生词

Audio

	Word	Pinyin	Meaning
1	国际	guójì	international
2	化	huà	(added after a word to indicate that something has become more [word], similar to -ize or -ization in English)
3	外国	wàiguó	foreign country
4	办公室	bàngōngshì	office
5	楼	lóu	multi-storied building, a floor (of a multi-level building)
6	合作	hézuò	to cooperate, to work together; cooperation
7	安静	ānjìng	quiet, peaceful

1c Puzzle It Out · 动动脑 PROGRESS CHECK

Complete the exercises that follow to check your understanding of what you learned in Section 1.

If you have questions, consult the Language Reference section.

Exercise 1 On a separate piece of paper, add 不但 and 而且 to the correct places in each sentence.

1 上海有很多外国公司，也有很多中国的公司。

2 我们要节约用水，也要节约用电。

3 我最近在学中文，我表哥最近也在学中文。

4 今天早上公交车上有很多人，地铁里也有很多人。

Exercise 2 Each sentence below states that something is easy to do or difficult to do. On a separate piece of paper, write a sentence that expresses how easy or difficult each activity (highlighted in gray) is to do, using 难 or 好.

1 他很快就学会怎么 做酸辣汤 了。

2 我已经参加过三次面试了，可是还没有 找到合适的工作 。

3 这个问题 ，我们已经讨论三天了，还没找到 解决 的办法。

4 她几分钟就把这些 数据分析 完了。

Language Reference · 语言注解

1 Two different people or things with a similar situation

In *Go Far with Chinese 2*, 不但 . . . 而且 . . . was introduced as meaning "not only...but also..." to state that two different things are true about someone or something.

1 马老师不但会吹笛子，而且还会弹吉他。

Not only can Mr. Ma play the flute, but he can also play the guitar.

不但 . . . 而且 . . . can also be used to express that two different people or things have something in common. The thing in common can be a specific situation or characteristic, or it can be two similarly positive or negative characteristics (as shown in example 4). In this case, the first person/thing comes after 不但, and the second person/thing comes after 而且. 也 must be added after the second person/thing.

2 我们学校有好几个老师会手语。不但刘老师会手语，而且白老师也会手语。

There are several teachers at our school who know sign language. Not only does Ms. Liu know sign language, Mr. Bai also knows sign language.

3 他们家的人都很高。不但他儿子很高，而且他女儿也很高。

Everyone in their family is very tall. Not only is his son tall, his daughter is also tall.

4 很多垃圾都是可以回收的。你看，不但这些杯子可以回收，而且那个不用的电脑也可以回收。

A lot of trash is recyclable. Look, not only are these cups recyclable, but that computer that's no longer in use can also be recycled.

5 我喜欢住在大城市，不但生活方便，而且大公司多，
工作也更好找。

I like living in a big city. Not only is life here convenient, but there are also a lot of large companies, so work is easier to find.

2 Describing something as easy to do or difficult to do

As mentioned in *Go Far with Chinese 1*, 好 can be added directly in front of a verb to indicate that something is easy to do.

1 家常豆腐很好做。

Home-style tofu is easy to make.

2 我刚买的手机特别好用。

The phone I just bought is really easy to use.

3 这些数据很好分析！

This data is really easy to analyze!

In the same way, 难 can be added before a verb to express that something is difficult to do.

4 很多人说历史特别难学。

Many people say that history is especially difficult to learn.

5 这个问题非常难解决。

This problem is extremely difficult to solve.

6 这几年工作很难找。

Work has been difficult to find these past few years.

Remember that there are exceptions to this usage; when 好 or 难 comes before verbs like 吃, 喝, 看, and 听, they express that the action is pleasant or unpleasant, rather than easy or difficult.

7 那本书非常好看。

That book is really good.

8 我不喜欢那个乐队，他们的歌很难听。

I don't like that band; their songs are really bad.

5Cs
COMPARISONS

COMMUNITIES
COMMUNICATION
CONNECTIONS
CULTURES

City living is a common experience for much of China's population. The process of 城市化 (chéngshì huà), or urbanization, in China increased rapidly after the Reform and Opening Up policies began in the late 1970s. The policies that promoted trade and the growth of new industries also resulted in the growth of cities — with many people from rural areas moving to urban areas to work. According to data from the seventh National Population Census of the People's Republic of China, the percentage of the population living in urban areas has increased significantly, as shown in the chart below.

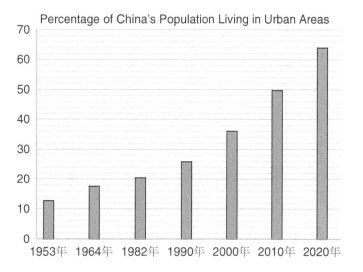

According to this census, there are 18 megacities where each has more than 1000 万 (ten million) permanent residents, including Chongqing, Shanghai, Beijing, and Chengdu. There are over 90 cities in China with populations over 100 万 (one million).

How many residents does the largest city in your country have? How many cities in your country have populations over one million?

People walking down a busy street in Shanghai

Imagine that an international company is looking for a place to build a new office. In pairs, propose a location that you think would work well for the company's new office.

Step 1: Read the list of features company executives want in their ideal location. Note that the list includes things they definitely need, things they would like, and things that it would be good to have but aren't necessary.

一定要……	要……	最好……
• 办公室够多 • 有一些大学 （更容易找到合适 的人来工作）	• 房租合适 • 有地铁和公交 • 有很多好学校 （方便在公司工作 的人的孩子上学）	• 气候和环境好 • 有一些商场 • 有很多外国餐厅

Step 2: Talk to your partner about places that have some or many of these characteristics. Can you think of any locations near where you live that might work? If not, you can also consider places farther away that you think would be especially suitable. This might include cities in your own country, or even foreign cities that you know a bit about! With your partner, choose one city that you think could work. Take notes about your choice and include your reasons.

Example:

我觉得我们住的城市就很合适。因为我们这儿有很多大楼，不但大楼里的办公室又多又新，而且这儿的房租也不贵。

Step 3: The teacher will call on one person from each pair to announce their choice and explain their reasons. Listen as your classmates give their reports. Are there certain locations that multiple pairs came up with? Did other groups mention reasons you and your partner hadn't considered?

Giving a final suggestion

2a Language Model · 语言范例 TARGET LANGUAGE INPUT

Your teacher will lead a discussion about the image below. Try to participate as much as you can. If there is anything you don't understand, let your teacher know.

Zhè　cì　huódòng　wǒmen　zìjǐ　jǔbàn　háishi　zhǎo
这 - 次 - 活动 - 我们 - 自己 - 举办 - 还是 - 找

Should we put this event on ourselves or

guójì　wénhuà　jùlèbù　yìqǐ　jǔbàn　ne?
国际 - 文化 - 俱乐部 - 一起 - 举办 - 呢？

[together] with the international cultures club?

Wǒmen　háishì　gēn　tāmen　hézuò　ba.
我们 - 还是 - 跟 - 他们 - 合作 - 吧。

(after some thought)　Let's work together with them after all.

🔊 Audio

Listen to the audio and try to understand as much as you can. Then read the dialogue, using the pinyin text and vocabulary list to figure out unfamiliar words.

 爱林，你的大学生活怎么样？

Àilín, nǐ de dàxué shēnghuó zěnmeyàng?

 挺好的。上大学以后，自己的时间更多了。你呢，春月？

Tǐng hǎo de. Shàng dàxué yǐhòu, zìjǐ de shíjiān gèng duō le. Nǐ ne, Chūnyuè?

 我也很好。第一个学期不是特别忙，每天只有两节课。我还找了一份工作。对了，你这个学期选了几门课？

Wǒ yě hěn hǎo. Dì yī gè xuéqī bú shì tèbié máng, měi tiān zhǐ yǒu liǎng jié kè. Wǒ hái zhǎo le yí fèn gōngzuò. Duì le, nǐ zhège xuéqī xuǎn le jǐ mén kè?

 这个学期我一共选了五门课。我没有选中文课，因为我们学校的中文课太简单了！

Zhège xuéqī wǒ yígòng xuǎn le wǔ mén kè. Wǒ méiyǒu xuǎn Zhōngwén kè, yīnwèi wǒmen xuéxiào de Zhōngwén kè tài jiǎndān le!

 是吗？我选中文课了。那你平常可以多听听中文录音，或者在网上看看中文视频。

Shì ma? Wǒ xuǎn Zhōngwén kè le. Nà nǐ píngcháng kěyǐ duō tīng ting Zhōngwén lùyīn, huòzhě zài wǎng shàng kànkan Zhōngwén shìpín.

 是啊！呀，春月，不好意思，请你等一下，好像有人找我。

Shì a! Ya, Chūnyuè, bù hǎoyìsi, qǐng nǐ děng yíxià, hǎoxiàng yǒu rén zhǎo wǒ.

 嗯。

Ǹg.

 是我同一个班的同学想跟我一起去还书。她说有几本书最好今天还。可是我们才聊了几分钟……我再去问问她明天还可以不可以。

Shì wǒ tóng yí gè bān de tóngxué xiǎng gēn wǒ yìqǐ qù huán shū. Tā shuō yǒu jǐ běn shū zuìhǎo jīntiān huán. Kěshì wǒmen cái liáo le jǐ fēnzhōng... Wǒ zài qù wèn wen tā míngtiān huán kěyǐ bù kěyǐ.

你还是现在跟她一起去还书吧。别还晚了。我们可以再约别的时间聊。

Nǐ háishi xiànzài gēn tā yìqǐ qù huán shū ba. Bié huán wǎn le. Wǒmen kěyǐ zài yuē biéde shíjiān liáo.

 也行。那我回来以后再跟你视频聊天儿。

Yě xíng. Nà wǒ huí lái yǐhòu zài gēn nǐ shìpín liáo tiānr.

Comprehension Check

		T	F
1	Isabella tells Ellen that she only signed up for two courses this semester.	○	○
2	Someone in the same class as Ellen is looking for her.	○	○
3	After considering the different options, Isabella suggests that Ellen go now.	○	○
4	Why was someone looking for Ellen?		

Vocabulary · 生词

Audio

	Word	Pinyin	Meaning
8	节	jié	(measure word for class periods)
9	一共	yígòng	altogether
10	录音	lùyīn	audio recording; to record
11	不好意思	bù hǎoyìsi	sorry; to feel embarrassed, to feel shy; embarrassing
12	嗯	ǹg	(word used to express agreement)
13	同	tóng	same, alike
14	班	bān	class
15	还	huán	to return (something), to give (something) back, to repay (a loan)
16	约	yuē	to make an appointment
17	行	xíng	all right, OK

In addition to meaning "okay," 行 (xíng) can also mean "to walk." Below is a famous Chinese saying, which originated with the philosopher Confucius. If 行 means "walk" and 必 (bì) means "certainly," can you guess what this saying means?

sān rén xíng,   bì yǒu wǒ shī

三人行，必有我师

Possible scenario: When you are introduced to someone, and even without knowing him/her, you believe there is something you can learn from him/her.

2c Puzzle It Out · 动动脑   PROGRESS CHECK

Complete the exercise below to check your understanding of what you learned in Section 2. If you have questions, consult the Language Reference section.

还是 can have several different uses. It can be used to ask for a choice between options, it can be used to mean "still," and it can be used to make a final suggestion. Read the examples below and identify how 还是 is being used.

1 **Q:** 我们找个时间一起去打球吧，我今天或者明天都有空。你呢?

   A: 我今天作业有点儿多。我们还是约明天吧。

(a) 还是 is being used to ask for a choice.

(b) 还是 is being used to mean "still."

(c) 还是 is being used to make a final suggestion.

2 **A:** 你更想买哪件衣服? 这件红的还是那件绿的?

   B: 我还是要那件红的吧，我觉得红的更好看。

(a) The first 还是 is being used to ask for a choice, and the second is being used to indicate B's final decision.

(b) The first 还是 means "still," and the second is being used to indicate B's final decision.

(c) The first 还是 is being used to ask for a final decision, and the second means "still."

3 **Q:** 这个问题我刚讲完，你没听懂吗?

   A: 不好意思，我还是不太明白。

(a) 还是 is being used to ask for a choice.

(b) 还是 is being used to mean "still."

(c) 还是 is being used to make a final suggestion.

3 Suggesting an alternative option

还是 . . . (吧) is a pattern used to suggest ultimately going with a particular option after some more thought or after a different suggestion has been proposed. Sometimes 还是 . . . (吧) is used as part of a compromise, after additional information to consider has been brought up (as shown in example 1). 还是 . . . (吧) can also be used to introduce one person's recommendation or choice after considering multiple options (as shown in example 2). 还是 . . . (吧) is a bit similar to how English uses "(how about)...after all" or "ultimately." The 吧 is optional but is used more often than not. Note that the person/people that the suggestion is directed at should come before 还是, not after.

1 **A:** 春假的时候我们一起出去旅行吧！

   Let's travel together during spring break!

B: 好啊。你想去哪儿旅行？

   Okay. Where do you want to travel?

A: 我想去纽约看看。

   I want to check out New York City.

B: 我也想去纽约，可是纽约有点儿远，而且我听说纽约什么东西都很贵。我们没有那么多钱啊。

   I also want to go to New York City, but it's a bit far. Also, I've heard everything is expensive there. We don't have that much money.

A: 你说的也对。那我们还是去附近的城市旅行吧。这样不需要很多钱。

   You're right. Then [ultimately], let's travel to a nearby city. That way, we won't need a lot of money.

2 **A:** 你看那条裤子怎么样？

   What do you think about those pants?

B: 挺漂亮的。

   They're beautiful.

A: 这条裤子呢？

   And these pants?

B: 也不错。

   They're also nice.

A: 那你想买哪条呢?

So which ones do you want to buy, then?

B: 我还是买这条裤子吧, 我觉得这条更好看!

I'll buy these pants after all; I think they look nicer!

3 A: 今天天气不错。我们不要坐公交车了,走路去上学吧。

The weather is pretty nice today. We shouldn't take the bus; let's walk to school.

B: 我担心时间不够了。我们还是坐公交车去学校吧。

I'm worried there's not enough time. How about we take the bus to school after all.

2d Using the Language · 语言应用 INTERPERSONAL

How good is your class at solving problems and giving advice?

Step 1: By yourself, think of a problem that you have encountered or that you might encounter. (For example, problems you encountered in class, in the cafeteria, with a sibling, etc.) If it is a made-up problem, make sure to think of some details: if there are other people involved, how did they react to the problem, or what might their feelings be? Did you already try to solve the problem, but your solution didn't work? Be prepared to discuss this problem and its details with your partner.

Example: 我昨天跟同学约好了, 今天晚上要去看电影。可是我忘了明天有一个考试, 我还没复习。怎么办呢?

Step 2: You will be assigned a partner. Present your problem to your partner and talk about the issue with him/her. Then listen to your partner's advice. When it is your turn to listen to your partner's problem, you should ask questions to get a better understanding of the situation. Give advice, including a few different possible solutions. Remember to use 还是 ... 吧 once you ultimately decide on what to suggest.

Example: 你还是复习功课吧。电影你们可以下个星期去看。

Questionnaires

3a Language Model · 语言范例 TARGET LANGUAGE INPUT

Your teacher will lead a discussion about the images below. Try to participate as much as you can. If there is anything you don't understand, let your teacher know.

Wǒ	zhèngzài	huídá	xuéxiào	fā	de	diàochá	wènjuàn	ne.
我	正在	回答	学校	发	的	调查	问卷	呢。

I'm filling out the survey that the school sent.

Nǐ	zài	zuò	shénme	ne?
你	在	做	什么	呢?

What are you doing?

1

diàochá

调查

to investigate, to survey; investigation, survey

2

wènjuàn

问卷

questionnaire

3b New Words in Context · 语境中学新词 INTERPRETIVE

Listen to the audio and try to understand as much as you can. Then read the dialogue, using the pinyin text and vocabulary list to figure out unfamiliar words.

可可，你在忙什么呢？

Kěkě, nǐ zài máng shénme ne?

写科学课的作业呢。科学课的作业真难，像这个题，我已经看了三遍了，还是不太懂。

Xiě kēxué kè de zuòyè ne. Kēxué kè de zuòyè zhēn nán, xiàng zhège tí, wǒ yǐjīng kàn le sān biàn le, hái shì bú tài dǒng.

赵老师也在图书馆，我刚才遇到他了。他说一会儿来找我们聊聊。你可以问问他。

Zhào lǎoshī yě zài túshūguǎn, wǒ gāngcái yù dào tā le. Tā shuō yí huìr lái zhǎo wǒmen liáo liáo. Nǐ kěyǐ wèn wen tā.

可可，天浩，你们都在这儿啊，太好了！我正在做一个调查问卷[1]呢。你们来帮我看一下，这些问题好回答吗？

Kěkě, Tiānhào, nǐmen dōu zài zhèr a, tài hǎo le! Wǒ zhèngzài zuò yí gè diàochá wènjuàn ne. Nǐmen lái bāng wǒ kàn yíxià, zhè xiē wèntí hǎo huídá ma?

赵老师，您为什么要做这个调查啊？

Zhào lǎoshī, nín wèishénme yào zuò zhège diàochá a?

因为我们想了解一下学生的想法，然后决定下个学期科学课怎么上，怎么考试，等等。

Yīnwèi wǒmen xiǎng liǎojiě yíxià xuéshēng de xiǎngfǎ, ránhòu juédìng xià gè xuéqī kēxué kè zěnme shàng, zěnme kǎo shì, děng děng.

赵老师，像这样做调查要用很多时间吧？

Zhào lǎoshī, xiàng zhèyàng zuò diàochá yào yòng hěn duō shíjiān ba?

是啊。不过，我觉得这样的调查很值得做，因为学生的想法对老师很重要。

Shì a. Búguò, wǒ juéde zhèyàng de diàochá hěn zhí dé zuò, yīnwèi xuéshēng de xiǎngfǎ duì lǎoshī hěn zhòngyào.

赵老师，您能把"你觉得科学作业难吗"写在问卷里吗？我想知道大家的想法是不是跟我一样。我觉得科学课的作业太难了。您看，这个题我已经看了三遍了，还是不会做啊。

Zhào lǎoshī, nín néng bǎ "nǐ juéde kēxué zuòyè nán ma" xiě zài wènjuàn lǐ ma? Wǒ xiǎng zhīdào dàjiā de xiǎngfǎ shì bú shì gēn wǒ yíyàng. Wǒ juéde kēxué kè de zuòyè tài nán le. Nín kàn, zhège tí wǒ yǐjīng kàn le sān biàn le, hái shì bú huì zuò a.

Comprehension Check

		T	F
1	Keke says she has seen three questions that are all the same type, but she doesn't understand them.	○	○
2	Tianhao just ran into Mr. Zhao in the library.	○	○
3	Mr. Zhao says that the survey is important and didn't take much time to make.	○	○

4 What question does Keke want Mr. Zhao to include in the survey, and why?

NOTE

1 调查 (diàochá) and 问卷 (wènjuàn) can often be used together in Chinese, unlike in English. 调查问卷 (diàochá wènjuàn) refers to a questionnaire that has an investigatory purpose. A similar but different term is 问卷调查 (wènjuàn diàochá), which refers to an investigation that uses questionnaires.

Vocabulary · 生词

	Word	Pinyin	Meaning
18	像	xiàng	to resemble, to be like
19	遍	biàn	(measure word for a completed action, indicates how many times in succession the action has been done)
20	遇到	yù dào	to run into, to encounter
21	调查	diàochá	to investigate, to survey; investigation, survey

Audio

	Word	Pinyin	Meaning
22	问卷	wènjuàn	questionnaire
23	想法	xiǎngfǎ	idea, opinion, way of thinking
24	决定	juédìng	to decide; decision
25	值得	zhí dé	to be worth, to deserve
	赵	Zhào	Zhao (a surname)

What a Character!

biǎn 扁

The word 遍 (biàn) contains the component 扁 (biǎn or piān). Characters that include this component are often pronounced as "bian" or "pian."

Each of the Chinese words below contains the 扁 component. Keeping in mind other components you have learned previously, can you match the Chinese word to its meaning in English?

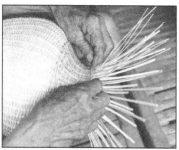

1 to weave

2 to pan-fry

3 plaque

a 煸 (biān)   b 编 (biān)   c 匾 (biǎn)

Complete the exercise below to check your understanding of what you learned in Section 3. If you have questions, consult the Language Reference section.

On a separate piece of paper, use 呢 to answer the following questions according to what's shown in the images.

1 他在做什么呢？

2 她刚才怎么没接电话？

3 你姐姐怎么没来？

Language Reference · 语言注解

4 Expressing an action in progress

In addition to 在 and 正在, 呢 is another way to indicate that an action is currently happening. 呢 can be used together with 在 or 正在, or it can appear by itself.

1 我弟弟看电视呢。
My younger brother is watching TV.

2 请你们安静点儿。学生们正在考试呢。
Please be quiet; the students are taking a test.

3 我们在玩儿游戏呢。
We're playing a game.

When the sentence includes the location of an action in progress, 在 is used to introduce the location, and only 呢 (not an additional 在 or 正在) is used to indicate that the action is currently happening.

4 老师在教室里准备明天的课呢。
The teacher is in the classroom preparing for tomorrow's lesson.

5 叔叔在厨房做晚饭呢。
My uncle is in the kitchen making dinner.

3d Using the Language · 语言应用 [INTERPERSONAL/PRESENTATIONAL]

Learn your classmates' opinions on a topic that interests you.

Step 1: With a partner, decide on a topic that you would like to know your classmates' thoughts on and that you are able to talk about in Chinese (possibilities include: environmental protection, sports, learning Chinese, etc.).

Example:

我想调查一下我们班同学对学习中文的想法。你想调查什么问题？

Step 2: With your partner, discuss the questions you want to ask about that topic and why. In Chinese, draft a brief questionnaire with three to five questions about the topic.

Sample discussion:

A: 做调查的时候，你想问哪些问题？为什么？

B: 我想问一下同学们，学习中文的时候，他们遇到过哪些问题？他们有没有找到解决问题的办法？我觉得这两个问题非常值得调查。如果他们找到的办法好用，可以告诉别的同学。如果他们不知道怎么办，我们可以想想怎么帮他们。

Step 3: Your teacher will assign each pair a "station" in the classroom. Your partner will stay at the station and be the questionee, while you go around to other people's stations as the questioner, asking others your survey questions. Once you have visited all the other stations, you will switch places with your partner and become the questionee while your partner becomes the questioner.

Step 4: Talk to your partner to gather your results together. What were the answers? Did they surprise you?

Step 5: Be prepared to give a brief presentation on your survey to the class. Your report should include what your questionnaire was about, what questions you asked and why, and the results.

Put the Pieces Together! · 融会贯通

A Listening and Reading · 阅读和听力 INTERPRETIVE

Passage 1 What's next for Martin and his friends? Read on...

最后一节课下课以后，天浩约马丁一起去图书馆。图书馆里很安静。马丁一到约好的房间，就看到了天浩、梅雅、可可、还有里奥……

 天浩，你不是说今天就我们两个人吗？……

 马丁，我没告诉你大家都会来吗？不好意思啊！

 好吧……那你们聊吧，我得去还几本书。

 等一下，马丁，我们刚才在讨论这次环保比赛的事呢。

 是啊，其实我们可以选一个别的环保问题。

 可是选别的问题有点儿麻烦吧……

 里奥，你决定参加环保比赛了？

 对！那你还参加吗，马丁？

 我……

 当然参加啊！

 是啊，马丁，你还是参加吧。对了，上次我们说到哪儿了？我们再一起讨论讨论吧！

 上次我们遇到了一点儿问题，大家的想法不太一样。有的人想选节约用水问题，有的人想选水污染问题。这个问题我们已经讨论了好几遍了。

然后关于节约用水的问题，梅雅已经找到了一些数据。水污染问题我们都不太了解……对了，我们一共有五个人。如果我们都对水污染不太了解，那别的同学会不会也不太了解呢？

 是啊！昨天我奶奶给我打电话了。她听说以后我们老家附近会有越来越多的高楼。城市化会污染水资源，她担心水污染会对茶叶和水果有一些不好的影响。我以前不知道这些……

 所以水污染的问题可能更值得宣传宣传？

 对。

 梅雅，你愿意换一个问题做报告啊？

 我觉得大家一起合作的时候，多听听别人的想法也不错。

 那我跟你一样，也换个想法！

 对了，我们先做一个问卷调查吧？

 什么问卷调查？

 我觉得我们可以找一些关于环境

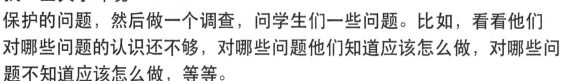

保护的问题，然后做一个调查，问学生们一些问题。比如，看看他们对哪些问题的认识还不够，对哪些问题他们知道应该怎么做，对哪些问题不知道应该怎么做，等等。

 然后我们可以选一个学生们认识还不太够的问题，讨论一下！

 对！我们做报告的时候，也可以讲一下我们做的这个调查。

 好主意！这次的校园环保比赛是一个国际化的比赛。不但我们学校别的班的学生能参加，而且很多在外国的学生也会参加。我们得认真准备一下……

 那我们多调查几个学校的学生吧？

行，春月和雪儿在同一个大学，我们还可以让她们帮我们把问卷发给她们学校里的学生。

 好。我们还可以请雪儿的表哥和美子帮我们在他们的学校里做一下调查！

 好。对了，调查的问题挺难写的，我想去问问科学课的赵老师有什么建议。

 我跟你一起去问问他吧。

在去赵老师办公室的路上，马丁和梅雅刚开始的时候都没有说话。后来……

 梅雅，上次我说了一些不太合适的话，让你不开心了。对不起……

 马丁，我也要跟你说对不起。我应该多听听你的想法。我们能像以前一样一起合作，我很开心。

 我也是！

Comprehension Check

		T	F
1	When Martin gets to the library, all his friends apologize to him.	○	○
2	Tianhao's grandmother is worried about the future urbanization of their hometown area because she thinks it will have a negative effect on the tea leaves and fruit.	○	○
3	Maya agrees with Martin that the issue of water pollution deserves publicity.	○	○
4	Keke suggests they conduct a survey to learn what students find interesting about environmental protection.	○	○
5	The environmental protection competition isn't just a campus-wide competition but an international one.	○	○
6	Martin tells Maya he is sorry for ignoring her.	○	○

Chapter 5 • Coming to an Agreement

Passage 2 The plaque in this school building shows which office is located on which floor. If you want to visit the office for international students, which floor should you go to? Give your answer using a complete Chinese sentence.

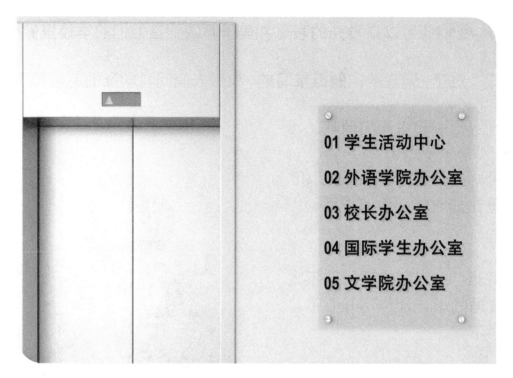

01 学生活动中心

02 外语学院办公室

03 校长办公室

04 国际学生办公室

05 文学院办公室

Passage 3 Listen to a student calling a counselor in the International Student Office. Are the statements that follow true or false?

		T	F
1	The student was calling for Mr. Li, but Ms. Zhao picked up the phone.	○	○
2	Ms. Zhao had just finished talking to a different student.	○	○
3	The student called because she wanted to make an appointment.	○	○
4	At one point during their call, Mr. Li suggested that the student call again later.	○	○
5	The student didn't know where the International Student Office was.	○	○

Passage 4 The report you will hear details some of the findings of a 2019 survey conducted by World Education Services on the thoughts of international students at universities in the United States.[1] You will need the information later, so take notes, and listen to the report multiple times if necessary. What are some of the problems mentioned in the report? If there are international students at your school, do you think they struggle with some of the same problems? Explain why or why not.

1 Skinner, M., Luo, N., and Mackie, C. (2019). Are U.S. HEIs meeting the needs of international students? New York: World Education Services. Retrieved from wes.org/ partners/research/

B   Speaking · 口语   INTERPERSONAL

Imagine that your school's administration has invited you and a partner to participate in an initiative to figure out how to make your school more welcoming for Chinese exchange students. The administration has already shared a report with you that explains some of the common problems faced by international students (Passage 4).

Step 1: Compare your notes about Passage 4 with the notes that your partner took. Try to create a complete list of all the problems mentioned in the passage. Ask your teacher for clarification if there are any parts of that passage that are unclear to you. If you have international students in your community, you can also add to the list any additional problems that you think they might have encountered.

Step 2: Look at your list and brainstorm some possible solutions to these problems. What specific actions could the students and teachers at your school take to help international students succeed and feel like part of your school community? Try to come up with at least five suggestions. Note: It is okay if the five suggestions consist of multiple solutions to a few problems, and no solutions to other problems.

Example:

如果我们学校的国际学生觉得自己在这儿没有好朋友，不太开心，我们可以约他们一起参加学校的活动，或者一起去运动，这样他们就能认识一些新朋友了。

C   Final Project · 结课项目   PRESENTATIONAL

Survey for International Students

Now that you have some ideas for possible solutions, you need to think about how to find out which solutions would be the most helpful to international students.

Step 1: Working in pairs, write a questionnaire asking international students for their opinions on the solutions that you brainstormed in the Speaking exercise. What format will you use for the questionnaire (agree/disagree, multiple choice)? Is there additional information that is important to gather from the international students to help you determine if your ideas will work?

Step 2: In Chinese, create a poster or a slide presentation of your survey.

Step 3: Your teacher will arrange a gallery walk in the classroom. One of you will present the poster to other teams while the other walks around and learns what the other teams' solutions are. Then switch roles so that both of you have the chance to present and to observe. Ask your classmates about their proposed solutions and suggest additional questions that they might want to add. Take note of any suggestions made by your classmates and use those suggestions to revise your survey.

Step 4: Submit the revised survey to your teacher. If possible, try to interview some international students in your community. Ask about their problems and think about how you could help them.

Can-Do Goals · 能力目标

Talk with your teacher if you have questions or if you are not certain you can do the following tasks:

- Describe some ways in which China has changed in the past several decades
- Express that two different people or things share a certain characteristic
- Say if something is easy or difficult to do
- Give others suggestions after some consideration
- Understand when someone talks about something that is currently happening

Cultural Knowledge · 文化知识

What is a special economic zone? Why are they important?

Container ships at the Shenzhen port

CONTEMPORARY SOCIETY

In Unit 3, you will learn to gather information to support a certain perspective. You will also learn how to discuss ways people use technology in their daily lives.

A woman uses her cell phone to buy street food in Chengdu, Sichuan Province

Essential Question
How is technology both the problem and the solution?

CHAPTER 7
Getting Things for Owen's New Place

Isabella, Xue'er, and Haisheng visit Owen to celebrate his recent move but end up helping him shop for furniture.

CHAPTER 8
Online Life

Martin and friends discuss the results of their survey and their lives online.

CHAPTER 9
The Day of the Competition

The group gives their presentation at the competition in Beijing, hoping to win a chance to go to Shanghai.

At the end of the unit, you will prepare a presentation arguing a certain position. You will:

● Research your presentation topic and prepare your argument

● Discuss your argument with you partner and decide how best to present your position

● Write a statement that supports your argument and addresses possible counterarguments

WORKING TOGETHER

In Unit 2, you will learn a bit about Taiwan and how to talk about jobs and internships. You will also learn to discuss things that two people have in common and more ways to describe the location of something.

People at a job fair in Chengdu

Essential Question
What affects the choices you make?

CHAPTER 4
Confidence Matters

Isabella, Haisheng, Owen, and Xue'er talk about looking for jobs and internships.

CHAPTER 5
Coming to an Agreement

Martin and his friends agree on how to pick a topic for the environmental protection competition.

CHAPTER 6
Miko's Life in Taipei

After seeking Miko's help for the competition, Martin and his friends watch a video that Miko posted online about living in Taipei.

UNIT 2 PROJECT

At the end of the unit, you will write an application essay for an imaginary summer immersion program. You will:

- Read the descriptions and requirements for several different programs

- Select one program and write your application

- Give one of your classmates feedback on how he/she could improve his/her application

Miko's Life in Taipei

马丁： 春月，我听梅雅说你上个
星期给她打电话了。

春月： 对，那你们参加环保比赛
遇到的问题，解决了吧？

马丁： 解决了！我们已经找到了
一个好办法，但是得请你、
雪儿，还有雪儿的表哥帮
我们在你们的学校里做做
调查。

春月： 我又要打工又要上课，很
忙啊。

马丁： 姐，我知道你很忙。不过，
如果我们能赢，就可以去
上海参加比赛了。你没忘
吧？

春月： 那好吧！

Can-Do Goals · 能力目标

In this chapter, you will learn to:

- Discuss how Taiwan's history has influenced its language and culture
- Describe something's location as being inside, outside, or between other things
- Indicate the direction of an action
- Express ideas such as "whoever," "wherever," and "whenever"
- Talk about how many times you have done something

Read the text and try to answer the Chinese questions.

Táiwān gàikuàng

台湾概况
Taiwan 101

Taiwan is a small island (岛, dǎo) with a complex history. The Qing dynasty, China's final dynasty, ruled Taiwan for centuries before Japan took control of it in 1895. The island returned to Chinese control in 1945, but, at the time, China was locked in a civil war between the Chinese Communist Party (CCP, 共产党, gòngchǎndǎng) and the Nationalist Party (国民党, guómíndǎng). In 1949, Chinese Communist forces defeated the Nationalists, many of whom fled the Mainland (大陆, dàlù) and moved the government to Taiwan.

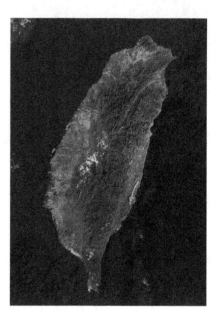

鯛魚鍋	$ 180
鮮蝦鍋	$ 190
海鮮鍋	$ 190

A menu posted in front of a hotpot restaurant in Taichung, Taiwan. The text 並ㄅㄧㄤˋ叫 uses both traditional characters and zhuyin to express the phrase bìnbiàng jiào, a Southern Min expression indicating that something is "great" or more literally "makes you want to shout." (Note that the currency in Taiwan is the Taiwanese dollar.)

The Chinese Language in Taiwan

Mandarin is the official language of both Taiwan and Mainland China, but there are some differences. More than half of the people living in Taiwan speak both Mandarin and Southern Min, a language that originated from Fujian Province. Taiwan uses an older set of characters, often referred to as "traditional" characters (繁体字, fántǐzì) — as opposed to the "simplified" character set (简体字, jiǎntǐzì) used in Mainland China. Additionally, people in Taiwan typically do not use pinyin (拼音, pīnyīn). Instead they use zhuyin (注音, zhùyīn), a system of symbols to represent the pronunciation of characters that is older than pinyin.

中国大陆和台湾现在用的汉字一样吗？人们用的是什么汉字？

A sign that says 国语日报 in traditional characters with zhuyin notation to the right of each character. This Taiwanese newspaper prints their materials with zhuyin to help children learn to read

Taiwanese Food

This history is visible in Taiwanese food, which is a unique blend of many influences, including food styles from Mainland China, Japan, and the aboriginal people of the island. One of the most famous examples of Taiwanese food is pearl milk tea (珍珠奶茶, zhēnzhū nǎichá), also known as bubble tea or boba tea. Invented in the 1980s, the drink has become popular across the globe.

All kinds of tea, including bubble tea, at a night market

台湾有什么有名的饮料？你喝过那种饮料吗？

Taiwanese People

The earliest arrivals to Taiwan came to the island several thousand years ago. They are the ancestors of the aboriginal people (原住民, yuánzhùmín). Additional waves of immigrants from different parts of the Chinese mainland brought to Taiwan a variety of languages and cultures. As a result, the modern population of Taiwan exhibits a mixture of heritages.

现在住在台湾的人都是从同一个地方来的吗？

By the Numbers

Busy streets of Taipei

Over 95 percent of the 23 million people living in Taiwan are Han Chinese (汉族, Hànzú).

A performance by the Amis, one aboriginal group

About 2 percent of Taiwan's population are aboriginal people.

在台湾，有百分之多少的人是汉族人？有百分之多少的人是原住民？

REFLECT ON THE ESSENTIAL QUESTION ●————— **What affects the choices you make?**

1 Based on what you learned, what would you choose to do if you visited Taiwan? Why?

2 What cultural and language groups exist in your community? How do you think your community is enriched by its diversity?

3 How does the history of your community affect the choices you make?

Shall we go in here?

1a Language Model · 语言范例 TARGET LANGUAGE INPUT

Your teacher will lead a discussion about the image below. Try to participate as much as you can. If there is anything you don't understand, let your teacher know.

Nà	jiā	diàn	wàimiàn	guà	zhe	de	yīfu	zhēn	hǎokàn!

那 — 家 — 店 — 外面 — 挂 — 着 — 的 — 衣服 — 真 — 好看!

The clothes hanging outside that store look really nice!

Nǐ	xiǎng	bù	xiǎng	zǒu	jìn	lǐmiàn	qù	kàn	kan?

你 — 想 — 不 — 想 — 走 — 进 — 里面 — 去 — 看 — 看?

Do you want to go inside and take a look?

A clothing shop in 中山 (Zhōngshān) district, Taipei

Listen to the audio of the email Miko sent to Ellen and try to understand as much as you can. Then read the email, using the pinyin text and vocabulary list to figure out unfamiliar words.

爱林：

　　好久不见[1]！你最近怎么样？我已经适应了在台湾的生活。我很喜欢在这里[2]买衣服。今天我买了一件黄色[3]的衣服，很漂亮！你看看我给你发的照片吧。对了，你还记得以前我们经常去学校附近的夜市吃晚饭吗？刚才我跟我们班的同学去这里的夜市了，我吃了好几种我同学推荐的美食。这个夜市里有很多家店，你看看第二张照片里中间的那家店，我觉得那家店的红烧牛肉面最好吃！我们走到那家店的时候，里面已经坐了很多人，所以我们就站在外面吃了。其实站在外面吃我也很开心，因为外面不但很舒服，而且可以看到夜市上挂着的很多红色的灯笼，特别漂亮！真希望你也在这里。什么时候我们可以再一起去夜市吃晚饭呢？

想你的美子

Àilín:

　　Hǎojiǔ bú jiàn! Nǐ zuìjìn zěnmeyàng? Wǒ yǐjīng shìyìng le zài Táiwān de shēnghuó. Wǒ hěn xǐhuan zài zhèlǐ mǎi yīfu. Jīntiān wǒ mǎi le yí jiàn huángsè de yīfu, hěn piàoliang! Nǐ kàn kan wǒ gěi nǐ fā de zhàopiàn ba. Duì le, nǐ hái jìde yǐqián wǒmen jīngcháng qù xuéxiào fùjìn de yèshì chī wǎnfàn ma? Gāngcái wǒ gēn wǒmen bān de tóngxué qù zhèlǐ de yèshì le, wǒ chī le hǎo jǐ zhǒng wǒ tóngxué tuījiàn de měishí. Zhège yèshì lǐ yǒu hěn duō jiā diàn, nǐ kàn kan dì èr zhāng zhàopiàn lǐ zhōngjiān de nà jiā diàn, wǒ juéde nà jiā diàn de hóngshāo niúròu miàn zuì hǎochī! Wǒmen zǒu dào nà jiā diàn de shíhou, lǐmiàn yǐjīng zuò le hěn duō rén, suǒyǐ wǒmen jiù zhàn zài wàimiàn chī le. Qíshí zhàn zài wàimiàn chī wǒ yě hěn kāixīn, yīnwèi wàimiàn búdàn hěn shūfu, érqiě kěyǐ kàn dào yèshì shàng guà zhe de hěn duō hóngsè de dēnglong, tèbié piàoliang! Zhēn xīwàng nǐ yě zài zhèlǐ. Shénme shíhou wǒmen kěyǐ zài yìqǐ qù yèshì chī wǎnfàn ne?

xiǎng nǐ de Měizǐ

Comprehension Check

		T	F
1	Miko opens her email by saying "long time no see."	◯	◯
2	Miko and her classmate ate red-cooked beef noodles inside a shop in the night market.	◯	◯
3	The shop where Miko and her classmate ate is the middle one in the second photo that she attached to the email.	◯	◯
4	Try writing the first line of Ellen's response.		

NOTE

1 好久不见 (hǎojiǔ bú jiàn) translates to "long time no see." The English expression may have come from Chinese speakers who immigrated to the United States in the 19th century.

2 The phrases 这里, 那里, and 哪里 have the same meaning as 这儿, 那儿, and 哪儿. They are more commonly used in Taiwan and southern Mainland China.

3 The character 色 (sè) means "color" and is added after words like 黄 (huáng), 红, and 绿 when referring to colors.

Vocabulary · 生词

Audio

	Word	Pinyin	Meaning
1	好久	hǎojiǔ	for a long time, quite a while
2	黄	huáng	yellow
3	夜市	yèshì	night market
4	晚饭	wǎnfàn	dinner
5	推荐	tuījiàn	to recommend
6	家	jiā	(measure word for businesses)
7	中间	zhōngjiān	between, middle, center
8	里面	lǐmiàn	inside, interior
9	外面	wàimiàn	outside, exterior

Complete the exercises below to check your understanding of what you learned in Section 1. If you have questions, consult the Language Reference section.

Exercise 1 Use the words in the list on the left to complete each sentence. Use each word only once.

到
出
回
进

1 请拿 _____ 一张纸写汉字。

2 我打算和姐姐一起从夜市走 _____ 家。

3 老师已经走 _____ 教室里了，我同学还在玩儿手机。

4 她们已经跑 _____ 外面的网球场了，我们也赶快过去吧。

Exercise 2 Rearrange the Chinese words and phrases in each row to translate the English sentences.

1 那家店 ｜ 里面！ ｜ 就在 ｜ 她

She is right inside that store!

2 很热，｜ 今天外面 ｜ 所以我们 ｜ 出去吃晚饭了。｜ 不打算

It's hot outside today, so we are not planning to go out for dinner.

3 最漂亮！｜ 那家 ｜ 咖啡馆 ｜ 我觉得 ｜ 中间的

I think that café in the middle is the prettiest!

Language Reference · 语言注解

1 Describing something's location as "inside," "outside," or "in the middle"

As you learned previously, 边 can be combined with location words such as 里 to give the location of a noun. 面 (miàn) can be used in essentially the same way and follows the same sentence structure. For example, "... 在 [noun] 里面" means "is inside of [noun]." 边 and 面 (miàn) can be used with a wide range of location and direction words, including 东, 南, 西, 北, 左, 右, 里, 外, 上, 下, 前, and 后.

jiā · lǐmiàn

1 你们在哪家店里面？

Which shop are you in?

2 我在外面等你吧！
wàimiàn

I'll wait for you outside!

3 我们小区的东面有一个很大的公园。
miàn

There's a big park to the east of our neighborhood.

To say that something is "in the middle" or "in between" two other things, the word 中间 (zhōngjiān) is most commonly used. This word can be used with the pattern "... 在 [noun] 和 [noun]（的）中间."

4 你坐在我和明明的中间吧。
zhōngjiān

How about sitting between me and Mingming?

Or, 中间 (zhōngjiān) can indicate that something is in the middle of a number of things, following the pattern "... 在 [number + MW + noun]（的）中间".

5 我们大学在两家医院中间。
jiā *zhōngjiān*

Our university is between two hospitals.

6 那个人就是她，站在她四个姐姐的中间。
zhōngjiān

That's her, standing right between her four older sisters.

It can also be used by itself to refer to being in the middle generally.

7 这张照片是在哪儿拍的？中间的那个人是谁啊？
zhōngjiān

Where was this photo taken? Who is the person in the middle?

2 **Expressing the direction of an action**

There are several words in Chinese that can be added to a verb to show the direction of an action. These words include 上, 下, 进, 出, 回, 过, 起, 到, 来, and 去. Add these direction words right after the verb when the action involves movement to another location.

1 我刚走进那家店，就看到了一条很好看的裤子。
jiā

I saw a very nice pair of pants right after I walked into that store.

2 刚才我看到一只黄色的猫跑到路那边了。
huáng

I just saw a yellow cat run to the other side of the road.

3 她拿起一个红色的包看了一下，然后又放下了。

She picked up a red bag, took a look, and then put it back down.

4 请选出你最喜欢的那个礼物。

Please select (lit. "pick out") the gift you like the most.

1d **Using the Language • 语言应用** INTERPERSONAL/PRESENTATIONAL

Design an obstacle course, creating a list of tasks for your classmates to complete as they move around the classroom.

Step 1: Your teacher will put you in groups. Work together to think of different obstacles for your classmates to navigate. Write each obstacle on a separate slip of paper. You should write at least four and no more than eight navigation tasks. Remember that all the tasks must be actions that all students can safely and comfortably complete.

Step 2: Your teacher will collect the slips of paper and put the class into two teams. Students on team 1 will take turns selecting and reading tasks while the students on team 2 take turns completing the tasks. Then, the two teams will switch roles. The teacher will assign one student the role of timekeeper — the team that completes its tasks the fastest will win!

5Cs

CULTURES

COMMUNITIES
COMMUNICATION
COMPARISONS
CONNECTIONS

One of the most popular night market snacks in Taiwan is 臭豆腐 (chòu dòufu), or stinky tofu. This fermented tofu side dish can be cold, steamed, or stewed, but it is perhaps most popular when deep fried. While the distinctive smell of stinky tofu may seem unpleasant to some, enthusiasts are happy to follow their nose to find a stall selling this pungent treat.

Can you think of any foods that smell bad to you but taste good?

I'll go wherever you want to go

2a Language Model · 语言范例　TARGET LANGUAGE INPUT

Your teacher will lead a discussion about the images below. Try to participate as much as you can. If there is anything you don't understand, let your teacher know.

Dǎoyóu　shuō,　wǒmen　xiǎng　qù　nǎlǐ,
导游 - 说，- 我们 - 想 - 去 - 哪里，

The tour guide says wherever we want to go,

tā　jiù　dài　wǒmen　qù　nǎlǐ.
她 - 就 - 带 - 我们 - 去 - 哪里。

she'll take us.

Nà　nǐ　xiǎng　qù　nǎlǐ　ne?
那 - 你 - 想 - 去 - 哪里 - 呢？

So, where do you want to go?

The Taipei Confucius Temple

Kǒng　(zǐ)　miào
孔（子）庙
Confucian Temple

The entrance to a popular night market in Taipei

2

夜 市
night market

Listen to the audio and try to understand as much as you can. Then read the dialogue, using the pinyin text and vocabulary list to figure out unfamiliar words.

 喂，王老师，我是美子。好久不见！您最近还好吗？

Wéi, Wáng lǎoshī, wǒ shì Měizǐ. Hǎojiǔ bú jiàn! Nín zuìjìn hái hǎo ma?

 我很好。你在台北怎么样啊？

Wǒ hěn hǎo. Nǐ zài Táiběi zěnmeyàng a?

 我也很好！我们班同学带我去了很多好玩儿的地方。

Wǒ yě hěn hǎo! Wǒmen bān tóngxué dài wǒ qù le hěn duō hǎowánr de dìfang.

 你们去了哪些有意思的地方？

Nǐmen qù le nǎ xiē yǒu yìsi de dìfang?

 我觉得台北的孔庙[1]很有意思。每次重要的考试以前，我们都会去那里。很多父母也会带着孩子一起去那里。

Wǒ juéde Táiběi de Kǒngmiào hěn yǒu yìsi. Měi cì zhòngyào de kǎoshì yǐqián, wǒmen dōu huì qù nàlǐ. Hěn duō fùmǔ yě huì dài zhe háizi yìqǐ qù nàlǐ.

 孔子是中国历史上最有名的老师，对中国的教育和传统文化都有很重要的影响。所以很多人希望去孔庙能给自己或者自己的孩子带来好运气。

Kǒngzǐ shì Zhōngguó lìshǐ shàng zuì yǒumíng de lǎoshī, duì Zhōngguó de jiàoyù hé chuántǒng wénhuà dōu yǒu hěn zhòngyào de yǐngxiǎng. Suǒyǐ hěn duō rén xīwàng qù Kǒngmiào néng gěi zìjǐ huòzhě zìjǐ de háizi dài lái hǎo yùnqi.

 您说得很对！其实日本也有很多孔庙。孔子对日本的教育和传统文化也有非常重要的影响。对了，王老师，您什么时候来台北玩儿啊？我最近学会开车了，我可以给您当导游。您想去哪里，我就开车带您去哪里！

Nín shuō de hěn duì! Qíshí Rìběn yě yǒu hěn duō Kǒngmiào. Kǒngzǐ duì Rìběn de jiàoyù hé chuántǒng wénhuà yě yǒu fēicháng zhòngyào de yǐngxiǎng. Duì le, Wáng lǎoshī, nín shénme shíhou lái Táiběi wánr a? Wǒ zuìjìn xué huì kāi chē le, wǒ kěyǐ gěi nín dāng dǎoyóu. Nín xiǎng qù nǎlǐ, wǒ jiù kāi chē dài nín qù nǎlǐ!

好啊，可能明年暑假吧！

Hǎo a, kěnéng míngnián shǔjià ba!

 太好了！我明年暑假应该也在台北。那明年夏天见！

Tài hǎo le! Wǒ míngnián shǔjià yīnggāi yě zài Táiběi. Nà míngnián xiàtiān jiàn!

Comprehension Check

		T	F
1	Miko seems to be having a great time in Taipei.	○	○
2	Miko has been to the Taipei Confucius temple once but didn't think it was very interesting.	○	○
3	Parents hope that bringing their children to a Confucian temple will bring them good luck.	○	○

4 What does Miko offer to do for Ms. Wang, and why?

NOTE

1 孔庙 (Kǒngmiào) is an abbreviated name for a temple of Confucius. These temples may also be called 孔子庙 (Kǒngzǐ miào) or 夫子庙 (Fūzǐ miào). Confucius' name was Kongqiu, but he is often called 孔夫子 (Kǒngfūzǐ). 孔 (Kǒng) is his family name, and 夫子 (fūzǐ) is a title meaning "master" or "scholar." The philosopher is also, more simply, referred to as 孔子 (Kǒngzǐ).

Vocabulary · 生词

Audio

	Word	Pinyin	Meaning
10	台北	Táiběi	Taipei (capital of Taiwan)
11	孔子	Kǒngzǐ	Confucius, a Chinese philosopher who lived from 551 to 479 BC, also known as 孔夫子 (Kǒngfūzǐ)
12	庙	miào	temple, shrine
13	教育	jiàoyù	education
14	传统	chuántǒng	tradition; traditional
15	运气	yùnqi	fortune, luck (good or bad)
16	开车	kāi chē	to drive a car
17	导游	dǎoyóu	tour guide

What a Character! guǎng 广

| 1 | 2 | 3 |

The words 庙 (miào) and 店 contain the component 广 (guǎng), which means "big house" or "broad." Many characters with this component have something to do with buildings. Can you match the following different kinds of buildings with their English definitions?

a courtyard

b garage

c plaza, (public) square

tíngyuán
1 庭园

chēkù
2 车库

guǎngchǎng
3 广场

2c Puzzle It Out · 动动脑 PROGRESS CHECK

Complete the exercise below to check your understanding of what you learned in Section 2. If you have questions, consult the Language Reference section.

Use the words and phrases in the list on the left to complete the exchange below. You will use each option more than once.

什么

怎么

什么时候

A: 今天晚上你想怎么去夜市？

B: 你想＿＿＿去，我们就＿＿＿去。

A: 那我们开车去吧！你想几点去呢？

B: 你想＿＿＿去，我们就＿＿＿去。

A: 那你想吃什么？

B: 你想吃＿＿＿，我就吃＿＿＿。

3 **Talking about "whoever," "whatever," "wherever," etc.**

In Chinese, the ideas of "whoever," "whatever," "whenever," "wherever," and "however" are expressed by combining two short phrases that use the same question word (highlighted in grey in the examples below). The word 就 is often added to the second phrase either just before the subject or at the beginning of the phrase if the subject is left out.

1 谁想去夜市，谁就跟我一起走吧。
   Whoever wants to go to the night market, come with me.

2 你想什么时候去图书馆，我们就什么时候去。
   We'll go to the library whenever you want.

3 你想吃什么，就吃什么吧。
   You can eat whatever you want.

4 你怎么说，我就怎么做。
   I'll do whatever you tell me to. (Lit. "I'll do however you say.")

5 暑假的时候，哪儿人少，我去哪儿玩儿。
   During summer vacation, I'll go visit wherever there are fewer people.

LANGUAGE CHALLENGE

The city of 台北 (Táiběi, Taipei) is not the only city in Taiwan whose name gives a hint about its location. The map shows the locations of the cities of 台中 (Táizhōng, Taichung), 台南 (Táinán, Tainan), and 台东 (Táidōng, Taitung). Can you label the cities correctly?

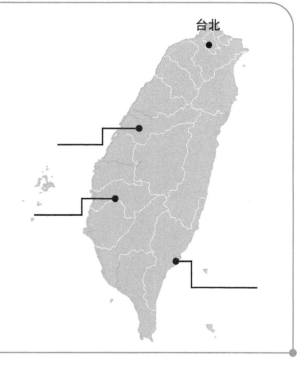

台北

Your goal in this activity is to agree on a travel itinerary for a day trip in Taipei with one of your classmates.

Step 1: Decide on where you want to go and what you want to do for two or three of the following time slots: morning, noon, afternoon, and evening. Leave the other one or two time slots open. Use the list of possible destinations below to help you.

Step 2: Search for a classmate whose itinerary complements yours. Ask what your classmate wants to do in a specific time slot and tell him or her what you want to do in that time slot. If you left that time slot open, indicate to your classmate that you'll do whatever he or she wants to do.

Example:

A: 你上午想去哪儿？

B: 我还没想好要去哪儿。你想去哪儿，我们就去哪儿吧。

A: 那我们去台北孔庙看看吧！

Step 3: Move around the classroom talking to different classmates until you find someone to take your day trip with. Then write your completed itinerary together. Share your itinerary with the class!

The Taipei Confucius Temple (台北孔子庙, Táiběi Kǒngzǐ Miào) attracts visitors who are interested in education, culture, history, and architecture.

士林夜市 (Shìlín Yèshì), located in the north of the city, is popular among both locals and tourists for its many shops and food stalls.

Bird watchers gather in Da'an Forest Park (大安森林公园, Dà'ān Sēnlín Gōngyuán) in hopes of catching a glimpse of local birdlife.

Visitors admire the artwork at Taipei Fine Arts Museum (台北市立美术馆, Táiběi Shìlì Měishùguǎn).

Doing something many times

3a Language Model · 语言范例　TARGET LANGUAGE INPUT

Your teacher will lead a discussion about the images below. Try to participate as much as you can. If there is anything you don't understand, let your teacher know.

Wǒmen　yǐjīng　kàn　le　sān　gè　chuántǒng　jiànzhù　le,
我们－已经－看－了－三－个－传统－建筑－了，

We have already seen three traditional buildings;

míngtiān　women　hái　yào　qù　kàn　liǎng　gè　xiàndài　jiànzhù.
明天－我们－还－要－去－看－两－个－现代－建筑。

and tomorrow we will go see two modern buildings.

1

zhōngshì chuántǒng jiànzhù
中式传统建筑

traditional Chinese-style architecture/building

2

xiàndài　jiànzhù
现代建筑

modern architecture/building

Listen to the audio and try to understand as much as you can. Then read the dialogue, using the pinyin text and vocabulary list to figure out unfamiliar words.

 喂，美子！你最近怎么样啊？在台北生活得开心吗？

Wéi, Měizǐ! Nǐ zuìjìn zěnmeyàng a? Zài Táiběi shēnghuó de kāixīn ma?

 很开心！你在上海怎么样啊，大文？我听雪儿说，你在跟她爸爸学做上海菜？

Hěn kāixīn! Nǐ zài Shànghǎi zěnmeyàng a, Dàwén? Wǒ tīng Xuěér shuō, nǐ zài gēn tā bàba xué zuò Shànghǎi cài?

 是啊，我已经跟雪儿的爸爸学做了好几个上海菜了！

Shì a, wǒ yǐjīng gēn Xuěér de bàba xué zuò le hǎojǐ gè Shànghǎi cài le!

 那下次见面，我一定要尝尝你做的上海菜！对了，上海的经济发展得那么好，工作应该挺好找的吧？

Nà xià cì jiàn miàn, wǒ yídìng yào cháng chang nǐ zuò de Shànghǎi cài! Duì le, Shànghǎi de jīngjì fāzhǎn de nàme hǎo, gōngzuò yīnggāi tǐng hǎo zhǎo de ba?

 不太好找。我其实已经去了好几个餐厅面试厨师的工作了，但是面试都没有成功。

Bú tài hǎo zhǎo. Wǒ qíshí yǐjīng qù le hǎojǐ gè cāntīng miànshì chúshī de gōngzuò le, dànshì miànshì dōu méiyǒu chénggōng.

 你别难过！我相信你是一个好厨师，多试几次，你一定可以！

Nǐ bié nánguò! Wǒ xiāngxìn nǐ shì yí gè hǎo chúshī, duō shì jǐ cì, nǐ yídìng kěyǐ!

 谢谢！我会继续努力的。你呢？听说你在学建筑设计？

Xièxie! Wǒ huì jìxù nǔlì de. Nǐ ne? Tīngshuō nǐ zài xué jiànzhù shèjì?

 是啊，以后我想当一个像林璎一样厉害的建筑设计师[1]。为了这个目标，除了在学校学习以外，我还去看了很多

Shì a, yǐhòu wǒ xiǎng dāng yí gè xiàng Lín Yīng yíyàng lìhai de jiànzhù shèjìshī. Wèile zhège mùbiāo, chúle zài xuéxiào xuéxí yǐwài, wǒ hái qù kàn le hěn duō

不同的建筑。有些是中式的
传统建筑，有些是现代建筑。
对了，其实我们宿舍的设计
也很有意思！

bùtóng de jiànzhù. Yǒuxiē shì zhōngshì de
chuántǒng jiànzhù, yǒuxiē shì xiàndài jiànzhù.
Duì le, qíshí wǒmen sùshè de shèjì
yě hěn yǒu yìsi!

听起来真不错！你会成功的！
我也要努力做一个好厨师！

Tīng qǐlai zhēn búcuò! Nǐ huì chénggōng de!
Wǒ yě yào nǔlì zuò yí gè hǎo chúshī!

嗯，我们一起加油吧！

Ǹg, wǒmen yìqǐ jiāyóu ba!

Comprehension Check

		T	F
1	Miko thinks that finding work should be easy because Shanghai is so economically developed.	○	○
2	Owen has already interviewed for a chef position at several restaurants.	○	○
3	Miko says that she has only visited modern buildings in Taiwan.	○	○

4   Do you think Miko likes studying architecture? Use details from the conversation to support your statement.

NOTE

1   The character 师 can convey the idea of "a master, a professional in a field." This idea can be found in the words 老师 and 厨师 (chúshī) and in terms like 设计师 (shèjìshī, designer), and 建筑师 (jiànzhùshī, architect).

Audio

Vocabulary · 生词

	Word	Pinyin	Meaning
18	经济	jīngjì	economy; economic
19	发展	fāzhǎn	to develop, to advance, to grow
20	厨师	chúshī	chef, professional cook
21	建筑	jiànzhù	building; architecture; to build, to construct

	Word	Pinyin	Meaning
22	设计	shèjì	design; to design
23	中式	zhōngshì	Chinese style
24	现代	xiàndài	modern, contemporary
25	宿舍	sùshè	dormitory, hostel
	林璎	Lín Yīng	Maya Lin, a Chinese American architectural designer

5Cs CONNECTIONS

COMMUNITIES
COMMUNICATION
CULTURES
COMPARISONS

林璎 (Lín Yīng), or Maya Lin, is a Chinese American architect, sculptor, and designer. Born in Ohio in 1959, 林璎 was a student at Yale University when her design for the Vietnam Veterans Memorial was chosen in a contest that attracted more than a thousand entries. Since then, she has designed many buildings and art installations, and her work can be seen in museums, national parks, and communities around the United States. Many of her works, such as the earthwork installation Storm King Wavefield in New York were inspired by her concern for the environment.

Think of a building that you consider to be beautiful, impressive, or inspiring. What aspects of the design appeal to you?

Visitors appreciate the Vietnam Veterans
Memorial in Washington, D.C.

The earthwork Storm King Wavefield in
New York blends seamlessly into the landscape.

3c Puzzle It Out • 动动脑 PROGRESS CHECK

Complete the exercise below to check your understanding of what you learned in Section 3. If you have questions, consult the Language Reference section.

Rearrange the Chinese words and phrases in each row to translate the English sentences.

1 设计了 | 她已经 | 了。 | 十件 | 中式衣服
She has already designed ten pieces of Chinese-style clothing.

2 跟这个厨师 | 三个菜了! | 我已经 | 学做了
I have already learned to cook three dishes from this chef!

3 三遍了。 | 这本关于 | 建筑设计的书, | 看了 | 我已经
I have read this book on architectural design three times already.

Language Reference • 语言注解

4 Expressing how many times

The chart below shows the sentence structure used when saying how many things you have done or how many times you have done something. The verb + 了 portion of this pattern expresses that the action is completed. The second 了 at the end of the pattern indicates that the number will continue to change in the future as you do the action again.

	verb + 了	number + MW	noun	了	
1 我已经	吃了	十个	饺子	了。	I've already eaten ten dumplings.
2 我们已经	看了	三个	zhōngshì jiànzhù 中式建筑	了。	We have already seen three Chinese style buildings.
3 我姐姐	看了	四本	jīngjì 经济学的书	了。	My older sister has read four economics books.
4 他已经	选了	五门	课	了。	He has already chosen five courses.

3d Using the Language · 语言应用 INTERPERSONAL

Play a card-collecting game with your classmates. For this game, imagine that you are attending a networking event and the cards you collect represent the people you have met at the event.

Step 1: Create a set of cards for the seven professions below.

Step 2: Your teacher will put you in groups. Combine your cards with those of your group, shuffle them, and redistribute them evenly among the group members.

Step 3: Look at your hand and decide which profession to focus on collecting. You might choose the profession that interests you the most, or the profession that you already have the most cards for.

Step 4: Take turns choosing one of your groupmates and telling him or her about how many people of a certain profession you have already met — if you have three furniture designer cards, for example, you will say you have met three furniture designers. If you have more of that profession than the other student, you may take a card from his or hand. If that student has more than you, then he or she will take a card from your hand. (No fibbing!) If you have the same number, no card is exchanged. Play moves clockwise to the next student.

Step 5: Try to collect as many cards of one profession as possible before your teacher calls time.

1 游戏设计师   5 设计医院的建筑师

2 app 设计师   6 设计校园的建筑师

3 家具设计师   7 设计大楼的建筑师

4 舞台设计师

Audio

A Listening and Reading • 阅读和听力 INTERPRETIVE

Passage 1 What's next for Martin and his friends? Read on...

马丁正在跟美子视频聊天……

 美子，好久不见！

 好久不见啊，马丁。你最近怎么样？

 还可以！你在台北怎么样啊？

 很好啊。春月没跟你说我在网上发了好几个视频了吗？很多是关于我在台北的大学生活的。你可以去看看！

 好啊！对了，我和梅雅他们要参加一个环保比赛。我们想先做个调查，看看学生们对哪些环保问题的认识还不够。你能不能帮我们在你的大学里也做一下调查呢？

 没问题！那你们别忘了去网上看我的视频啊。

 谢谢！那我一会儿把调查问卷发给你。下午下课以后我们一起去看你的视频！

下课以后，马丁、天浩、梅雅、可可和里奥一起在中文教室里看美子的视频。

 大家好！我是美子，现在在台北上大学，后面就是我的宿舍。我的专业是建筑设计。虽然我现在还不会做设计，但是我希望毕业以后可以像林璎一样，当一个很棒的建筑设计师。除了对建筑有兴趣以外，我还很喜欢做视频。在今天的这个视频里，我给大家当一次导游。我们一起去台北几个特别的建筑，和有名的夜市看看吧！

现在我已经到第一个地方了。你们一定听说过孔子吧？孔子是中国历史上最有名的老师，这里就是台北的孔庙。现在请跟我一起走进孔庙看看吧。我在北京住过几年，一直对中式传统建筑很有兴趣。你们看，孔庙就是传统的中式建筑。建筑师们

在这里用了红色和黄色等颜色。孔子对教育有特别大的影响，所以有一些父母喜欢带孩子来孔庙。他们觉得来这里会给孩子带来好运气，孩子考试的时候会有一个好成绩。

看完了传统的中式建筑，现在我们去台湾最高的现代建筑——台北 101 看看吧！台北 101 就在孔庙的东南边，从这里开车过去只要十几分钟。

现在我们看到的就是台北 101。它不但非常高，而且还是绿色建筑。台湾的经济发展很快，所以这里有很多国际公司的办公室。这里也有一些餐厅和商店。如果你不怕高，也可以到台北 101 上面去看看外面漂亮的台北。

在台北 101 里面有很多有名的餐厅和厨师，但是如果你跟我一样是学生，可能会觉得那里的菜特别贵。那你可以去美食中心看看，那里的吃的会便宜很多。现在，我带你们去台北有名的夜市看看吧，那里也有很多又好吃又便宜的东西。

刚来台北的时候，我还不太清楚应该在夜市里买些什么。所以我们班同学去哪家店，我就去哪家店。他们点什么，我就点什么。不过，现在我已经知道哪家店的饮料最好喝，哪家店的东西最好吃了。我还能给朋友们推荐一些新的美食！你们看，中间的这家店……

 等一下，我好像饿了……

 我也饿了。

 可是现在还没到回家吃晚饭的时间……

 我们先去吃点儿零食，再回来看美子的视频吧？

 好啊！

Comprehension Check

		T	F
1	Martin and Miko haven't seen each other in a long time.	○	○
2	Miko says she will only help Martin and his friends if they watch her videos.	○	○
3	Miko wants to be an architectural designer like Maya Lin, and she has already designed several buildings.	○	○
4	In her video, Miko brings viewers to a modern-style Confucian temple.	○	○
5	According to Miko, you can eat food made by famous chefs at Taipei 101.	○	○
6	When Miko first visited a Taiwanese night market, she just went wherever her classmates did.	○	○
7	What do you think Miko was about to say when Martin and the others stopped watching the video?		

Passage 2 The restaurant shown below specializes in a dish that is popular in many parts of Asia. Can you tell what it is? Choose the set of simplified Chinese characters that corresponds to the traditional characters shown on the sign.

(a) 清真黄牛肉面馆 (b) 清真黄牛肉饺子 (c) 清真红烧牛肉面

A halal restaurant in Taipei, Taiwan

Passage 3 Listen to the conversation between a student named Qingqing and a teacher. Are the statements that follow true or false?

		T	F
1	This is most likely the first time Qingqing and Ms. Bai have met.	◯	◯
2	Qingqing asks Ms. Bai about the school trip to Taipei this year.	◯	◯
3	Last year, the tour guide brought the students to see a traditional Chinese-style skyscraper.	◯	◯
4	Ms. Bai seems to think that the food in Taiwan isn't very good.	◯	◯

Passage 4 Listen to a radio advertisement. Are the statements that follow true or false?

		T	F
1	The advertisement is for a part-time job opportunity in Taipei.	◯	◯
2	The students who sign up will stay in a dormitory at Taipei University.	◯	◯
3	The students will take a class about traditional Chinese architecture.	◯	◯
4	On weekends, students will visit different cities in Taiwan.	◯	◯

Speaking · 口语

Imagine that your school's Chinese department is planning a trip to Taiwan, and the teachers want to know which cities students are interested in visiting.

Step 1: Look at the options below and choose all that interest you. You may choose just one or even all four. Think about why you are interested in each option.

Step 2: Your teacher will put you in small groups. Tell your group members how many options you chose, what they are, and why you chose them.

Example:

我选了三个城市。我选的第一个地方是台北。我对传统中式建筑很有兴趣，在台北可以看到很多这种建筑。

Step 3: After you have listened to your group members' thoughts, ask each member at least one follow-up question. For instance, you might ask when the person would like to visit the site, how he or she would like to get there, or how many people he or she would like to go with. If you are asked a follow up question and don't have an opinion, simply express that you'll do whatever others want to do.

Example:

Q: 你想跟几个人一起去？
A: 谁想去，谁就一起去吧。

台北

台南 (Táinán, Tainan)

在台北你可以在现代的高楼里买东西，也可以在传统的庙里找好运气。你不但可以在台北的中心看到一些很有意思的博物馆，而且可以在城市附近的山上看到很漂亮的花。

台南是一个很特别的城市！在台南可以看到中式孔庙，也可以看到传统的西式 (xīshì, Western style) 建筑，还可以看到现代的高楼。台南的日本菜也很有名！从别的城市开车到台南也很方便。

垦丁 (Kěndīng, Kenting)

花莲 (Huālián, Hualien)

垦丁有很多很漂亮的海滩 (hǎitān, beach)、一个特别有名的夜市和很多便宜的旅馆。你可以住在海滩 和夜市中间的旅馆：什么时候想游泳，就什么时候走到海滩去游泳；什么时候想吃晚饭，就什么时候走到夜市去吃晚饭！

花莲是在台湾西部的一个小城市。花莲在山和海 (hǎi, sea) 的中间，很漂亮。在那里可以了解丰富的原住民 (yuánzhùmín, aboriginal people) 文化，也可以看看原住民的建筑。因为花莲离山很近，从那儿开车去山里玩儿也很方便。

C Final Project · 结课项目 PRESENTATIONAL

Taiwan Tour

Imagine that a travel agency has asked you to design a tour of Taiwan that will appeal to students. Use the opinions and ideas from your conversation with your group in the Speaking activity to design and present your tour.

Step 1: Review the cities you read about for the Speaking activity, or do some research to learn about other interesting destinations in Taiwan.

Step 2: Decide on at least three destinations for your Taiwan tour plan. Research how far they are from Taipei by car and what the best route would be to see them all. Consider how each destination might appeal to different people. For instance, are there interesting outdoor activities? Indoor activities? Local delicacies to try?

Step 3: Mark the travel destinations on a map of Taiwan. Include photos and a bit of information about each destination on the map. Create an outline of a presentation explaining your tour and why you chose each destination. Include travel information in your presentation.

Step 4: Give your presentation to the class and be ready to answer questions from your classmates.

Can-Do Goals · 能力目标

Talk with your teacher if you have questions or if you are not certain you can do the following tasks:

- Discuss how Taiwan's history has influenced its language and culture
- Describe something's location as being inside, outside, or between other things
- Indicate the direction of an action
- Express ideas such as "whoever," "wherever," and "whenever"
- Talk about how many times you have done something

Cultural Knowledge · 文化知识

What do you know about Taiwan?

Getting Things for Owen's New Place

CHAPTER 7

第 dì 七 qī 课 kè

康大文

#打工

康大文
找到工作和新家了，开始新生活！

林马丁
大文，你真厉害！

二村美子
太棒了

刘海生
我知道你一定行！

东方雪儿
你真棒，大文！

林春月
我们一定要给你庆祝庆祝！

197 16 8

Write a comment...

Can-Do Goals • 能力目标

In this chapter, you will learn to:

- Describe some of the ways technology affects how people buy and sell things in China
- Understand complex numbers when used to represent prices
- Estimate a quantity by providing an approximate number
- Express whether someone can afford something or not
- Describe certain quantities of different types of objects
- Compare products and living spaces according to price and quantity

zhìnéng   kējì   yǔ   diànzǐ   shāngwù

智能科技与电子商务
Smart Technology and E-commerce

An unstaffed convenience store where people can pay by cell phone

In China, as in many other countries today, the relationship between commerce and technology has grown extremely close. Smartphones and e-commerce platforms help people buy whatever they want, whenever they want.

你喜欢在网上买东西吗？

Paying with Technology

Credit and debit cards were not popular in China at the beginning of the 21st century; people used cash (现金, xiànjīn) for most purchases. Cell phone use took off rapidly in China after 2010, and now the apps on smartphones (智能手机, zhìnéng shǒujī) can be used for many kinds of purchases — from picking up a bite to eat to paying rent. Not everyone has adjusted to mobile payments, however. Since so many businesses prefer using mobile payments, people who don't have smartphones or don't know how to make mobile payments sometimes have difficulty paying for things they need.

A fruit stall in Shenzhen displays a QR code. Customers scan this code with their phone app to pay.

在中国，人们买东西付钱的时候，更喜欢刷卡、用现金，还是用智能手机？为什么？

你觉得这会给人们的生活带来哪些方便和不方便的地方？

172

Straight to the Customer

E-commerce (电子商务, diànzǐ shāngwù) platforms in China allow consumers to skip going to the store and buy products from home. Some major platforms even allow customers to purchase fruits and vegetables directly from farmers. These platforms can increase farmers' incomes (收入, shōurù) and give customers the benefit (好处, hǎochù) of accessing fresher food. However, the growth of delivery services that support these platforms has also led to new problems. For example, delivery drivers are under a lot of pressure to deliver large numbers of packages quickly, which has resulted an increase in traffic accidents (交通事故, jiāotōng shìgù).

A group of delivery drivers wait for the light to change in Chengdu, Sichuan Province.

电子商务的发展给人们带来了哪些好处和问题？

By the Numbers

According to a survey from one major Chinese e-commerce platform, food delivery (外卖, wàimài) is especially popular with younger generations. However, ordering (订, dìng) food for delivery can create unnecessary waste. A 2017 study estimated that over 60 million plastic containers and cups from food delivery were being thrown out every day.

如果人们订的外卖太多，对环境会有什么影响？

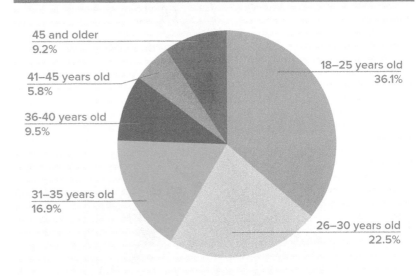

Food Delivery Customers in China by Age

- 45 and older 9.2%
- 41–45 years old 5.8%
- 36-40 years old 9.5%
- 31–35 years old 16.9%
- 18–25 years old 36.1%
- 26–30 years old 22.5%

Source: Meituan Research Institute, 2020

REFLECT ON THE ESSENTIAL QUESTION

How is technology both the problem and the solution?

1. In your community, what kinds of online platforms and apps do people rely on to get things done in their daily lives?

2. Do you or your friends and family members use apps to make purchases? If so, what apps do you use and how often do you use them?

3. How do you feel about technology acting as an intermediary between people?

Talking about prices

1a Language Model · 语言范例 TARGET LANGUAGE INPUT

Your teacher will lead a discussion about the image below. Try to participate as much as you can. If there is anything you don't understand, let your teacher know.

Zhè   tào   yùndòngfú   shāngchǎng   lǐ   mài   sān   bǎi   duō   kuài,
这 — 套 — 运动服 — 商场 — 里 — 卖 — 三 — 百 — 多 — 块，

This set of athletic wear costs more than three hundred yuan at the mall,

dànshì   zài   wǎngshàng   zhǐ   yào   jiǔshí   duō.
但是 — 在 — 网上 — 只 — 要 — 九十 — 多。

but it only costs a little over ninety online.

1b New Words in Context · 语境中学新词 INTERPRETIVE

Audio

Listen to the live stream of Ellen's infomercial for her online store and try to understand as much as you can. Then read the passage, using the pinyin text and vocabulary list to figure out unfamiliar words.

你们好！欢迎来到我的网店[1]。我的店里有很多最近最受欢迎的衣服和鞋。这些衣服和鞋不但样子好看，而且一点儿都不贵！你们看这套运动服[2]，它的设计特别有个性，也很受欢迎。很多号都已经卖完了，只有两套中号的了。所以你们要是想买，得赶快买。我再给你们推荐一下这双鞋，穿起来非常舒服。这双鞋如果你们在商场里买，打折的时候也要一百多。在我的店里只要六十块〇六毛。我的店里还有一些小东西，比街上的"一元店[3]"卖得更便宜。你们在我的店里买，还可以节约时间，我会把东西送到你们家。要是你们有什么问题，可以在视频下面告诉我，我很快就会回答你们的问题。

Nǐmen hǎo! Huānyíng lái dào wǒ de wǎng diàn. Wǒ de diàn lǐ yǒu hěn duō zuìjìn zuì shòu huānyíng de yīfu hé xié. Zhèxiē yīfu hé xié búdàn yàngzi hǎokàn, érqiě yì diǎnr dōu bú guì!Nǐmen kàn zhè tào yùndòng fú, tā de shèjì tèbié yǒu gèxìng, yě hěn shòu huānyíng. Hěn duō hào dōu yǐjīng mài wán le, zhǐ yǒu liǎng tào zhōng hào de le. Suǒyǐ nǐmen yàoshi xiǎng mǎi, děi gǎnkuài mǎi. Wǒ zài gěi nǐmen tuījiàn yíxià zhè shuāng xié, chuān qǐ lái fēicháng shūfu. Zhè shuāng xié rúguǒ nǐmen zài shāngchǎng lǐ mǎi, dǎzhé de shíhou yě yào yì bǎi duō. Zài wǒ de diàn lǐ zhǐ yào liùshí kuài líng liù máo. Wǒ de diàn lǐ hái yǒu yìxiē xiǎo dōngxi, bǐ jiē shàng de "yì yuán diàn" mài de gèng piányi. Nǐmen zài wǒ de diàn lǐ mǎi, hái kěyǐ jiéyuē shíjiān, wǒ huì bǎ dōngxi sòng dào nǐmen jiā. Yàoshi nǐmen yǒu shénme wèntí, kěyǐ zài shìpín xiàmiàn gàosu wǒ, wǒ hěn kuài jiù huì huídá nǐmen de wèntí.

Comprehension Check

		T	F
1	The athletic clothing at Ellen's store is sold out.	◯	◯
2	Ellen says that the shoes she is selling cost less than they would at a mall.	◯	◯

3 If you were going to ask a question or leave a comment on Ellen's video, what would you say?

NOTE

1 网店 means "online store."

2 运动服 means "athletic clothing," "sportswear."

3 一元店 is similar to a dollar store; a store that sells items for one yuan or for a very low price.

Audio

Vocabulary · 生词

	Word	Pinyin	Meaning
1	鞋	xié	shoes
2	样子	yàngzi	style, appearance
3	套	tào	(measure word for things that come in sets)
4	号	hào	size, number
5	中	zhōng	medium; middle
6	双	shuāng	(measure word for a pair)
7	商场	shāngchǎng	shopping mall, shopping center, department store
8	毛	máo	(measure word for one tenth of a unit of currency)
9	元	yuán	(measure word for Chinese currency, most often used in written communication)

COMPARISONS

COMMUNITIES
COMMUNICATION
CULTURES
CONNECTIONS

Some Chinese people use slang words to refer to currency from other countries. For example, the word 刀 (dāo) literally means "knife" or "blade," but some people use it as slang for U.S. currency because "dāo" sounds similar to "dollar."

Can you think of slang words used for money in English? How would you explain these words to someone in Chinese?

1c Puzzle It Out · 动动脑

Complete the exercises below to check your understanding of what you learned in Section 1. If you have questions, consult the Language Reference section.

Exercise 1 Use the words in the list on the left to complete the equations below. You may use some words more than once.

元
毛
百

₁ 5   + 5 毛 = 1 元

₂ 1 百 + 2 百 = 3

₃ 5   + 5 元 = 10 元

₄ 50 元, 打八折 = 40

₅ 1 元 – 7   = 3 毛

Exercise 2 Choose the best option to complete each sentence.

1 A: 参加这种考试需要多少钱？

　 B: 三十块一定够，好像需要 　　　　 钱。

　　 a 二十多块　　　　　 b 三十多块　　　　　 c 三十一块

2 A: 你们今天的比赛几点开始？

　 B: 三点。现在是一点半，还有 　　　　 就开始了。

　　 a 一个小时　　　　 b 一个多小时　　　　 c 两个多小时

3 A: 我们班有 　　　　 个学生。

　 B: 是吗？我们班也有二十多个学生。

　　 a 十九　　　　　　 b 二十五　　　　　　 c 二十

4 A: 我认识三百多个汉字，你呢？

　 B: 我认识的比你少，我只认识 　　　　 。

　　 a 三百个　　　　　 b 三百二十个　　　　 c 三百多个

Language Reference · 语言注解

1 Denominations of currency

Chinese money is called 元 (yuán). Both 元 (yuán) and 块 can be used as measure words for Chinese money, but 元 (yuán) is often used in written language, and 块 is often used in spoken Chinese. The word 钱 is not included when giving a price in writing but may or may not be included when doing so in spoken Chinese.

1 ¥9 = 九块钱 (spoken) = 九块 (spoken) = 九元 (written)
   [yuán above 元]

The measure words 毛 (máo) and 分 are used for smaller units of money: 毛 (máo) is used for tenths of a unit (such as a dimes or ten cents in US currency), and 分 is used for one-hundredths of a unit (such as pennies in US currency). The way money is expressed in Chinese differs from English for amounts like "$9.99" because the "dimes" and the "pennies" are said separately. So, "$9.99" is 九块九毛 (máo) 九分钱 , literally "nine dollars, nine tenths of a dollar, and nine hundredths of a dollar."

Note that if 钱 is omitted, the last measure word is often omitted as well, as shown in the table below.

	Amount	Full expression in Chinese	Omitting 钱	Omitting 钱 + last measure word
2	$4.70	四块七毛钱	四块七毛	四块七
3	¥0.65	六毛五分钱	六毛五分	六毛五
4	$8.25	八块两毛五分钱	八块两毛五分	八块两毛五
5	$119	一百一十九块钱[1]	一百一十九块	一百一十九
6	¥205	两百〇五块钱[2]	两百〇五块	两百〇五

[1] Note that if the amount in the tens place is one, it is read 一十, not 十.

[2] The word 零 (or 〇) may also be added if necessary to clarify that the value of one unit is zero. For example, ¥11.07 is read 十一块〇七分. The 〇 helps clarify that there are 块 and 分 but no 毛 (máo). That is, the value of the tenths place is zero. In this case, the word 分 should not be omitted.

2 Indicating an approximate number using 多

The word 多 can be used in more than one way to give an estimate or state an approximate amount. Depending on how 多 is used, it can indicate that there is a little more than the number given, or it can indicate a range higher than the number given.

Pattern #1: [number] + [measure word] + 多 + [noun]

This pattern indicates that there is more of the noun than the number given, but less than one higher than the number given. Note that this pattern can only be used for things that can be divided into smaller units or pieces, like weeks, days, hours, dollars, or yuan. It cannot be used for things like people or animals because they cannot be divided.

1	两个多小时	more than two hours (more than two but less than three)
2	八块多钱	more than eight yuan (more than eight but less than nine)
3	三个多月	more than three months (more than three but less than four)
4	两年多	more than two years (more than two but less than three)
5	五岁多	more than five years old (more than five but less than six)

Pattern #2: [number that ends with 十 / 百 / 千 / 万] + 多 + [measure word] + [noun]

This pattern indicates a range between the number given and a number that is ten, one hundred, one thousand, or ten thousand higher.

6	十多个朋友	more than ten friends (more than ten but less than twenty)
7	五百多个学生	more than five hundred students (more than five hundred but less than six hundred)
8	两千多年	more than two thousand years (more than two thousand but less than three thousand)
9	一万多块钱	more than ten thousand yuan (more than ten thousand but less than twenty thousand)

Note that some words, like 天, 岁, 年, and 分钟, can function as measure words, so they come before 多 in pattern 1 and after 多 in pattern 2 (see examples 4 and 8).

Imagine that you and your partner found part-time jobs promoting an online store.

Step 1: With your partner, decide what kind of online store you would like to promote, such as a 鞋店, 包店, 宠物店, or 乐器店. You can pick a store that you both like or create your own.

Step 2: Create an advertisement with your partner. You and your partner can decide on the format of the advertisement, such as a poster, video, or audio recording. Your advertisement should feature items sold at the store and mention how much the items cost.

Step 3: Be prepared to present your advertisement to the class.

5Cs
CULTURES
COMMUNITIES
COMMUNICATION
COMPARISONS
CONNECTIONS

You may have noticed that many of the characters used for writing numbers in Chinese are simple and easy to write. Although using simple characters is convenient for reading and writing, it can also cause problems because they are easily mistaken for other characters, or even intentionally falsified. For example, it's very easy to add a stroke to 二 and make it 三 . For this reason, complicated versions of the characters for numbers were developed to prevent these kinds of errors on important documents.

一 二 三 四 五 六 七 八 九 十
壹 贰 叁 肆 伍 陆 柒 捌 玖 拾

This set of alternate characters still appears today in official documents and notes, such as money. Can you think of ways other currencies are protected from being altered or forged?

Not being able to afford something

2a Language Model• 语言范例 TARGET LANGUAGE INPUT

Your teacher will lead a discussion about the images below. Try to participate as much as you can. If there is anything you don't understand, let your teacher know.

Nǐ kàn, zhège shūjià zěnmeyàng?
你 - 看, - 这个 - 书架 - 怎么样?

What do you think of this bookshelf?

Tài guì le, wǒ mǎi bù qǐ.
太 - 贵 - 了, - 我 - 买 - 不 - 起。

It's too expensive. I can't afford it.

1 桌子

yǐzi
2 椅子
chair

shūjià
3 书架
bookcase, bookshelf

Audio

Listen to the audio and try to understand as much as you can. Then read the dialogue, using the pinyin text and vocabulary list to figure out unfamiliar words.

叔叔，谢谢您和阿姨这些天的照顾！我已经找好房子了。这个星期五就可以搬过去了。

Shūshu, xièxie nín hé āyí zhèxiē tiān de zhàogù, wǒ yǐjīng zhǎo hǎo fángzi le. Zhège xīngqī wǔ jiù kěyǐ bān guò qù le.

你这么快就要搬走啊，大文！你找的房子怎么样？

Nǐ zhème kuài jiù yào bān zǒu a, Dàwén! Nǐ zhǎo de fángzi zěnmeyàng?

挺不错的。市中心¹的房子太贵了，我租不起。我租的那个房子离市中心有点儿远，所以房租不太贵，而且还带²一些家具。有桌子、椅子等等。您看，这是我新家的照片。

Tǐng búcuò de. Shì zhōngxīn de fángzi tài guì le, wǒ zū bù qǐ, wǒ zū de nàge fángzi lí shì zhōngxīn yǒu diǎnr yuǎn, suǒyǐ fángzū bú tài guì, érqiě hái dài yìxiē jiājù. Yǒu zhuōzi, yǐzi děng děng. Nín kàn, zhè shì wǒ xīn jiā de zhàopiàn.

看起来真不错！对了，那星期五我们帮你搬家吧？

Kàn qǐ lái zhēn búcuò! Duì le, nà xīngqī wǔ wǒmen bāng nǐ bān jiā ba?

不用麻烦您和阿姨了，叔叔。我的东西不多，也不重，只有衣服和书架上的一些书。

Búyòng máfan nín hé āyí le, shūshu. Wǒ de dōngxi bù duō, yě bú zhòng, zhǐ yǒu yīfu hé shūjià shàng de yìxiē shū.

那你找工作的事怎么样了？

Nà nǐ zhǎo gōngzuò de shì zěnmeyàng le?

刚找到，是在一个国际餐厅。

Gāng zhǎo dào, shì zài yí gè guójì cāntīng.

新家和新工作，恭喜啊！我们得给你庆祝庆祝³，大文！

Xīn jiā hé xīn gōngzuò, gōngxǐ a! Wǒmen děi gěi nǐ qìngzhù qìngzhù, Dàwén!

哈哈，谢谢叔叔！

Hāha, xièxie shūshu!

别客气！欢迎你以后有时间再来家里玩儿！

Bié kèqi! Huānyíng nǐ yǐhòu yǒu shíjiān zài lái jiā lǐ wánr!

Comprehension Check

		T	F
1	Owen is moving to an apartment in the center of the city.	○	○
2	Owen needs a lot of help moving his things.	○	○
3	Why does Xue'er's dad want to celebrate?		

NOTE

1 市中心 means "downtown, city center."

2 When talking about renting apartments and other living spaces, 带 is used to describe what is included in the rental. 带家具 means that the rental space is furnished.

3 In order to specify whom a celebration is for, 给 can be added before 庆祝.

Vocabulary • 生词

Audio

	Word	Pinyin	Meaning
10	房子	fángzi	house, apartment, building
11	搬	bān	to move (furniture, large items); to move (from one living space to another)
12	租	zū	to rent
13	房租	fángzū	rent (for an apartment, house, etc.)
14	家具	jiājù	furniture
15	椅子	yǐzi	chair
16	重	zhòng	heavy, severe
17	书架	shūjià	bookcase, bookshelf
18	恭喜	gōngxǐ	congratulations; to congratulate

LANGUAGE CHALLENGE

In Chinese, there is a particular kind of saying called 歇后语 (xiēhòuyǔ) that consists of two parts. Here is an example:

Kǒng fūzǐ bān jiā   jìng shì shū
孔夫子搬家 —— 净是书。

When Confucius moves (to a new house), there is nothing but books.

This saying is used when someone loses continuously or keeps failing at something. The saying could be used to describe a football team on a losing streak, for example. Can you guess why this saying would be used in that kind of situation? (Hint: The answer relates to the pronunciation of the final word.)

The picture on the right is in the style of 剪纸 (jiǎnzhǐ), a traditional Chinese art form that involves cutting paper. It shows Confucius being pulled in a cart by a water buffalo.

2c Puzzle It Out · 动动脑   PROGRESS CHECK

Complete the exercise below to check your understanding of what you learned in Section 2. If you have questions, consult the Language Reference section.

Match the first part of each sentence with the option on the right that best completes the thought.

1 酸辣鱼好像比以前贵多了，   a 我喝不起了。

2 这种饮料今天不打折了，   b 我吃不起了。

3 虽然我很喜欢那双鞋，
但是我的钱不够，   c 我们买不起，
也租不起。

4 这里的房子非常贵，   d 所以我买不起那双鞋。

Language Reference · 语言注解

3 Understanding the different meanings of 不起

There is more than one possible meaning for 不起. When it is paired with certain verbs, such as 买, 租, 吃, 穿, and 付, it means that the subject cannot afford to do the action that the verb indicates.

1 那套运动服太帅了！我很想买，但是买不起。

That [exercise] outfit is so cool! I'd love to buy it, but I can't afford it.

2 我很想去那场演唱会，可是门票太贵了，我买不起。

I really want to go to that concert, but the tickets are too expensive. I can't afford it.

3 他很想住在市中心，可是那里的房子他租不起。

He'd really like to live downtown, but he can't afford the rent for those apartments.

看不起 means that the subject disdains or looks down on someone or something.

4 有时候，住在大城市的人看不起住在山里的人，这是不对的。

Sometimes people who live in the city look down on people who live in the mountains, and that is wrong.

Note that the positive form of these verb phrases, 买得起 and 看得起, are not often used unless asking a question, responding to a question, or when saying something contrary or unexpected.

5 Q: 这个蛋糕这么大，我们买不起吧？

This cake is so big. We can't afford it, can we?

A: 买得起。我最近打工刚赚了一点儿钱。

We can afford it. I recently made some money working part time.

6 Q: 你看这双鞋太好看了，可是这么贵！谁买得起啊？

Check out this pair of shoes. They look absolutely beautiful, but they are so expensive! Who could afford them?

A: 这双鞋真的很贵！我买不起……

These shoes really are expensive! I can't afford them...

7 Q: 我们只有一块钱，能买得起什么啊？

We only have one dollar. What can we possibly buy with that?

A: 一块钱虽然不多，可是也能买得起一些东西，比如：小零食。

Although one dollar isn't much, it can buy some things, like small snacks.

2d Using the Language · 语言应用 INTERPERSONAL

For this game, the class will be divided into customers and salespeople. The goal for the customer is to buy everything on his/her list, and the goal for salespeople is to sell as many items as possible.

	Buyers	Salespeople
Step 1:	Imagine that you are redesigning your room. Look at the items below and write a list of five items that you want to buy.	Write down six objects from the items below that you will sell at your store. (Note: This means that your "inventory" will be a total of six things.) Decide how to price them.
Step 2:	You have ¥1,000. Go around the classroom to different salespeople and "buy" the items on your list. If the price is too high, be ready to say "我买不起" and ask for discounts so that you don't spend too much money on any one item. Example: 太贵了，我买不起。 便宜点儿吧！	Buyers will come to your store. If you have what they want, try to sell them the item. Try to get as much money as you can, but consider offering discounts, or the buyers may go to a different store. Example: 好吧！要是你买两个，可以给你打八折！
Step 3:	The buyer who has bought the most items from his/her list wins. If it is a tie, the buyer with the most money left over wins.	The salesperson who sells the most items wins. If it is a tie, the salesperson who brings in the most money wins.

Quantities of things

3a Language Model · 语言范例　TARGET LANGUAGE INPUT

Your teacher will lead a discussion about the image below. Try to participate as much as you can. If there is anything you don't understand, let your teacher know.

Wǒmen　jiàoshì　lǐ　yǒu　èrshí　bǎ　yǐzi,　shíjiǔ　zhāng　zhuōzi.
我们－教室－里－有－二十－把－椅子，－十九－张－桌子。

In our classroom, there are twenty chairs and nineteen desks.

Nǐmen　jiàoshì　lǐ　ne?
你们－教室－里－呢？

How about your classroom?

A high school classroom in Beijing

3b New Words in Context · 语境中学新词 INTERPRETIVE

Listen to the audio and try to understand as much as you can. Then read the dialogue, using the pinyin text and vocabulary list to figure out unfamiliar words.

 昨天雨下得真大啊！

Zuótiān yǔ xià de zhēn dà a!

 是啊！我回家的时候才知道，厨房的窗户我们忘了关！而且我家没电了，雨和冰箱里的水进到客厅和我的房间了。

Shì a! Wǒ huí jiā de shíhou cái zhīdào, chúfáng de chuānghu wǒmen wàng le guān! Érqiě wǒ jiā méi diàn le, yǔ hé bīngxiāng lǐ de shuǐ jìn dào kètīng hé wǒ de fángjiān le.

 啊？水还进到你的房间了啊？你的东西没事吧？

À? Shuǐ hái jìn dào nǐ de fángjiān le a? Nǐ de dōngxi méi shì ba?

 哎，很多东西都不能用了。我得换一张床，买几本新书。我们还得再买几把椅子。真的太麻烦了！哎，昨天晚上我和爸爸妈妈花了好几个小时收拾房子。

Āi, hěn duō dōngxi dōu bù néng yòng le. Wǒ děi huàn yì zhāng chuáng, mǎi jǐ běn xīn shū. Wǒmen hái děi zài mǎi jǐ bǎ yǐzi. Zhēnde tài máfan le! Āi, zuótiān wǎnshàng wǒ hé bàba māma huā le hǎojǐ gè xiǎoshí shōushi fángzi.

 那你们把房子收拾干净了吗？

Nà nǐmen bǎ fángzi shōushi gānjìng le ma?

 还没有……所以昨天晚上我们住在旅馆里了。

Hái méiyǒu... Suǒyǐ zuótiān wǎnshàng wǒmen zhù zài lǚguǎn lǐ le.

 那你的床买好了吗？

Nà nǐ de chuáng mǎi hǎo le ma?

 也没有。我爸爸说，这个周末我们一起去家具店看看。

Yě méiyǒu. Wǒ bàba shuō, zhège zhōumò wǒmen yìqǐ qù jiājù diàn kàn kan.

 对了，我最近看到了几个网上家具店的广告，很多东西在打折。他们还会直接把东西送到家里。你要不要看看？

Duì le, wǒ zuìjìn kàn dào le jǐ gè wǎng shàng jiājù diàn de guǎnggào, hěn duō dōngxi zài dǎzhé. Tāmen hái huì zhíjiē bǎ dōngxi sòng dào jiā lǐ. Nǐ yào bú yào kàn kan?

好！我只在网上买过小东西，还没买过家具。我得多看几条评价，选一张好点儿的床！

 是啊，在网上买东西真的得先看看评价怎么样。

Hǎo! Wǒ zhǐ zài wǎngshàng mǎi guò xiǎo dōngxi, hái méi mǎi guò jiājù. Wǒ děi duō kàn jǐ tiáo píngjià, xuǎn yì zhāng hǎo diǎnr de chuáng!

Shì a, zài wǎng shàng mǎi dōngxi zhēnde děi xiān kàn kan píngjià zěnmeyang.

Comprehension Check

		T	F
1	Sanjay and his parents forgot to close the window yesterday.	○	○
2	Sanjay needs a new bed and a new desk due to some water damage.	○	○
3	Martin suggested that Sanjay buy replacement furniture online.	○	○

4 Based on what Sanjay said, why do you think he wanted to read some reviews before shopping online?

Vocabulary · 生词

Audio

	Word	Pinyin	Meaning
19	厨房	chúfáng	kitchen
20	窗户	chuānghu	window
21	冰箱	bīngxiāng	refrigerator
22	客厅	kètīng	living room
23	花	huā	to spend
24	广告	guǎnggào	advertisement
25	直接	zhíjiē	direct, immediate
26	评价	píngjià	evaluation, appraisal; to evaluate, to appraise

Complete the exercise below to check your understanding of what you learned in Section 3. If you have questions, consult the Language Reference section.

Choose the word from the list on the left that best completes each sentence. Use each word only once. (Hint: these sentences can be sung to the tune of "Twinkle, Twinkle, Little Star.")

张
把
家
双

1 一 ___ 桌子两杯茶，三 ___ 椅子四把花。

2 五 ___ 商场六条街，七件衣服八 ___ 鞋。

What a Character!

 xué 穴

1 穴 2 穴 3 穴 4 穴 5 穴

The word 窗户 **(chuānghù) contains the component** 穴 **(xué), which means "cave." It is used in many words that relate to caves and enclosed spaces, but it is used in a wide variety of other words as well.**

Each of the Chinese words below contains the 穴 component. Use this knowledge to match the words with the correct image and English meaning.

chuānglián
1 窗帘

zhǎi xiǎo
2 窄小

niǎo wō
3 鸟窝

a a bird's nest

b narrow and small

c window drapes, curtains

Language Reference · 语言注解

4 Measure words

In *Go Far with Chinese 1*, *Go Far with Chinese 2*, and previous chapters, you learned many measure words. 个 is the most common measure word and can sometimes be used as a substitute for other measure words. However, overusing 个 or using the wrong measure word can confuse people or interrupt the flow of conversation, so it is important to use the most appropriate measure word whenever possible. The table below reviews many of the measure words you have learned so far:

Measure word	Used with	Measure word	Used with
把	椅子、花、吉他	本	书
场	比赛、演唱会、考试、面试	份	饺子、工作、计划、报告、申请、调查
家	旅馆、咖啡馆、餐厅、商场、医院、公司	件	衣服、事、礼物
节	课	块	钱、肉、蛋糕
门	课、考试、才艺	盘	菜、家常豆腐、红烧鱼
双	筷子、鞋	条	裤子、路、街、短信、狗、鱼
碗	面条、凉皮、米饭、酸辣汤	位	老师、同学、厨师、师傅、医生
张	门票、桌子、照片、床、地图、海报	只	宠物、猫、狗、鸟

Note that some nouns can use different measure words depending on the situation. For example, the measure word 只 is used for animals, so the word for dog can use the measure word 只. However, the measure word 条 is used for long, thin things, so 条 can also be used for dogs that are long and thin (see example 1 below).

1 我家有三只狗。   vs.   那条狗很可爱！
   My family has three dogs.   vs.   That dog is cute!
                                       (The speaker is pointing to a long, thin dog.)

Both 次 and 遍 can be used as measure words for verbs, indicating the number of times a person does something. 次 can be used with most verbs and in a variety of situations. 遍 is used to emphasize that an action is performed from start to finish, and it is usually used for actions that don't have to be completed all at once, such as reading a book or singing a song.

2 她去过四次西安。   She has been to Xi'an four times.

3 请再说一遍。   Please say that one more time.

Imagine that your friend's older sibling was looking for an apartment for next year to share with two other people. Your friend's sibling asked you and your partner to help him/her decide which apartment to rent.

Step 1: Look at the listings for apartments below and read their descriptions.

Step 2: Discuss which apartment(s) you like best and why. With your partner, decide which apartment you will recommend to your friend's sibling.

Step 3: Report your decision to the class. Did the other groups make the same choice as your group?

天远小区：一个客厅，三个房间，一个厨房，一个洗手间。离地铁站非常近，走路只需要 5 分钟。离商场也很近。带家具（一个冰箱、一张桌子、四把椅子、三张床）。房租：¥2,900/月。

国际公园：一个客厅，五个房间，一个厨房，两个洗手间。离公交车站很近，走路才 20 分钟。附近有很多公园。不带家具。房租：¥3,200/月。

东方花园：四个房间，一个厨房，两个洗手间。离市中心很近，坐地铁只要十分钟。带家具（一个冰箱、四张床）。房租：¥3,400/月。

香梅园：一个客厅，两个房间，一个厨房，一个洗手间。离大学很近。带家具（一个冰箱、一张桌子、四把椅子、三张床）。房租：¥1,800/月。

Put the Pieces Together! · 融会贯通

A Reading and Listening · 阅读和听力 INTERPRETIVE

Audio

Passage 1 What's next for Isabella and her friends? Read on...

周末下午，春月、雪儿和海生来到了大文的新家，庆祝他找到了工作。

 恭喜你找到了工作，大文！

 大文，恭喜啊！

 是啊，恭喜恭喜！我们给你买了点儿水果、蛋糕，还有花。

 谢谢你们！你们太客气了！我家比较小，没有客厅，你们先坐椅子上吧。我把蛋糕放到厨房的冰箱里。

 好。大文，你的新家虽然不大，但是特别舒服！窗户外面能看到那么多绿绿的树。

 是啊！你已经买了这么多家具了啊？

 没有，我租的房子是带家具的，有桌子、椅子和床。对了，还有电视。

 那房租贵不贵啊？

不贵！因为这儿离市中心比较远。来，这是我给你们准备的饮料和零食。不好意思，我其实开始的时候想请你们在我家吃晚饭。但是我最近太忙了，还没去买做饭要用的东西……

 别客气！对了，你今天不用去工作，我们几个也有空。我们跟你一起去商场里买做饭要用的东西吧？

 春月，你想吃大文做的菜了吧？

 哈哈！想吃是想吃，不过大文自己一个人住，也很需要这些东西啊。这样他才能照顾好自己。

 你说得也对。

 那在网上买吧？又方便又便宜。

 我们还是一起去商场买吧？我在药店打工得站着，所以也想去买一双舒服点儿的鞋。

 鞋也可以在网上买啊。你可以找一双评价好一点儿的鞋。

 不行，在网上买鞋不能试，可能会不合适。而且网上很多东西的评价不是真的……

大家讨论了一会儿，决定一起去商场买东西。海生先买了一双打折的鞋，花了一百多块钱。然后，春月建议大家去家具店，帮大文看看有什么要买的东西。大文看到春月为了让他的新家更舒服，一直在帮他选东西。他想，虽然有的时候春月说话有点儿直接，但是她其实对朋友很好……

 大文，你看这个书架怎么样？我记得你好像很喜欢看书。

 对！我的书现在还没地方放。这个书架真的挺不错的，但是太贵了，我买不起啊。

 这个书架真的很贵，而且还不打折！

而且这个书架有点儿太大了吧，看起来也很重。我们没有车，怎么搬回去啊？

 是啊，我们再看看别的书架吧。

 你们先在这儿看看。我在网上找找有没有合适的书架，在网上买可以送到家。

 好啊。你们看，那个不错！只要一百一十块九毛九。

 可以，可是这个今天好像不打折……

 没关系，我可以拍张照片，看看网上有没有一样的……找到了！这个在网上只要九十八块九毛八！

 这家店的评价怎么样？

 我看了一下，这是一家七、八年的老店。评价挺不错的！而且这些评价应该是真的。

 那你在网上买吧，大文？

 好，那我们现在去买做饭要用的东西吧！

 哎，等等，前面那家店的广告上写着今天运动服打五折！你们能不能等我一下？我想进去看看。

 行。

 雪儿，这套运动服我穿着怎么样？

 不错！你觉得呢？

195

样子我挺喜欢的，但是好像有点儿小，我想买一套中号的。我去问问售货员。

春月想让售货员帮她拿一套中号的运动服，可是……

 不好意思，中号的太受欢迎了，已经卖完了。不过我们的网店里还有，你可以去看看。

 好吧……谢谢。对了，雪儿，你有什么想买的衣服吗？

 没有。其实我已经有点儿饿了……

 我也是。糟糕，已经六点多了，我们还没有买到做饭要用的东西……

 在商场里时间过得太快了！

 是啊，而且花了三个多小时，很多东西我们还得在网上买。

 没关系。我们在商场里一边买东西一边聊天儿很开心啊！那边有个美食中心，好吃的东西又多又便宜，我们去那儿吃晚饭吧？

 好主意！我们就在这儿给你庆祝，就不用你自己做饭了！

Comprehension Check

		T	F
1	Isabella, Xue'er, and Haisheng helped Owen move to his new apartment.	◯	◯
2	Haisheng wanted to go to the mall to buy shoes because he wanted to try them on before he bought them.	◯	◯
3	Owen bought a bookshelf at the mall because it is on sale for ¥98.98.	◯	◯
4	Isabella found clothes that she liked at the mall, but her size was all sold out.	◯	◯
5	After Owen, Isabella, Xue'er, and Haisheng finished shopping, they went back to Owen's apartment to have dinner.	◯	◯
6	Summarize the story in three to five sentences. Why did Isabella, Xue'er and Haisheng go to visit Owen? Where did they go and what did they do?		

Passage 2 This advertisement was posted on the street in the Wangjing district of Beijing. What is this advertisement for? How do you know?

Passage 3 Listen to the conversation between two college students and answer the following questions.

1 Where is the boy living now?

   (a) in a room at his friend's place, close to the school

   (b) in an apartment that is not very close to the school

   (c) in the school's dormitory

2 How much is the monthly rent?

   (a) less than eight hundred yuan

   (b) more than eight hundred yuan

   (c) eight hundred yuan

3 How will the boy buy furniture for his apartment?

   (a) He will buy the furniture online.

   (b) His parents will buy him furniture for his birthday.

   (c) He and the girl will go to the mall this weekend to buy furniture.

Passage 4 Below are pictures of some items that a student searched for online. Listen to him describe his online shopping experience. On a separate piece of paper, write down which items he purchased. For the items he purchased, write down how much he spent on each item. For the items he did not purchase, explain why he did not purchase them.

B Speaking · 口语 INTERPERSONAL

Imagine that an exchange student from the south of China has just arrived at your school and wants to buy some new things to adjust to life in your area. He/she has asked you and your group for advice on items to buy and where to get the best deals.

Step 1: With your group, make a list of the top five things that you think most students in your school need or want. Consider the climate and environment of where you live and how they might be different from where the exchange student came from.

Step 2: For each item on your list, do you think it is better to go to a store to buy the item or to buy the item online? What stores or 网店 would you recommend, and why? You can make more than one recommendation if your group doesn't agree or if you think there is more than one good way to buy the item.

Step 3: Be prepared to share your recommendations with the class.

C Final Project · 结课项目 `PRESENTATIONAL`

Ideal Apartment

Imagine that you have just landed your dream internship in Shanghai. The company where you will be working will help you relocate and cover the cost of your housing, but you need to give them a description of your ideal apartment.

Step 1: On your own, brainstorm a list of things that you think are important when choosing a place to live. Consider the following:

- type of apartment (full apartment, single room with shared common spaces, shared room)
- layout/design of the apartment (number of rooms, bathrooms, etc.)
- type of building (tall apartment building, traditional-style building, what floor, etc.)
- number of roommates
- design of rooms (size of rooms, windows, view, etc.)
- furniture/amenities (bed, TV, internet, kitchen, etc.)
- location (close to subway, parks, stores, offices, etc.)

Use your notes to write a description of the apartment you would like.

Step 2: Your teacher will ask you and a classmate to exchange descriptions. Take on the role of property agent. Search online to find apartments that match the description you have been given. Be sure to find three to five different options.

Step 3: Show the apartments that you found to your classmate and discuss. Which apartment does your classmate like the best? Of all the apartments that your classmate found, which do you like the best? Your teacher will lead a discussion and ask about everyone's ideal apartments. Be prepared to show the apartment that your partner chose and explain why he or she likes that apartment.

Can-Do Goals · 能力目标

Talk with your teacher if you have questions or if you are not certain you can do the following tasks:

- Describe some of the ways technology affects how people buy and sell things in China
- Understand complex numbers when used to represent prices
- Estimate a quantity by providing an approximate number
- Express whether someone can afford something or not
- Describe certain quantities of different types of objects
- Compare products and living spaces according to price and quantity

Cultural Knowledge · 文化知识

What are some of the businesses that take payment via apps in China? Can you use apps to pay for things at similar places in your community?

A 24-hour automated store with no sales staff in Shenzhen, China

Online Life

春月他们帮马丁做完关于环保
比赛的调查了。这个星期三下
午四点，除了美子以外，春月
他们都没有课，大文也放假。
所以春月、雪儿和海生来到了
大文家，准备跟马丁他们视频
聊天儿。中文教室下午没有人，
所以马丁他们约好了就在那儿
见面，要跟春月他们讨论一下
关于环保比赛的事。

Can-Do Goals · 能力目标

In this chapter, you will learn to:

- Analyze how Chinese people do or do not benefit from spending time online
- Discuss your thoughts about the internet
- Express that something began and continued on
- Understand when others indicate the motion and direction of an action
- Briefly describe news related to a familiar topic

wǎngluò   yúlè   shēnghuó

网络娱乐生活
Going Online for Fun

As of 2021, China had over 900 million internet users. While many use the internet (网络, wǎngluò) for work or school, many also go online for fun! In China, as in many other countries, the explosion of online content has created new forms of entertainment while also raising concerns about the effects of spending increasing amounts of time online.

China's Digital World

The online environment in China is dominated by apps and platforms that were developed there and conform to the requirements of the Chinese government. However, digital life in China shares many features that are common to the internet environments in countries across the globe. Some of the most popular online activities in China are chatting with friends, watching videos, reading the news (新闻, xīnwén), listening to music, and playing games.

中国人的网络生活跟你的网络生活有哪些不一样的地方？有哪些一样的地方？

Creating content for the internet — a woman live streams by the Bell Tower in Xi'an

New Forms of Media

Digital distribution channels have pros and cons for content creators. One benefit is that publishing stories (故事, gùshi) online as web novels (网络小说, wǎngluò xiǎoshuō) allows authors to reach a broader audience, and to do so fairly quickly. Sometimes these web novels become so popular that they are adapted into movies or TV shows! Many authors complain, however, that it can be difficult to get credit and compensation for their work because of digital theft: web novels are sometimes reposted without permission or even republished under other names by unscrupulous readers.

网络小说在中国有多受欢迎？
你看过网络小说吗？

Many web novels are in the fantasy, romance, and historical genres. Here, a model dresses in a costume based on the clothing worn in China during imperial times.

Playing Games

The video game (电子游戏, diànzǐ yóuxì) industry in China makes billions of dollars annually, with many people enjoying mobile games (手游; from 手机游戏) and online games (网游; from 网络游戏). Some of the most popular games are even translated into other languages and can be played outside of China. Given the popularity of gaming, many people have raised concerns that video games can damage children's eyes (眼睛, yǎnjing) and take time away from their studies. There are now rules in place that require game companies to put time and spending limits in place for players under the age of 18.

中国的孩子每个星期能玩儿很长时间的手游或者网游吗？

People in Chongqing play games at an internet café. Some gamers go to internet cafés to play because the cafés have dependably fast internet connections.

By the Numbers

There are over 700 million gamers in China! Here are some notable facts.

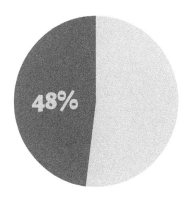

48% of gamers in China are women

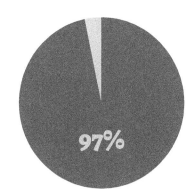

97% of 18- to 24-year-olds are gamers

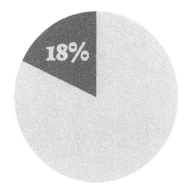

18% of gamers play more than 30 hours a week

Source: Niko, 2020

REFLECT ON THE ESSENTIAL QUESTION

How is technology both the problem and the solution?

1 What makes it appealing to do things online instead of in person?

2 What are the advantages and disadvantages of sharing content online?

3 Should young people be allowed to manage their own internet usage? Why or why not?

Discussing internet use

1a Language Model · 语言范例 TARGET LANGUAGE INPUT

Your teacher will lead a discussion about the images below. Try to participate as much as you can. If there is anything you don't understand, let your teacher know.

Wǒ jiā de wǎngluò bú tài hǎo, shàng wǎng hěn màn.
我 家 的 网络 不太 好, 上 网 很 慢。
The internet at my house isn't very good; going online is very slow.

Yǒu duō màn?
有 多 慢?
How slow is it?

1

大楼：高

2

山：远

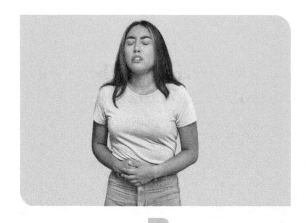

3

肚子：疼

4

他：累

Audio

Listen to the audio and try to understand as much as you can. Then read the dialogue, using the pinyin text and vocabulary list to figure out unfamiliar words.

同学们，会写汉字对学习中文很重要。今天我们要练习手写第八课的生词。请大家把纸和笔准备好。

Tóngxuémen, huì xiě hànzì duì xuéxí Zhōngwén hěn zhòngyào. Jīntiān wǒmen yào liànxí shǒu xiě dì bā kè de shēngcí. Qǐng dàjiā bǎ zhǐ hé bǐ zhǔnbèi hǎo.

不好意思，王老师，我有一个问题。会写汉字有多重要呢？您看，我们现在做什么事都用手机或者电脑，学校和家里也有网络。如果我需要什么信息，可以直接上网找。跟朋友联系的时候，我会发电子邮件¹或者短信。我已经很长时间不用纸和笔写字了。我觉得我会打字² 就行了。我们为什么还要练习手写汉字呢？

Bù hǎoyìsi, Wáng lǎoshī, wǒ yǒu yí gè wèntí. Huì xiě hànzì yǒu duō zhòngyào ne? Nín kàn, wǒmen xiànzài zuò shénme shì dōu yòng shǒujī huòzhě diànnǎo, xuéxiào hé jiā lǐ yě yǒu wǎngluò. Rúguǒ wǒ xūyào shénme xìnxī, kěyǐ zhíjiē shàng wǎng zhǎo. Gēn péngyou liánxì de shíhou, wǒ huì fā diànzǐ yóujiàn huòzhě duǎnxìn. Wǒ yǐjīng hěn cháng shíjiān bú yòng zhǐ hé bǐ xiě zì le. Wǒ juéde wǒ huì dǎ zì jiù xíng le. Wǒmen wèishénme hái yào liànxí shǒu xiě hànzì ne?

这个问题非常好，也很值得讨论。要不然³，大家都说说自己的想法吧，怎么样？

Zhège wèntí fēicháng hǎo, yě hěn zhí dé tǎolùn. Yàobùrán, dàjiā dōu shuō shuo zìjǐ de xiǎngfǎ ba, zěnmeyàng?

Comprehension Check

T   F

1. Ms. Wang tells the students to prepare paper and a pen because they will be writing characters by hand. ○ ○

2. Martin wonders how important it is to know how to write characters by hand. ○ ○

3. Martin says he writes by hand only when sending letters to his friends. ○ ○

4. What are your thoughts on practicing writing Chinese characters by hand?

NOTE

1 电子邮件 (diànzǐ yóujiàn) can be abbreviated to 电邮 (diàn yóu), or to just 邮件 (yóujiàn) if the context makes it clear that you are talking about email and not physical mail.

2 打字 (dǎ zì) means "to type."

3 In addition to meaning "otherwise, or else," 要不然 can also be used to express "how about." When used this way, 要不然 can also be abbreviated to 要不.

Audio

Vocabulary · 生词

	Word	Pinyin	Meaning
1	手	shǒu	hand
2	纸	zhǐ	paper
3	笔	bǐ	pen
4	网络	wǎngluò	internet, network
5	信息	xìnxī	information
6	上网	shàng wǎng	to go online, to use the internet
7	联系	liánxì	to contact, to get in touch; connection, relation
8	电子邮件	diànzǐ yóujiàn	email
9	字	zì	character

1c Puzzle It Out · 动动脑 PROGRESS CHECK

Complete the exercise below to check your understanding of what you learned in Section 1. If you have questions, consult the Language Reference section.

Come up with a possible follow up question using 多 for each of the sentences below.

Example: 纽约的冬天很冷。 → 纽约的冬天有多冷?

1 我哥哥很高。

2 我家离学校很近。

3 我们学校很大。

4 那条裤子挺贵的。

5 北京的夏天很热。

6 那个饭馆的凉皮做得很好吃。

Language Reference • 语言注解 ●━━━━━━━━━━━━━━━━━━━━━━━━━━━

1 Using 多 to ask questions about the amount or the degree

多 can be combined with descriptive words to ask questions. In *Go Far with Chinese* 1 and 2, 多长, 多大, and 多少 were covered.

1 你学了多长时间的笛子了？　　How long have you been studying the flute?

2 她穿多大的 T 恤衫？　　What size T-shirt does she wear?

3 这个电脑多少钱？　　How much does this computer cost?

However, using 多 to ask questions goes beyond those few specific examples. 多 can be combined with any descriptive word to ask questions about the measurement or degree of something. Below are some exchanges that use 多 to ask questions.

4 A: 你家离图书馆多远？　　How far is your house from the library?

　 B: 不太远。走路只要十五分钟。　It's not far, only a fifteen minute walk.

5 A: 这个问题很重要。你看一下。　This topic is very important. Take a look.

　 B: 多重要？　　How important is it?

　 A: 明天的考试老师可能会考！　The teacher might test us on it in tomorrow's exam!

When 多 is used to ask a question, sometimes 有 is added in front of 多.

6 A: 你弟弟现在有多高？　　How tall is your younger brother now?

　 B: 跟我一样高了。　　He's the same height as me.

7 A: 你说你累了，你有多累？　　You say you're tired—how tired are you?

　 B: 我累得站不起来了。　　I'm so tired, I can't stand up. (Literally: I'm tired to the point of not being able to stand up.)

Technology is a big part of our lives, but there are also some downsides to spending so much time plugged in. Would you be willing to spend a full day "unplugged"?

In groups, use Chinese to discuss the following questions and any other questions that may come up in the course of your conversation.

- Is the internet important to you? How important is it?
- What do you usually do online?
- Are you willing to spend a day without watching TV or movies, using a cell phone, or using a computer?
- Do you think spending a day without a phone, computer, and TV is good? Why or why not?
- What would you do differently if you had no phone and no internet/computer for a day? Would anything be more difficult? Would anything be easier?

The teacher will call on one person from each group to summarize their group's discussion. Be prepared to give your report.

5Cs

CULTURES
COMMUNITIES
COMMUNICATION
COMPARISONS
CONNECTIONS

For much of China's history, scholars considered four items to be especially important to their work: a brush, paper, ink, and an inkstone. These four items were so highly regarded that they gained the title 文房四宝 (wénfáng sì bǎo), or "The Four Treasures of the Study." There's even a quick way to talk about these four items— 笔墨纸砚 (bǐ mò zhǐ yàn).

笔 (bǐ) refers to 毛笔 (máo bǐ), the calligraphy or painting brush.

墨 (mò) means "inkstick." Although today ink is usually bought in liquid form, in ancient China it was traditionally purchased as a stick—a mixture of soot and glue. To use the ink, the inkstick would be ground against the stone and mixed with water.

纸 (zhǐ) describes paper—a must-have for writing or painting! Xuan paper (a type of paper famed for its smoothness, absorptive properties, and durability) is especially desirable and is often used for calligraphy.

砚 (yàn) refers to an inkstone. An inkstone is a flat slab of stone designed for the inkstick to be ground against. Inkstones also often have a hollowed-out section to hold the water or freshly mixed ink.

Although nowadays writing is rarely done using brush and ink, 笔墨纸砚 are still used by calligraphers and are viewed as important products in Chinese culture.

Have you used any or all of these 文房四宝 before?

Expressing that something begins and continues on

2a Language Model · 语言范例　TARGET LANGUAGE INPUT

Your teacher will lead a discussion about the images below. Try to participate as much as you can. If there is anything you don't understand, let your teacher know.

Dì　yī　gè　nǚshēng　wèishénme　kū　qǐ　lái　le?

第－一－个－女生－为什么－哭－起来－了?

Why has the first girl started crying?

Biéde　rén　xīnqíng　zěnmeyàng?　Nǐ　zěnme　zhīdào?

别的－人－心情－怎么样?－你－怎么－知道?

What are other people's moods like? How do you know?

2b New Words in Context · 语境中学新词 INTERPRETIVE

Listen to the audio and try to understand as much as you can. Then read the dialogue, using the pinyin text and vocabulary list to figure out unfamiliar words.

哈哈……

Hāha...

春月，你不是在做作业吗？
怎么看着电脑笑起来了？

Chūnyuè, nǐ bú shì zài zuò zuòyè ma?
Zěnme kàn zhe diànnǎo xiào qǐ lái le?

雪儿，我休息一会儿，正在
看《李山的快乐生活》呢。
这个电视剧¹太有意思了。
你看，那个大眼睛、小脸的
大学生²就是李山。他养了
一只特别聪明的小鸟。早上
李山跟它说："我要去比赛
了。"然后那只小鸟说："祝
你好运³！"可是李山一回
家，它就说："你的房间太
乱了，快收拾一下！"李山
觉得很奇怪，这只鸟是跟谁
学的。

Xuěér, wǒ xiūxi yíhuìr, zhèng zài
kàn "Lǐ Shān de kuàilè shēnghuó" ne.
Zhège diànshìjù tài yǒuyìsi le.
Nǐ kàn, nàge dà yǎnjing, xiǎo liǎn de
dàxuéshēng jiù shì Lǐ Shān. Tā yǎng le
yì zhī tèbié cōngmíng de xiǎo niǎo. Zǎoshàng
Lǐ Shān gēn tā shuō: "Wǒ yào qù bǐsài
le." Ránhòu nà zhī xiǎo niǎo shuō: "Zhù
nǐ hǎo yùn!" Kěshì Lǐ Shān yì huí
jiā, tā jiù shuō: "Nǐ de fángjiān tài
luàn le, kuài shōushi yíxià!" Lǐ Shān
juéde hěn qíguài, zhè zhī niǎo shì gēn shéi
xué de.

我知道！跟李山的妈妈学的！

Wǒ zhīdào! Gēn Lǐ Shān de māma xué de!

啊？你怎么知道？

Á? Nǐ zěnme zhīdào?

我以前看过这个小说。你想
不想知道后来李山怎么了？

Wǒ yǐqián kàn guò zhège xiǎoshuō. Nǐ xiǎng
bù xiǎng zhīdào hòulái Lǐ Shān zěnme le?

不，不。别告诉我！要不然
电视剧就没意思了。

Bù, bù. Bié gàosu wǒ! Yàobùrán
diànshìjù jiù méi yìsi le.

Comprehension Check

		T	F
1	Xue'er asks why Isabella stopped laughing.	○	○
2	The main character of the TV series has big eyes and a small face.	○	○
3	Every day when Li Shan gets home, his bird tells him to go to sleep.	○	○

4   How did Xue'er know that the bird had learned that phrase from Li Shan's mother?

NOTE

1   电视剧 (diànshìjù) refers to series that are aired on television; for web series, which only appear online, 网剧 (wǎng jù) is used.

2   大学学生 is typically abbreviated to 大学生. Similarly, 高中学生 can be abbreviated to 高中生.

3   祝你好运 means "(I wish you) good luck." 好运 is an abbreviation of 好运气.

Vocabulary · 生词

Audio

	Word	Pinyin	Meaning
10	笑	xiào	to laugh, to laugh at, to smile
11	起来	qǐ lái	(word added after an action or state of being to indicate that it began suddenly or unexpectedly)
12	电视剧	diànshìjù	TV drama, TV series
13	眼睛	yǎnjing	eyes
14	脸	liǎn	face
15	养	yǎng	to raise, to care for (plants or animals)
16	乱	luàn	messy, random, arbitrary; messily, randomly, arbitrarily
17	小说	xiǎoshuō	novel, fiction book

The sentences below each include an expression that has 眼 (yǎn) (short for 眼睛 (yǎnjing)) in it. Based on the context, can you guess the meanings of these two expressions? Hint: the first expression has a negative meaning, and the second expression has a positive meaning.

1 他有些眼高手低，毕业以后
只想去有名的大公司，可是
他一点儿经验都没有，所以
一直没找到合适的工作。

(Note: 低 (dī) means "low.")

2 他眼明手快，乒乓球打得非
常好。一看见球过来了，他
马上就能准备好，然后把球
打回去。

2c Puzzle It Out · 动动脑　PROGRESS CHECK

Complete the exercise below to check your understanding of what you learned in Section 2. If you have questions, consult the Language Reference section.

Choose the phrase from the list on the left that best completes each sentence. Use each option once.

1 A: 你看，她的脸　　　　了。

　B: 是啊，她可能觉得有点儿不好意思了。

紧张起来

红起来

唱起歌来

2 A: 他今天好像看起来跟平常不太一样。

　B: 他一听到要考试就　　　　了。

3 A: 他怎么　　　　了？

　B: 因为他很高兴。他一高兴就喜欢唱歌。

COMMUNICATION

COMMUNITIES
CULTURES
COMPARISONS
CONNECTIONS

Previously you learned a few ways to wish someone well: 祝你生日快乐, 祝你身体健康, and 祝你好运. Another fairly common expression to wish someone well is 祝你笑口常开 (xiào kǒu cháng kāi). 笑口常开 conveys the wish that someone will often find himself or herself smiling, entirely happy and without any concerns. You might use this phrase on a birthday card, or a card to wish someone a happy new year.

Can you think of other common phrases for well-wishes that you like to use? Consider asking your teacher or looking up whether there's an equivalent expression in Chinese!

Language Reference · 语言注解

2 Indicating the beginning of an action or state with 起来

In *Go Far with Chinese* 1 and 2 a few different usages of 起来 were introduced: 起来 meaning "to get up"; 起来 coming before a description to indicate an impression; and 起来 added after a verb to express an upward or rising motion. In addition to these usages, 起来 can also come after an action or a state of being to indicate that it began—often suddenly or unexpectedly—and continued on.

1 他吃了那个水果以后，嗓子就痒起来了。
After he ate that fruit, his throat began to itch.

2 到了说再见的时候，我和朋友都哭起来了。
When the time came to say goodbye, my friend and I both started crying.

3 冬天到了，天气冷起来了。
Winter has arrived; the weather has started getting cold.

Often the pattern 一 . . . 就 . . . is used together with 起来.

4 我弟弟一看到那个视频就笑^{xiào}起来了。

As soon as my younger brother sees that video, he starts laughing.

5 赵医生一到医院就忙起来了。

As soon as Dr. Zhao arrives at the hospital, she becomes busy.

6 我一听到那种音乐头就疼起来了。

As soon as I hear that type of music, I start getting a headache.

When describing the start of an action that has an object (highlighted in grey in the examples below), the object is placed in between 起 and 来. Occasionally, the object can simply be omitted, as shown in example 9.

7 我朋友一坐下就玩儿起手机来了。

As soon as my friend sits down, she starts playing around on her phone.

8 她一听到音乐就跳起舞来。

The moment she hears music, she starts dancing.

9 他们一见面就聊起天儿来了。/ 他们一见面就聊起来了。

They started chatting as soon as they met up.

2d Using the Language · 语言应用 INTERPERSONAL/PRESENTATIONAL

What can you do to help make your classmates' days better?

Step 1: In groups, talk about what others can do to make you feel better when you are unhappy. Take note of your groupmates' responses.

你不开心的时候，别人做什么会让你的心情好起来？

Step 2: Looking at your notes, are there certain activities or things that a few different classmates say would make them feel better? As a group, create a list of five things you can do to improve someone's mood, so that, if you notice that a person seems unhappy, you can help him/her feel better.

Example:

有的同学说，把不开心的事说出来，他们的心情就会好起来。所以有人不开心的时候，我会跟她/他聊聊天儿。

Step 3: Present your list to the class, and pay attention when other groups present their lists. Did other groups list any of the same things to make someone feel better? If so, take note of them: the more commonly listed methods may be the most effective!

Talking about news

Language Model · 语言范例 TARGET LANGUAGE INPUT

Your teacher will lead a discussion about the images below. Try to participate as much as you can. If there is anything you don't understand, let your teacher know.

Wǒmen	yīnggāi	bǎ	fàng xué	yǐhòu	de	shíjiān

我们 - 应该 - 把 - 放学 - 以后 - 的 - 时间

yòng	zài	shénme	huódòng	shàng	bǐjiào	hǎo	ne?

用 - 在 - 什么 - 活动 - 上 - 比较 - 好 - 呢?

What activities would be a good use of our after-school time?

Qǐng	bǎ	nǐ	de	xiǎngfǎ	shuō	chū	lái	ba.

请 - 把 - 你 - 的 - 想法 - 说 - 出 - 来 - 吧。

Please express your opinion.

1

yóu yǒng

游泳

to swim; swimming

2

pá shān

爬山

to hike (in the mountains), to climb a mountain; hiking

Audio

Listen to the audio and try to understand as much as you can. Then read the text conversation between Sanjay and Martin, using the pinyin text and vocabulary list to figure out unfamiliar words.

马丁，这个周末我们去爬山或者游泳吧？

Mǎdīng, zhège zhōumò wǒmen qù pá shān huòzhě yóu yǒng ba?

马丁？我已经等了你两个多小时了，你怎么还不回我的短信啊？收到我的短信，回我一下。你又在练二胡，没看手机吗？

Mǎdīng? Wǒ yǐjīng děng le nǐ liǎng gè duō xiǎoshí le, nǐ zěnme hái bù huí wǒ de duǎnxìn a? Shōu dào wǒ de duǎnxìn, huí wǒ yíxià. Nǐ yòu zài liàn èrhú, méi kàn shǒujī ma?

不好意思啊，赛吉！我放学以后跟梅雅他们去讨论环保比赛的事了。我刚看到你给我发的短信！

Bù hǎoyìsi a, Sàijí! Wǒ fàng xué yǐhòu gēn Méiyǎ tāmen qù tǎolùn huánbǎo bǐsài de shì le. Wǒ gāng kàn dào nǐ gěi wǒ fā de duǎnxìn!

好吧……对了，环保比赛的问卷调查你们做完了吗？

Hǎo ba... Duì le, huánbǎo bǐsài de wènjuàn diàochá nǐmen zuò wán le ma?

都做完了！

Dōu zuò wán le!

那这个周末你应该有时间跟我去运动了吧？

Nà zhège zhōumò nǐ yīnggāi yǒu shíjiān gēn wǒ qù yùndòng le ba?

这个周末可能不行……明天跟春月他们讨论完问卷的调查结果以后，我们还得分析一下收到的数据。而且最近有几条关于环保话题的新闻，我想看看能不能把新闻里的一些信息放进环保比赛的报告里。

Zhège zhōumò kěnéng bù xíng... Míngtiān gēn Chūnyuè tāmen tǎolùn wán wènjuàn de diàochá jiéguǒ yǐhòu, wǒmen hái děi fēnxī yíxià shōu dào de shùjù. Érqiě zuìjìn yǒu jǐ tiáo guānyú huánbǎo huàtí de xīnwén, wǒ xiǎng kàn kan néng bù néng bǎ xīnwén lǐ de yì xiē xìnxī fàng jìn huánbǎo bǐsài de bàogào lǐ.

马丁，环保比赛重要是重要，可是你不能把时间都花在准备比赛上啊。你也要多关心关心自己，也多运动运动啊。

Mǎdīng, huánbǎo bǐsài zhòngyào shi zhòngyào, kěshì nǐ bù néng bǎ shíjiān dōu huā zài zhǔnbèi bǐsài shàng a. Nǐ yě yào duō guānxīn guānxīn zìjǐ, yě duō yùndòng yùndòng a.

你说得对。我好久没去爬山了。那这个周末我们去爬山吧！

Nǐ shuō de duì. Wǒ hǎojiǔ méi qù pá shān le. Nà zhège zhōumò wǒmen qù pá shān ba!

Comprehension Check

		T	F
1	Sanjay asks Martin if he wants to go swimming or hiking after school.	○	○
2	Sanjay asks Martin to respond to his text once he gets it.	○	○
3	Sanjay advises Martin to take better care of himself, and exercise more.	○	○

4 Initially, what reason does Martin give for not being able to hang out?

Vocabulary · 生词

Audio

	Word	Pinyin	Meaning
18	爬山	pá shān	to hike (in the mountains), to climb a mountain; hiking
19	游泳	yóu yǒng	to swim; swimming
20	收	shōu	to receive, to accept
21	放学	fàng xué	to be finished with the school day
22	结果	jiéguǒ	result; as a result
23	话题	huàtí	topic
24	新闻	xīnwén	news
25	关心	guānxīn	to care about; concern

Complete the exercise below to check your understanding of what you learned in Section 3. If you have questions, consult the Language Reference section.

With help from the images, select the direction words that best complete each sentence.

Direction words: 上去，进来，下来

1 把东西搬＿＿＿＿。 2 把信息写＿＿＿＿。 3 把包拿＿＿＿＿。

Language Reference · 语言注解

3 Expressing placement and motion towards/away

把 sentences are often used with words that indicate a motion. In some cases, 把 sentences include words that give more detailed information about the motion of the item being handled: one word that indicates the direction, like 下, 上, 过, 出, 进, and another word (either 去 or 来) that indicates whether the motion is away from or toward the speaker.

1 能不能麻烦您帮我把那本书拿下来？
  Could you please help get that book down for me?

2 请把那个冰箱搬进来。
  Please move that refrigerator in here.

3 明天聚会的时候，把你们的乐器都带过来。
  Bring your musical instruments with you for the party tomorrow.

4 离开教室的时候，请把垃圾也带出去扔了。
  When you leave the classroom, please also take the trash out.

In addition to being used to talk about doing something to particular items, 把 can also be used with more abstract concepts, like time.

5 出去旅行以前，最好先把时间计划好。

Before going on a trip, it's best to first plan out your time.

6 他把放学以后的时间都花在网上了，所以他妈妈很生气。

He spent all of his after-school time on the internet, so his mother is very angry.

把 sentences can also be used to express that someone didn't or shouldn't do something to an item. In these cases, the word that negates the action (such as 没, 别, 不用, 不能, 不可以) should come before 把.

7 她还没把照片发给我。

She still hasn't sent the photos to me.

8 别把可回收垃圾和不可回收垃圾放在一起。

Don't put the recyclable and the non-recyclable trash together.

3d Using the Language · 语言应用 INTERPERSONAL/PRESENTATIONAL

Briefly report on a news story to inform your classmates about something that's going on.

Step 1: Get into groups based on which of the following news topics you find interesting: current events (in your town or school), an environmental issue, the economy, music, dance, movies, online games, or sports. If one group has more than five people, split it into smaller groups.

Example: 我比较关心关于经济的新闻话题。你们呢？

Step 2: With your groupmates, discuss any news that you have read recently about your group's chosen topic. (If time allows, your teacher may ask you to research news articles about the topic.) As a group, decide what news about the topic is most important to share with the class.

Example: 我看到一条新闻说，在今年毕业的大学生里，找到工作的人比去年多了 30%。我觉得这条信息对大家挺重要的。我们把它写下来吧！

Step 3: Organize the information you've found to create a simple news report on the topic you chose. Prepare to present to the rest of the class. Be sure to have visual support if your report includes words that are not familiar to other students. Plan your report so that each student in your group will deliver part of the presentation.

Example: 大家好！在今天的新闻里，我们要介绍一下……

What a Character!

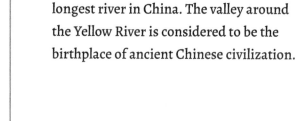

The component 氵 (shuǐ) appears in both characters of the word 游泳. This component, often referred to as 三点水, appears in many characters related to water or liquid.

Below are the names of four famous bodies of water in China. You'll notice that each word for "lake" or "river" has the 氵 component in it. Based on the other components you know, can you match the Chinese name to the English name?

长江

洞庭湖

黄河

青海湖

a Yellow River (Huáng Hé): The second longest river in China. The valley around the Yellow River is considered to be the birthplace of ancient Chinese civilization.

b Qinghai Lake (Qīnghǎi Hú): The largest inland saltwater lake in China, located in Qinghai province. Qinghai Lake is an important habitat for many species of birds and also a popular tourist destination.

c Yangtze River (Cháng Jiāng): The longest river in Asia—its Chinese name is simply "long river"!

d Dongting Lake (Dòngtíng Hú): One of the largest freshwater lakes in China. It is the lake referenced in the names of Hunan and Hubei, and is located near the border of those two provinces.

Put the Pieces Together! · 融会贯通

A Listening and Reading · 阅读和听力 INTERPRETIVE

Passage 1 What's next for Martin, Isabella, and their friends? Read on...

大家在网上一见面，就聊起来了。因为好久没有这么多人一起聊天儿了，大家都笑得很开心。

 不好意思，我家有点儿乱。

 没有没有，大文，你养了那么多花，很漂亮！

 是啊！那我先说一下我们在高中里调查的结果吧。我们一共收到了一百多份问卷。在问卷里，大家说，听到最多的是气候问题，了解最少的是水资源污染问题。

 很多同学经常看到关于气候变化的新闻，也经常能在学校里或者很多别的地方看到关于节约用水的宣传。

 不过，也有很多同学说，虽然经常有人告诉他们要节约用水，但是他们觉得水资源很丰富。所以，他们其实没有节约用水的习惯。

所以节约用水和水资源污染问题都值得我们多宣传？

 好像是……

大家讨论了一会儿在高中里的调查结果，觉得有好几个问题都值得宣传。然后，春月说了一下他们和美子在大学里的调查结果……

 看起来你们的调查结果跟我们的差不多。

 是啊！

 对了，我们拿纸和笔把这些数据写下来吧？天浩，你字写得好，你来写怎么样？

 好呀！

 你们不用手写了，我们一会儿用电子邮件把这些数据和信息发给你们。

 那太好了！谢谢！

 那你们选哪个话题去参加比赛呢？

 是啊，没想到做调查问卷也没有帮我们解决问题……

 我在想……"保护水资源"怎么样？我们不但可以让大家认识到节约用水很重要，也可以让大家多了解关于水资源污染学生能做些什么。

 好主意！

 对！做这个调查以前，虽然我们的想法不一样……

 但是其实我们关心的问题是一样的——怎么保护水资源。

 可可，你真聪明，你解决了我们的一个大问题！

 可可好像脸红了。

没有没有，这都是大家一起努力的结果。

 你太谦虚了，可可。

 对了，我记得可可和马丁还说过，后面几个问题的调查结果会决定你们在哪儿和怎么做宣传。是吗？

 对，关于后面的几个问题，我们调查的结果是，学生们有的时候会看看学校里的宣传。

 不过，大家都更喜欢在网上了解和讨论他们有兴趣的话题。有 60% 的人每天放学以后会花两三个小时在网上。

 嗯，现在大家好像都是这样。虽然我的新家里有电视，但是我不太看。如果有想了解的信息或者新闻，我会直接在网上看视频。

 在我家，我爸爸妈妈经常在电视上看电视剧。但是我跟你一样，更喜欢在网上看视频或者看网剧。而且我还要在网上学习、听音乐、玩儿游戏，和看网络小说，所以我有的时候会把放学以后的时间都花在网上。

 嗯，我也是。对了，里奥今天没来，因为他的眼睛不舒服，去看医生了。我觉得可能是他玩儿手机游戏的时间太长了，所以眼睛不舒服。

 我不太喜欢玩儿游戏，但是不知道为什么，我每次一上网，时间就过得特别快……

哈哈，是啊！所以我们也需要在网上做一下宣传。对了，那你们调查的大学生每天花多长时间上网呢？

比高中生花的时间更多，很多人每天要花五六个小时。

大家会花很多时间在网上聊天儿，但是和朋友经常见面、一起玩儿的时间越来越少了……

是啊。我觉得我们应该少花点儿时间在网上跟朋友聊天，多见面聊聊。有空的时候，我们还可以一起去爬山、游泳、看电影，或者吃饭。

大文，春月打工的公司和你工作的餐馆挺近的。你们没有经常一起吃饭吗？

啊？我和春月？嗯……吃过几次……对了，那关于调查结果，我们还有什么要讨论的吗？

没有了，我们五个人再讨论讨论吧。谢谢你们！

别客气！

祝你们比赛成功！

祝你们好运！

加油！有空多联系呀！

Comprehension Check

		T	F
1	Survey respondents hadn't heard much about climate change but were interested in it.	◯	◯
2	The respondents said that there seems to be plenty of water, so they haven't actually made a habit of saving water.	◯	◯
3	At Keke's suggestion, the group chooses "Protecting Water Resources" for their topic.	◯	◯
4	Although Owen's new apartment has a TV in it, he doesn't really watch TV.	◯	◯
5	Leo is too tired from staying up late playing computer games, so he didn't come to the meeting today.	◯	◯
6	What are Isabella's thoughts about talking with friends online?		

Passage 2 Imagine you see this flyer posted at Martin's school. What is it advertising? What is it asking for?

你笑起来真好看

欢迎您参加摄影俱乐部的笑脸活动!

我们想收集一百张笑脸照片。
如果您有这样的照片,请发
给我们。如果您没有,我们
可以帮您拍,不要钱。

拍照片的时间:4月28日下午
拍照片的地点:篮球馆

Passage 3 There are websites that work as directories, pointing internet users to a variety of different websites in a certain category. Below is an example of what might be included on such a directory website. Based on this list, what are some websites you could visit if you wanted to read the news?

类别	网站名字				
小说	原创小说	获奖小说	网络小说	文学之家	更多》
游戏	99小游戏	游戏超市	大玩家	玩吧	更多》
视频	我爱看电影	kk电视剧	天天影视	拍拍网	更多》
音乐	古典音乐欣赏	现代音乐	音乐人	音乐会	更多》
新闻	国际关系	新闻天下	今日新闻	时事纵横	更多》
美食	五星餐厅	下厨房	南北美食	美食家	更多》
旅游	在路上	带你去旅行	驴友俱乐部	导游网	更多》
汽车	汽车天下	赛车网	二手车	汽车之友	更多》
购物	每日生活网	好物推荐	打折啦	买卖	更多》
体育	最新赛事	运动俱乐部	体育世界	爱运动	更多》

Passage 4 Listen to the conversation. Answer the questions on a separate piece of paper.

1 According to the girl, what did the boy and his classmates start to do as soon as class was dismissed?

(a) play on their phones

(b) listen to music

(c) chat

2 Why does the boy say the girl ought to know about the gathering?

(a) because Zhao Xiaopeng sent everyone an email about it

(b) because Zhao Xiaopeng advertised the gathering online, and the girl goes online often

(c) because Zhao Xiaopeng said he had already texted the girl about it

3 What doesn't the girl understand?

(a) why she was the only one in her class to complete the survey

(b) who Zhao Xiaopeng is asking to take the survey and where to take the survey

(c) what the survey is about and how the results will be useful

4 What does the girl say about how people spend their time after school?

(a) She spends four to five hours online and thinks other classmates might do the same.

(b) She spends four to five hours online but thinks most of her classmates spend more time online.

(c) She thinks most people spend four to five hours online, which is too much.

Passage 5 Listen as a woman describes her internet habits. Then mark the following statements true (T) or false (F).

		T	F
1	The speaker thinks the internet is very important.	○	○
2	The speaker spends all her time online.	○	○
3	The speaker cares about sports news and international issues.	○	○
4	The speaker watches TV series online every day for hours, until her eyes start to hurt.	○	○
5	The speaker often takes her dog with her when she goes hiking.	○	○

B Speaking · 口语 INTERPERSONAL

In pairs, take turns describing two series of events: a typical school day for you (including after school activities) and a news story you read or heard about. As your partner is speaking, listen and draw what you hear—you will likely need several pictures to convey the events. After your partner has finished speaking, show your drawings to him/her to check that you understood the events correctly.

Examples:

1 我每天早上七点半起床，八点半开始上课，下午三点半放学。放学以后我会……

2 我今天看到一条新闻，下个月有一个国际美食比赛……

C Final Project · 结课项目 INTERPERSONAL/PRESENTATIONAL

Plan a Summer School for Students Who Want to Unplug

Work in groups to create a weekly schedule or itinerary for a summer school program that is a mix of fun and academics—with little to no screen time.

Step 1: In your group, discuss what activities and classes you might want for your summer school program. Why do you think having those particular activities/classes would be good?

Step 2: Decide on a weekly schedule for those classes and activities.

Step 3: Brainstorm what rules the program should have. Will cell phones be allowed? Will participants be allowed to watch TV? How can they get in touch with family? May they bring pets? As you discuss, make sure to explain to your groupmates why you think the rules you suggest are important to have.

Step 4: Create a flyer to encourage students to sign up for your summer school program. Include a short paragraph describing the camp, and make sure to highlight the things you think will be most exciting using text and images.

赶快申请快乐夏校吧！

广告设计、写小说、舞台表演⋯⋯
你对这些课有兴趣吗？

我们的老师经验丰富，如果你的作业完成得很好，
会有机会参加国际比赛。

游泳、打篮球、跑步⋯⋯
下课以后你可以选自己喜欢的活动。
每个周末大家会一起出去爬山或者看电影。

要求：
- 不能上网
- 不能看电视，宿舍里没有电视
- 可以带宠物，我们有人帮你照顾

如果你想了解更多信息，请跟我们联系。
我们的电子邮件: _____@____.com

Chapter 8 · Online Life

Can-Do Goals · 能力目标

Talk with your teacher if you have questions or if you are not certain you can do the following tasks:

- Analyze how Chinese people do or do not benefit from spending time online
- Discuss your thoughts about the internet
- Express that something began and continued on
- Understand when others indicate the motion and direction of an action
- Briefly describe news related to a familiar topic

Cultural Knowledge · 文化知识

What are some online activities that Chinese people enjoy?

People playing video games in an exhibit booth at the China International Exhibition of Digital Interactive Entertainment in Shanghai

马丁准备了一会儿明天的环保比赛，觉得压力挺大的。然后他在手机上发了一条信息……

 林马丁

明天就要比赛了，有点儿紧张！

#环保比赛

 杨天浩
你还好吧，马丁？

 林春月
别紧张，你们一定行！

 杨梅雅
我们一定能赢！不要紧张呀。

 二村美子
我在台湾给你们加油！

 姜大文
马丁，今天晚上睡个好觉。加油！

Can-Do Goals · 能力目标

In this chapter, you will learn to:

- Talk about ways in which technology can impact the environment for the better
- Describe how an action is performed
- Give detailed information about the direction of an action
- Understand and express that an action was done by someone or something
- Identify formal transition words that indicate a sequence

Read the text and try to answer the Chinese questions.

kējì   zài huán bǎo zhōng de   juésè

科技在环保中的角色
Technology's Role in Protecting the Environment

The goal of technology has historically been to make life more convenient and comfortable, and until recently, the environmental impact of innovation has often been an afterthought. However, people across the globe are increasingly turning to new technologies to discuss and solve environmental issues caused by old ones.

Tourists having dinner at a restaurant in Yunnan Province

Raising Awareness Through Social Media

The Chinese government (政府, zhèngfǔ) has used social media (社交媒体, shèjiāo méitǐ) to discourage food waste. When eating at a restaurant in China, it is common to order more food than the group can eat as a way both to show generosity and to show off wealth. The government hopes discussions of the issue on social media will discourage people from ordering — and wasting — excess food.

中国政府希望用社交媒体实现什么目标？

Using Apps to Change Habits

In 2019, the United Nations awarded a Chinese app its Champions of the Earth" award. The app, called Ant Forest, allows players to log their daily activities and earn points (得分, défēn) for doing things that are good for the environment, such as taking public transportation. Users can share their activities and compete with their friends. Once a user has earned enough points, the app pays for a real tree to be planted in an area of China affected by desertification (沙漠化, shāmòhuà). Because of this app, over 100 million trees were planted in just the first few years after its release.

用这个手机app的人怎么得分？
你怎么评价这个app？

Ant Forest has supported conservation work in the Tengger Desert, Ningxia Province

This train zips along the Beijing-Shanghai High-speed Railway at over two hundred miles per hour.

Changes to Infrastructure

The burning of fossil fuels for transportation is a major source of pollution in China. To try to solve this problem, the Chinese government has expanded its network of high speed trains. High speed trains (高铁, gāotiě) run on electricity and are more energy efficient than airplanes or cars. The hope is that, as China generates more electricity through renewable sources, this mode of transportation will become even more environmentally friendly.

高铁在中国为什么受欢迎?

如果你在中国,想从北京到上海去玩儿,你会开车还是坐高铁? 为什么?

By the Numbers

In an effort to use greener sources of energy, many nations are investing in solar power (太阳能, tàiyáng néng). To do this, they install panels that absorb the power of the sun and convert it into electricity.

Countries with the Largest Solar Energy Capacity	
Country	**Solar Capacity (gigawatts)**
China	205
United States	62
Japan	62
Germany	49
India	38

Source: International Renewable Energy Agency, 2019

Solar panels installed on the river near the Pudong, Shanghai

REFLECT ON THE ESSENTIAL QUESTION

How is technology both the problem and the solution?

1. Do you know of any apps that help people change their habits? What features of these apps make them effective (or not)?

2. Can you think of one way that upgrading technology can help solve environmental problems?

3. If you could invent any app to solve a problem in your community, what problem would your app address? Why?

Describing actions

1a Language Model · 语言范例 TARGET LANGUAGE INPUT

Your teacher will lead a discussion about the images below. Try to participate as much as you can. If there is anything you don't understand, let your teacher know.

Tā　zài　rènzhēn　de　zuò　gōngkè.　Tāmen　ne?
他 — 在 — 认真 — 地 — 做 — 功课。他们 — 呢?
He is studying diligently. How about them?

1

de
认真地

2

de
安静地

3

de
高兴地

4

de
紧张地

Audio

Listen to the audio and try to understand as much as you can. Then read the dialogue, using the pinyin text and vocabulary list to figure out unfamiliar words.

里奥，告诉你一个好消息！我不用去参加俱乐部明天的聚会了。所以我明天可以去环保比赛给你加油了！

Lǐ'ào, gàosù nǐ yí gè hǎo xiāoxi! Wǒ bú yòng qù cānjiā jùlèbù míngtiān de jùhuì le. Suǒyǐ wǒ míngtiān kěyǐ qù huán bǎo bǐsài gěi nǐ jiā yóu le!

太好了！对了，我们一边走一边聊吧。我手机上有一个 app 提醒我今天走路走得太少了。

Tài hǎo le! Duì le, wǒmen yìbiān zǒu yìbiān liáo ba. Wǒ shǒujī shàng yǒu yí gè app tíxǐng wǒ jīntiān zǒu lù zǒu de tài shǎo le.

什么 app 啊？

Shénme app a?

看，就是这个很有用的健康 app，效果特别好！我每天都用它记录我有没有运动，喝了几瓶水，睡得怎么样，等等。然后它会给我一个得分！如果我想得高分，就得更健康地生活。

Kàn, jiù shì zhège hěn yǒuyòng de jiànkāng app, xiàoguǒ tèbié hǎo! Wǒ měi tiān dōu yòng tā jìlù wǒ yǒu méiyǒu yùndòng, hē le jǐ píng shuǐ, shuì de zěnmeyàng, děng děng. Ránhòu tā huì gěi wǒ yí gè défēn! Rúguǒ wǒ xiǎng dé gāo fēn, jiù děi gèng jiànkāng de shēnghuó.

所以你最近晚上不玩儿游戏了，还这么认真地做运动啊？

Suǒyǐ nǐ zuìjìn wǎnshàng bù wánr yóuxì le, hái zhème rènzhēn de zuò yùndòng a?

嗯！每年的 4 月 7 号是世界健康日[1]。如果我在那天以前每天都能得两千分，就能收到一份礼物！

Ǹg! Měi nián de sì yuè qī hào shì shìjiè jiànkāng rì. Rúguǒ wǒ zài nà tiān yǐqián měi tiān dōu néng dé liǎng qiān fēn, jiù néng shōu dào yí fèn lǐwù.

是吗？你刚说这个 app 叫什么？我也想下[2]一个！

Shì ma? Nǐ gāng shuō zhège app jiào shénme? Wǒ yě xiǎng xià yí gè!

Comprehension Check

		T	F
1	Sanjay shares the good news that he will participate in the environmental competition.	◯	◯
2	Leo suggests that they walk and talk because of a reminder from an app on his phone.	◯	◯
3	The app gives a score based on how many bottles you recycle in a day.	◯	◯
4	Do you think the app Leo describes is useful? Why or why not?		

> **NOTE**
>
> 1 In the phrase 世界健康日 (shìjiè jiànkāng rì), the character 日 means "day on which something is observed" or "special day." This usage of 日 is seen in the names of many observances and also in the word 生日.
>
> 2 下载 (xiàzǎi, download) is often abbreviated as 下 in daily conversation.

Vocabulary · 生词

Audio

	Word	Pinyin	Meaning
1	消息	xiāoxi	news, information
2	提醒	tí xǐng	to remind, to warn; reminder
3	有用	yǒuyòng	useful
4	效果	xiàoguǒ	result, effect, efficacy
5	记录	jìlù	to take notes, to keep records; notes, records
6	瓶	píng	(measure word for bottles)
7	得分	dé fēn; défēn	to earn points; score
8	地	de	(word that connects a descriptive word to a verb)
9	世界	shìjiè	world

Complete the exercise below to check your understanding of what you learned in Section 1. If you have questions, consult the Language Reference section.

Use the words in the list on the left to complete each sentence. You will use some words more than once.

的
得
地

1 这是一个非常棒 ____ 消息。

2 这个中文学习 app ____ 效果特别好!

3 今天 ____ 晚饭我们吃 ____ 很开心!

4 我要把这件事好好 ____ 记录下来。

5 我妹妹每天都会认真 ____ 做功课。

Language Reference · 语言注解

1 Describing an action

The word 地 (de), highlighted in gray in the examples below, is used to link action words to descriptive words and phrases. 地 (de) is often confused with 得, since both words are used in descriptions of how an action is done. Unlike 得, 地 (de) comes after the descriptive word, connecting it to the verb that follows. In addition, in sentences with 地 (de) the emphasis falls more on the action, but in sentences with 得, the emphasis falls more on the descriptive word or result of the action.

1 弟弟开开心心^{de}地吃了他的生日蛋糕。
My little brother happily ate his birthday cake.

2 上次的考试我认真^{de}地准备了,所以成绩很好。
I prepared conscientiously for the last test, so I did well on it.

3 她正在安静^{de}地看书呢。你别说话了。
She's reading quietly now. Stop talking.

4 你需要把你的想法清清楚楚^{de}地告诉他。
You need to tell him your thoughts clearly.

Your teacher will put you in pairs. Read the four prompts below, and together select one to use in a short skit.

Step 1: Spend time brainstorming an interesting or surprising series of events. As you write, be sure to describe the actions of the characters in your skit as specifically and vividly as possible.

Step 2: Your teacher will collect the skits and display them. As you circulate around the room reading the skits, take note of any that you think are interesting. With your partner, choose two or three that you are willing to act out. Your teacher will assign you to one (or more) of these skits.

Step 3: Each pair will act as the narrator and take turns reading their own skit out loud. The actors selected by the teacher will act out the skit while you read. Read your skit as dramatically as you can, and when it is your turn to act, be sure to ham it up!

1 他紧张地走进了赵老师的办公室。

2 这场比赛她认真地准备了半年，可是……

3 他高兴地做了好几个菜，有红烧鱼、家常豆腐和炒青菜。

4 她正在安静地看网络小说，然后听到有人叫她。

5Cs
CONNECTIONS
COMMUNITIES
COMMUNICATION
COMPARISONS
CULTURES

There's a day for everything! Try to match the Chinese and English names of the four international observances listed below. Is there any you'd like to observe in Chinese class?

shuìmián
1 世界睡眠日, 3月21日

wǔdǎo
2 国际舞蹈日, 4月29日

3 国际手语日, 9月23日

4 世界动物日, 10月4日

a International Dance Day

b World Animal Day

c International Day of Sign Languages

d World Sleep Day

Action toward or away from someone

2a Language Model · 语言范例 TARGET LANGUAGE INPUT

Your teacher will lead a discussion about the image below. Try to participate as much as you can. If there is anything you don't understand, let your teacher know.

Wǒ	biǎomèi	yí	kàn	dào	wǒ	jiù	xiào	zhe	pǎo	guò	lái	le.
我	表妹	一	看	到	我	就	笑	着	跑	过	来	了。

My cousin ran over smiling the moment she saw me.

Tā	shì	bú	shì	yǒu	hǎo	xiāoxi	yào	gēn	wǒ	fēnxiǎng?
她	是	不	是	有	好	消息	要	跟	我	分享?

Does she have good news to share with me?

Listen to the audio and try to understand as much as you can. Then read the dialogue, using the pinyin text and vocabulary list to figure out unfamiliar words.

这个咖啡馆是我表哥推荐的。
怎么样？不错吧？

Zhège kāfēiguǎn shì wǒ biǎogē tuījiàn de.
Zěnmeyàng? Búcuò ba?

嗯，看起来真不错！

Ǹg, kàn qǐlái zhēn búcuò!

那你别看手机了。我有点儿
饿了，我们一边等大文，一
边先吃点儿东西吧。

Nà nǐ bié kàn shǒujī le. Wǒ yǒudiǎnr
è le, wǒmen yìbiān děng Dàwén, yìbiān xiān chī diǎnr dōngxi ba.

好啊，我们最好不要点太多
了，要是吃不完就浪费了。

Hǎo a, wǒmen zuìhǎo búyào diǎn tài duō
le, yàoshi chī bù wán jiù làngfèi le.

同意。刚才我走进来的时候，
看到一张桌子上还有很
多吃的喝的，但是吃饭的人
已经走了，太浪费了！

Tóngyì. Gāngcái wǒ zǒu jìn lái de shíhou,
kàn dào yì zhāng zhuōzi shàng hái yǒu hěn
duō chī de hē de, dànshì chīfàn de rén
yǐjīng zǒu le, tài làngfèi le!

嗯，现在很多国家都有浪费
资源的问题。可是世界上还
有很多人常常吃不饱饭，
或者喝不到干净的水。所以
我觉得这样做很不好。

Ǹg, xiànzài hěn duō guójiā dōu yǒu làngfèi
zīyuán de wèntí. Kěshì shìjiè shàng hái
yǒu hěn duō rén chángcháng chī bù bǎo fàn,
huòzhě hē bú dào gānjìng de shuǐ. Suǒyǐ
wǒ juéde zhèyàng zuò hěn bù hǎo.

你说得对！我们每个人都应
该学会节约。好了，别看手
机了，我们赶快点东西吃吧。

Nǐ shuō de duì! Wǒmen měi gè rén dōu yīnggāi xué huì jiéyuē. Hǎo le, bié kàn shǒujī le, wǒmen gǎnkuài diǎn dōngxi chī ba.

好！哎，我觉得我现在每天
都离不开¹手机！除了跟家人
和朋友联系以外，我还要用

Hǎo! Āi, wǒ juéde wǒ xiànzài měi tiān
dōu lí bù kāi shǒujī. Chúle gēn jiārén
hé péngyou liánxì yǐwài, wǒ hái yào yòng

手机上的 app 学习和找资料。
另外，我还用手机分享信息，
或者在网上表达自己的想法。

shǒujī shàng de app xuéxí, hé zhǎo zīliào. Lìngwài, wǒ hái yòng shǒujī fēnxiǎng xìnxī, huòzhě zài wǎng shàng biǎodá zìjǐ de xiǎngfǎ.

嗯，我也经常用手机在网上
买东西。不过，手机重要
是重要，现在我们还是先
点菜吧！我快饿死了……

Ňg, wǒ yě jīngcháng yòng shǒujī zài wǎng shàng mǎi dōngxi. Búguò, shǒujī zhòngyào shì zhòngyào, xiànzài wǒmen háishi xiān diǎn cài ba! Wǒ kuài è sǐ le...

好，好，好。对了，我想起来
我昨天在网上看到，现在
世界上有五十多亿人用手机。
很多人像我一样，每天都离
不开手机。

Hǎo, hǎo, hǎo. Duì le, wǒ xiǎng qǐlái wǒ zuótiān zài wǎng shàng kàn dào, xiànzài shìjiè shàng yǒu wǔshí duō yì rén yòng shǒujī. Hěn duō rén xiàng wǒ yíyàng, měi tiān dōu lí bù kāi shǒujī.

是吗？哎？大文怎么还没来？
他是不是走到别的咖啡馆去
了啊？你赶快给他发个短信
问问吧。

Shì ma? Āi? Dàwén zěnme hái méi lái? Tā shì bú shì zǒu dào biéde kāfēi guǎn qù le a? Nǐ gǎnkuài gěi tā fā gè duǎnxìn wèn wèn ba.

Comprehension Check

		T	F
1	Xue'er saw a lot of wasted food and drinks on a table as she walked into the café.	◯	◯
2	Isabella thinks she can't live without her computer.	◯	◯
3	Xue'er doesn't like phones and doesn't think they're very useful.	◯	◯

4 What did Isabella suddenly remember toward the end of the conversation?

NOTE

1 Adding 不 in between the first and second characters of some words, such as 离开 and 想起来 (xiǎng qǐlái), indicates that the speaker cannot do the action. So 离不开 means "cannot get away from" or "cannot live without." Similarly, 想不起来 means "cannot remember, cannot recall."

Audio

	Word	Pinyin	Meaning
10	浪费	làngfèi	to waste
11	国家	guójiā	nation, country
12	另外	lìngwài	in addition, besides
13	分享	fēnxiǎng	to share; (the action of) sharing
14	表达	biǎodá	to express (feelings, thoughts); expression (of a thought or feeling)
15	想起来	xiǎng qǐlái	to suddenly remember, to recall
16	亿	yì	hundred million

2c Puzzle It Out · 动动脑 PROGRESS CHECK

Complete the exercise below to check your understanding of what you learned in Section 2. If you have questions, consult the Language Reference section.

Based on the image, choose the phrase that best completes each sentence.

她 ＿＿＿＿ 了。　他们 ＿＿＿＿ 了。他 ＿＿＿＿ 了。

a 走下来
b 走进来
c 跑上去

Language Reference · 语言注解

2 Using 来 and 去 to describe an action moving toward or away from someone

The words 来 and 去 can be combined with other direction words to give additional detail about whether the action is moving toward or away from the speaker. Notice that in the sentences below, 来 and 去 are added after the location.

1 我看到一只猫跑进教室了。

I saw a cat run into the classroom.

2 我看到一只猫跑进教室去了。

I saw a cat run into the classroom (away from me, since I am not in the classroom).

3 我看到一只猫跑进教室来了。

I saw a cat run into the classroom (towards me, since I am in the classroom).

4 他们一起开车去台北了。

They drove together to Taipei.

5 他们一起开车到台北去了。

They drove together to Taipei (away from me, since I am not in Taipei right now).

6 他们一起开车到台北来了。

They drove together to Taipei (towards me, since I am in Taipei right now).

It is not always necessary to add a location or destination for the action.

7 我看到一只猫跑进来了。

I saw a cat run in (towards me, wherever I am).

8 他们一起开车过去了。

They drove there together (away from me, wherever I am right now)

Additionally, the relative directions of "toward" and "away" may not always refer to the speaker.

9 他从桌子上把一张照片拿起来了。

He picked up a photo from the table. [Here, the motion of the photo is toward the subject 他 and not the speaker.]

10 然后他把那张照片放下去了。

Then he put the photo back down. [Here, the motion of the photo is away from the subject 他 and not the speaker.]

Figure out the route that Jingjing's dog took around her neighborhood.

Step 1: Your teacher will assign seven students to play the role of a bystander at each of the locations pictured on the map below. Each bystander will be given a slip of paper indicating when they saw Jingjing's dog and what it did.

Step 1: Your teacher will put the remaining students in pairs. Work together with your partner to interview all the bystanders about when and where they saw Jingjing's dog. Make sure to take notes!

Example:

Student: 你什么时候、在哪儿看到了静静的小狗？

Bystander: 今天下午快五点的时候，我在公园看见一只小狗跑到我这边来了。

Step 3: Once you have interviewed everyone, work with your partner to map out the route Jingjing's dog took around the neighborhood. Share your results with the class. Did everyone figure out the correct route?

Step 4: Play another round with a different route! Your teacher will choose seven different students to play the role of bystanders. Pairs will be rearranged as necessary.

LANGUAGE CHALLENGE

The poem below is titled 悯农 (mǐn nóng), meaning "Pity the Farmers." It is attributed to 李绅 (Lǐ Shēn), a poet who lived during the Tang dynasty (608–907CE). In the poem, 李绅 reflects on the work done by farmers to put food on everyone's plates. A translation of the first half of the poem has been given to you. Can you translate the second half?

chú hé dāng   hàn dī hé tǔ.
锄 禾 日 当 午， 汗 滴 禾 下 土。
Tilling the land under the noon sun, sweat drips on seedlings on the ground.

                lì lì jiē
谁 知 盘 中 餐， 粒 粒 皆 辛 苦。
粒 = grain; measure word for grain-like things   皆 = all, each and every

A farmer plants rice by hand

Saying what was done

3a Language Model· 语言范例 TARGET LANGUAGE INPUT

Your teacher will lead a discussion about the image below. Try to participate as much as you can. If there is anything you don't understand, let your teacher know.

Tā	shàng kè	wánr	shǒujī	bèi	lǎoshī	fāxiàn	le.
他	上课	玩儿	手机	被	老师	发现	了。

He was playing with a cell phone in class and got caught by the teacher.

Nǐ	rènwéi	tā	yīnggāi	zhèyàng	zuò	ma?
你	认为	他	应该	这样	做	吗？

Do you think that he should have done that?

Audio

Ellen is attending college in her home country, the United Kingdom. Listen to the audio of Ellen's recent blog post and try to understand as much as you can. Then read the passage, using the pinyin text and vocabulary list to figure out unfamiliar words.

以前在北京上高中的时候，我特别想赶快去上大学，因为我觉得这样我就会有更多的时间去做自己想做的事。现在我上大学上了几个月了，才发现课少了有好处，也有坏处¹。好处大家都知道！坏处呢？就是我发现我很容易浪费时间，做一些没有意思的事。后来有一次，我朋友带我去参加了一次志愿者活动。我认为那次活动对我的影响非常大，所以现在我每个星期都去做志愿者。做了志愿者以后，我被问了好几次，为什么我的变化这么大？在这儿，我想把自己做志愿者的经验分享给大家。首先，我帮到了很多有需要的人。比如：我和我同学会去教一些刚搬到我们国家，英文还说得不太好的人学英文。其次，我学到了很多在教室里学不到的东西。另外，我还认识了新的朋友。我回国²以后认识的几个朋友都是在做志愿者的时候认识的！

Yǐqián zài Běijīng shàng gāozhōng de shíhou, wǒ tèbié xiǎng gǎnkuài qù shàng dàxué,
Yīnwèi wǒ juéde zhèyàng wǒ jiù huì yǒu gèng duō de shíjiān qù zuò zìjǐ xiǎng zuò
de shì. Xiànzài wǒ shàng dàxué shàng le jǐ gè yuè le, cái fāxiàn kè shǎo le
yǒu hǎochù, yě yǒu huàichù. Hǎochù dàjiā dōu zhīdào! Huàichù ne?
Jiù shì wǒ fāxiàn wǒ hěn róngyì làngfèi shíjiān, zuò yìxiē méiyǒu yìsi de
shì. Hòulái yǒu yí cì, wǒ péngyou dài wǒ cānjiā zuò le yí cì zhìyuànzhě
huódòng. Wǒ rènwéi nà cì huódòng duì wǒ de yǐngxiǎng fēicháng dà, suǒyǐ
xiànzài wǒ měi gè xīngqī dōu qù zuò zhìyuànzhě. Zuò le zhìyuànzhě yǐhòu,
wǒ bèi wèn le hǎojǐ cì, wèishénme wǒ de biànhuà zhème dà? Zài zhèr,
wǒ xiǎng bǎ zìjǐ zuò zhìyuànzhě de jīngyàn fēnxiǎng gěi dàjiā. Shǒuxiān, wǒ
bāng dào le hěn duō yǒu xūyào de rén. Bǐrú, wǒ hé wǒ tóngxué huì qù jiāo
yìxiē gāng bān dào wǒmen guójiā, yīngwén hái shuō de bú tài hǎo de rén xué yīngwén. Qícì, wǒ xué dào le hěn duō zài jiàoshì lǐ xué bú dào de dōngxi.
Lìngwài, wǒ hái rènshi le xīn de péngyou. Wǒ huí guó yǐhòu rènshi de
jǐ gè péngyou dōu shì zài zuò zhìyuànzhě de shíhou rènshi de!

Comprehension Check

		T	F
1	Ellen says that there are advantages and disadvantages to taking fewer classes.	◯	◯
2	Ellen says the first benefit of volunteering is that you can make new friends.	◯	◯
3	Ellen volunteered to help new immigrants study English.	◯	◯
4	Write a final sentence to complete Ellen's blog post.		

NOTE

1 坏处 (huàichù) is the opposite of 好处 (hǎochù) and means "disadvantage, bad point, con."

2 回国 (huí guó) means "to return to one's home country."

Vocabulary · 生词

	Word	Pinyin	Meaning
17	发现	fāxiàn	to realize, to discover, to find out
18	好处	hǎochù	advantage, benefit, good point, pro
19	坏	huài	bad, harmful; broken
20	志愿者	zhìyuànzhě	volunteer
21	认为	rènwéi	to think, to consider, to have an opinion
22	被	bèi	(word that indicates that an action was done to someone or something)
23	首先	shǒuxiān	first (of all), above all
24	其次	qícì	next, secondly; secondary

Complete the exercise below to check your understanding of what you learned in Section 3. If you have questions, consult the Language Reference section.

Choose the option that best matches the meaning of each sentence.

1 这个问题我被妹妹问了好几次。
  (a) 这个问题妹妹问了我好几次。
  (b) 这个问题我问了妹妹好几次。

2 我最喜欢喝的绿茶被我哥哥拿走了。
  (a) 我哥哥给我买了一杯我最喜欢的绿茶。
  (b) 我哥哥把我最喜欢的绿茶拿走了。

3 那个志愿者做的好事被大家发现了。
  (a) 大家发现了那个志愿者做的好事。
  (b) 那个志愿者发现了大家做的好事。

What a Character!

yī
衤

1	2	3	4	5
衤	衤	衤	衤	衤

The words 被 (bèi) and 裤 contain the component 衤 (yī), which means "clothing." Many words with this component have something to do with clothing. The 衤 (yī) component is easy to confuse with 礻 (shì), which is often used in words related to worship, temples, or religious activities, such as 庆祝.

Look carefully at the words below. Which words have the 衤 component, and which words have the 礻 component?

1 袖子 (xiùzi)
sleeve

2 社会 (shèhuì)
society, community

3 补 (bǔ)
to repair, to patch, to mend

3 Expressing that an action was done (by someone)

The word 被 (bèi), highlighted in gray in the examples below, can be used in sentences where the focus is on the person or thing that is acted upon — and not on who is doing the action. In some sentences with 被 (bèi), the actor is not stated. In these sentences, the verb comes after 被 (bèi) and is always followed by another word that describes the result of the action, such as 到, 走, 下来, or 了. 被 (bèi) is more often used to express a negative or neutral feeling. It is less often used to express positive developments.

1 我同学的书^{bèi}被拿走了。
My classmate's book was taken away.

2 糟糕！上次的调查结果没有^{bèi}被记录下来！
Oh no! The survey results from last time were not recorded!

3 那份报告已经^{bèi}被找到了。
That report has already been found.

4 饭馆里那些没吃完的饭菜都^{bèi}被浪费了，这样很不好。
Those leftovers in the restaurant were all wasted; that's really not good.

When the person doing the action is stated, the person is added in between 被 (bèi) and the verb.

5 我同学的书^{bèi}被老师拿走了。
My classmate's book was taken away by the teacher.

6 糟糕！调查结果好像^{bèi}被明明带回家了！
Oh no! The survey results seem to have been taken home by Mingming!

7 那个蛋糕^{bèi}被我弟弟吃了。
That cake was eaten by my younger brother.

8 饭馆里那些没吃完的菜都^{bèi}被服务员收走了。
Those leftovers in the restaurant were taken away by the waiters.

Imagine that a group of student volunteers has helped your teacher move to a new classroom, but some things need to be rearranged. With a partner, search the image below for the items on the list. When you find one, tell your partner where the object had been placed. You might say something like:

老师的电脑被放到左边的那张桌子上了。

Once you have found all the items on the list, pick a few items that you think ought to be placed somewhere else. State the disadvantages of the item's current location and where you think it should be put instead. Be prepared to share your thoughts with the class.

List of items:

地图、 时钟 (shízhōng, clock)、 电脑、 植物 (zhíwù, plant)、
老师的包、 红色的笔、 花、 金鱼 (jīnyú, goldfish)、
地球仪 (dìqiúyí, globe)、 黑板 (hēibǎn, blackboard)

Example:

老师的电脑被放在了左边的桌子上。我觉得这样做的坏处是电脑离黑板有点儿远。我觉得电脑应该离黑板近一点儿。

墙 (qiáng, wall)

Put the Pieces Together! • 融会贯通

Audio

A **Listening and Reading • 阅读和听力** `INTERPRETIVE`

Passage 1 What's next for Martin and his friends? Read on...

今天和明天的"校园环保比赛"要在篮球馆举办，来参加比赛和看比赛的学生们已经走进篮球馆来了。这次比赛一共有八个小组参加。每个小组要先做报告，然后老师们会问一些问题。在做报告和回答问题的时候，每个小组能不能清楚地表达他们的想法，会影响最后的比赛成绩。马丁他们是第一个做报告的小组。

 大家好！我们小组选的话题是保护水资源。我们在几个高中和大学里做了一个问卷调查。首先，请大家看看我们的调查结果。有 72% 的同学对水资源污染的问题不太了解。有 65% 的同学知道要节约用水，但是他们没有这个习惯。这会对我们的生活有什么影响呢？

 我们每个人每天都要喝水。除了人以外，树也离不开水。我家在陕西有一个茶园，那儿的茶树也要经常"喝"水，而且要"喝"干净的水。干净的水资源很重要，可是很多国家的水资源都不够用。现在有 20 亿人生活在有水资源压力的国家。不但这 20 亿人的生活可能会被影响，而且在他们生活的国家里，经济发展可能也会被影响。所以，我们小组做的是关于保护水资源的宣传计划。

我们想用不同的方法做宣传。在学校里，很多人不知道，每年的 3 月 22 日是"世界水日"。我们的计划是：首先，在那天以前，做一些海报在校园里宣传。我们要在海报上跟大家分享一些数据，建议大家不要浪费水。比如：不用水的时候要把水关了，洗澡不要洗太长时间，等等。

其次，我们要举办一个志愿者活动，请同学们一起宣传"世界水日"和怎么保护水资源。另外，我们还在问卷里问了一些别的问题。我们发现很多学生每天花很长时间上网。所以，我们也会在网上宣传。我们想和别的志愿者一起拍一些关于水资源保护的视频，发到网上，让更多的人能看到这些信息。

最后，我们计划再设计一个关于水资源保护的 app。大家可以用 app 记录自己的环保习惯，也可以看看朋友们是怎么保护环境的。如果他们想有更高的得分，就得多看一些关于水资源保护的视频，多分享几个自己保护水资源的好办法，多回收一些垃圾等等。这个 app 还会给大家发一些消息，提醒大家在不同的地方和时间应该怎么去保护水资源。这些就是我们小组的宣传计划。

谢谢你们的报告。我先问你们一个问题。你们为什么决定做这个问卷调查呢？

我们认为，用数据可以让大家更清楚地了解一些信息，比如学生们的想法和生活习惯。这对我们做宣传计划很有用。我们做完这次关于水资源保护的宣传以后，还希望再做一次调查，看看我们宣传的效果怎么样。

好。那关于水资源保护，人们其实有很多事可以做，你们为什么要做关于水资源保护的 app 呢？

现在的学生每天都要花很多时间在网上，他们习惯从网上了解信息。我们认为，用 app 提醒大家保护环境可以带来很多好处。如果学生们觉得这个 app 很有意思，我们就可以让他们多了解一些有用的信息。

好，谢谢你们的回答。现在我们请下一个小组做报告。

比赛的第二天还有另外四组做报告，所以结果第二天才能出来。马丁那天有事，没有去参加。下午，他紧张地给梅雅打了一个电话。

 梅雅，结果怎么样？

 马丁，我们有一个好消息和一个坏消息。你想先听哪一个？

 啊？那……我先听坏消息吧……

 坏消息是老师们说，我们还应该在报告里多讲讲关于防止水污染的问题。

 啊……那我们输了吗？

 但是好消息是，我们组的报告比别的小组的更好，所以我们赢了！老师提醒我们，去上海比赛的时候，要多讲一下那个问题。

 真的吗？！太好了！我现在就去告诉春月他们！

Comprehension Check

T　　F

1　At the beginning of the story, Martin's group hasn't entered the basketball court yet.　○　○

2　Keke reports that the first part of the group's plan is to make posters together on World Water Day.　○　○

3　Leo reports that the second part of the group's plan is to work with volunteers to make videos raising awareness of water resource issues.　○　○

4　According to Keke, they want to make an app because no one in their group likes making posters.　○　○

5　What is the good news and the bad news that Maya has for Martin?

6　Toward the beginning of the presentation, Tianhao states that two billion people live in countries whose water resources are "under pressure." In this context, what do you think "under pressure" means?

Passage 2 Below is an advertisement for a school celebration of a Chinese holiday. What holiday is it? Based on the context, what do you think 音乐会 means?

今年中秋节除了赏月、
吃月饼、
看花灯以外，
还可以怎么过？

快来参加 **中秋节网络音乐会** 吧!

Passage 3 Listen to the conversation and mark the following statements true (T) or false (F).

		T	F
1	The boy has come to tell Sisi to go to the teacher's office.	○	○
2	The girl thinks Sisi will definitely get bad news.	○	○
3	The girl thinks that a World Culture Day activity sounds pretty interesting.	○	○
4	The boy notices Sisi running over to them with a smile.	○	○
5	Sisi says she wants to share her plans for a World Culture Day activity with them.	○	○
6	The boy wants to volunteer to help out Sisi's club, but the girl doesn't.	○	○

Passage 4 Listen to Sisi's announcement at the beginning of her club meeting and answer the questions that follow.

1 According to the announcement, the club's World Culture Day activity
  (a) was a great success.
  (b) is ready to begin.
  (c) was approved by the school.

2 Why does Sisi lay out some requirements for the meeting?
  (a) so that the meeting can end quickly
  (b) so that the discussion can be more productive
  (c) so that everyone has a chance to speak

3 First, Sisi welcomes all the members to share their thoughts and says she will
  (a) give a score to everyone's suggestions.
  (b) record everyone's suggestions.
  (c) take a vote on everyone's suggestions.

4 Sisi asks everyone to
  (a) simply and clearly express their thoughts.
  (b) simply and conscientiously express their thoughts.
  (c) conscientiously and clearly express their thoughts.

B Speaking · 口语 INTERPERSONAL

Imagine that you are being surveyed by Martin and his team regarding the water resource protection app that they are developing.

Step 1: With your partner, brainstorm possible features that you would like to see in the app. What would you like the app to do for you? Remind you of something? Teach you something? Something else?

Example: 我希望这个 app 可以提醒我不要浪费水。

Step 2: Discuss with your partner one or two features that you think are important for the app.

Step 3: When your teacher calls on you, share the feature or features that you think are most important and give reasons to support your opinion.

Example:

我觉得提醒大家不要浪费水是最重要、最有用的，因为我们每天都会用水，可是有的时候我们可能没有发现自己其实已经用了太多的水了。如果这个app可以发消息提醒大家，就能更好地帮我们养成 (yǎngchéng, to form) 节约用水的好习惯。

C Final Project · 结课项目 PRESENTATIONAL

Celebrate with the World

Imagine that your local government has decided to participate in a world celebration. The goal is to raise awareness about a global issue that has a connection to your community. The mayor is organizing discussion groups to present on which "world day" to choose, and your class will participate.

Step 1: You will work in pairs, and your teacher will assign a world celebration for you and your partner to research. Your goal will be to make the most convincing argument possible for your assigned day.

Some possible holidays include the ones listed below, which were established by the United Nations:

世界水日   世界家庭 (jiātíng, family) 日

世界环境日   世界读 (dú, reading) 书日

国际手语日   世界盲文 (mángwén, braille) 日

国际志愿者日

Step 2: Meet with your partner and review what you learned about the holiday you have been assigned. What makes the day appropriate for your community? What reasons could you give to encourage people to support this day as a new holiday for your community? Decide which points you each want to make and who will speak first at the panel. Be sure to include basic information about the day and statistics that show its importance.

Step 3: To give everyone a chance to speak, there will be multiple discussions taking place at once. Your teacher will assign you and your partner to a group, which will consist of yourselves and another pair of students who will argue for a different possible "world day." During the discussion, each person will be given two minutes to speak. (Your teacher will let you know which pair will start and will keep time for the whole class.) While the opposing group members are speaking, be sure to take notes.

Step 4: Once your discussion has finished, write a brief statement to support your assigned position. Give reasons that support your position and offer counterpoints to the arguments in favor of the other "world day." Use your notes from the discussion to help you. (Remember to use the formal transition words you have learned as you make your points.)

Step 5: Submit your statement to your teacher. Your teacher will post or share the statements so that you can read arguments that your classmates made to support other possible days. Once you have had a chance to read some of the statements, your teacher will lead a class discussion about the best "world day" for your community. Be prepared to share your real preference — you don't need to keep to your assigned position!

我们一起庆祝吧!

Can-Do Goals • 能力目标

Talk with your teacher if you have questions or if you are not certain you can do the following tasks:

- Talk about ways in which technology can impact the environment for the better
- Describe how an action is performed
- Give detailed information about the direction of an action
- Understand and express that an action was done by someone or something
- Identify formal transition words that indicate a sequence

Cultural Knowledge • 文化知识

How is China using technology to help solve environmental problems?

SOCIAL IDENTITY AND GLOBAL RESPONSIBILITY

In Unit 4, you will learn to discuss your own identity while learning more about Shanghai as a diverse, complex city. You will also learn to express your perspective and respond to other people's ideas.

Street art in Shanghai

Essential Question
What makes the identity of people and places unique and complex?

CHAPTER 10
Advocating for Yourself and Others

Xue'er, Isabella, Owen, and Haisheng discuss differences in their family dynamics.

CHAPTER 11
Touring Shanghai

After Martin and his friends arrive in Shanghai, Isabella and her friends show them some of the best sights in the city.

CHAPTER 12
Looking Back, Looking Ahead

The whole group meets up for New Year's Eve on the Bund in Shanghai, and the friends share their hopes for the new year.

257

At the end of the unit, you will develop a plan to create a welcoming environment for all students at school. You will:

- Read a school's online forum to learn about different students' perspectives

- Brainstorm ways to help address the issues and challenges that students face

- Write an action plan to make a more welcoming school environment

Advocating for Yourself and Others

CHAPTER

10

第 dì

十 shí

课 kè

马丁他们很快就要来上海了，大家都特别开心。春月今天约了大文、雪儿、和海生一起吃午饭，他们还讨论了一下要带马丁他们去哪儿玩儿。大家讨论完以后，雪儿说她有事，得先走了。大家问她要去哪儿……

Can-Do Goals · 能力目标

In this chapter, you will learn to:

- Explain some ways in which gender equality has changed in China over the last century
- Identify the basic structural elements of a letter or email
- Express your opinion on a familiar subject
- Summarize someone else's perspective on a familiar subject
- Respond to other people's opinions with your own perspective
- Discuss the effects of common stereotypes

biànhuà zhōng de Zhōngguó yǔ xìngbié píngděng

变化中的中国与性别平等

Gender Equality in a Changing China

Women's rights (女性权利, nǚxìng quánlì) have been severely restricted in China for most of
its history, as they have been in most societies throughout the world. However, China has made
major strides over the past century towards gender equality (性别平等, xìngbié píngděng).

This stamp from 1991 commemorates Qiū Jǐn (秋瑾, 1875–1907),
a staunch supporter of women's rights in the early 1900s.

Reshaping Traditional Views of Gender

In the early 1900s, China was changing dramatically, and
both men and women explored ways to transform their
society. Many people began to advocate for women's rights
and gender equality. As people's attitudes changed, laws
(法律, fǎlǜ) were passed that granted new rights for women,
such as the right to own property—in the past, women's right
to own and inherit property had been very restricted.

法律对性别平等的发展重要吗？ 为什么？

Changes under the Communist Party

The Chinese Communist Party (CCP) was
founded in 1921, and one of its earliest ideas
was that women should have greater rights.
After coming to power in 1949, the CCP enacted
legislation that declared women to be equal to
men and ended arranged marriages. Women
started taking on new roles in the workforce, and
the party famously promoted the phrase "women
hold up half the sky (妇女能顶半边天, fùnǚ
néng dǐng bàn biān tiān)."

你怎么理解"妇女能顶半边天"这句话的
意思？

新生事物春满园 妇女顶起半边天

This 1976 poster was created by the Chinese government to support women's
involvement in agricultural work. It includes a variation on the saying "women
hold up half the sky."

21st Century Challenges

In China, as in many other countries, debates over gender equality have shifted from basic rights to broader issues of inequality, like sexism (性别歧视, xìngbié qíshì), representation, and discrimination. Activists are also drawing people's attention to other serious proplems, such as sexual harassment and domestic violence. However, while people who identify as feminists are supported by many, they are also attacked online. Despite significant advancements over the last century, there are still many barriers to gender equality.

现在在中国，人们比较关心哪些关于性别平等的问题？

Vice Premier Wu Yi meets with Secretary of State Colin Powell in 2004. Although Wu Yi was one of the most powerful women in the world, relatively few Chinese women have reached the highest levels of government.

By the Numbers

Statistics across many aspects (方面, fāngmiàn) of life in China show both the progress (进步, jìnbù) that has been made toward women's equality and also the challenges that remain.

	Politics	In 2021, only 28.8% of the members of the CCP were women, but this is an increase from 2011, when only 23.3% were women.
	Education	University and college enrollment for women has grown. In 2010, 50.9% of college students were women, a number that increased to 51.7% in 2019.
	Labor force	In 2019, more than 60% of women ages 15 and older contributed to China's labor force. This was a decline from 1990, when more than 73% contributed to the labor force.

Xinhua News Agency, 2021, 2012; The Central People's Government of the People's Republic of China, 2012; National Bureau of Statistics of China, 2020; The World Bank, 2021; International Labour Organization 2021

最近这些年性别平等在哪些方面有进步？哪些方面还需要继续进步？

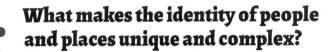

REFLECT ON THE ESSENTIAL QUESTION

What makes the identity of people and places unique and complex?

1 Do you think different generations have different ideas about gender roles? If so, what are some of those differences?

2 What is the history of gender equality like in your country? How have people's rights changed over the decades?

3 What ideas affect how different genders are viewed in your community?

Expressing agreement

1a Language Model · 语言范例 TARGET LANGUAGE INPUT

Your teacher will lead a discussion about the images below. Try to participate as much as you can. If there is anything you don't understand, let your teacher know.

Tīngshuō nǐ xǐhuan kàn lǎo jiànzhù.
听说 - 你 - 喜欢 - 看 - 老 - 建筑。
I heard that you like old buildings.

Shì hěn xǐhuan, wǒ juéde lǎo jiànzhù hěn yǒuyìsi
是 - 很 - 喜欢，- 我 - 觉得 - 老 - 建筑 - 很 - 有意思。
I do. I think that old buildings are very interesting.

1

看网剧

2

爬山

3

xìn
写信
to write a letter

4

gùshi
讲故事
to tell a story

Listen to the letter Martin's team received from the university in Shanghai and try to understand as much as you can. Then read the email, using the pinyin text and vocabulary list to figure out unfamiliar words.

同学们：

　　你们好！恭喜你们小组赢了这场校园环保比赛！我们给你们写这封信，是想跟你们分享一些关于在上海举办的下一场比赛的信息。

　　首先，你们到上海以后，我们大学的志愿者会去接你们。他们会带你们去我们大学的学生宿舍。参加这次比赛的同学都会住在那里。学生宿舍就靠着老图书馆和学校的餐厅。你们可以用餐票¹去餐厅吃饭，很方便！另外，比赛的那天晚上，我们会一起去看一场表演。那场表演讲的是一个关于环保的故事，是我们大学的学生演的。要是你们有朋友或者家人想来看比赛或者看表演，他们需要在网上订票和选位子。

　　最后，希望你们不要太紧张。比赛成绩是很重要，但是更重要的是，你们能让更多人关心环保，让大家认识到环保是每个人都可以做的事！

上海环境科学大学
11月5日

Tóngxué men:

　　Nǐmen hǎo! Gōngxǐ nǐmen xiǎo zǔ yíng le zhè chǎng xiàoyuán huán bǎo bǐsài. Wǒmen gěi nǐmen xiě zhè fēng xìn, shì xiǎng gēn nǐmen fēnxiǎng yìxiē guānyú zài Shànghǎi jǔbàn de xià yì chǎng bǐsài de xìnxī.

　　Shǒuxiān, nǐmen dào Shànghǎi yǐhòu, wǒmen dàxué de zhìyuànzhě huì qù jiē nǐmen. Tāmen huì dài nǐmen qù wǒmen dàxué de xuéshēng sùshè. Cānjiā zhè cì bǐsài de tóngxué dōu huì zhù zài nàlǐ. Xuéshēng sùshè jiù kào zhe lǎo túshūguǎn hé xuéxiào de cāntīng. Nǐmen kěyǐ yòng cān piào qù cāntīng chī fàn, hěn fāngbiàn! Lìngwài, bǐsài de nà tiān wǎnshàng, wǒmen huì yìqǐ qù kàn yì chǎng biǎoyǎn. Nà chǎng biǎoyǎn jiǎng de shì yí gè guānyú huán bǎo de gùshi, shì wǒmen dàxué de xuéshēng yǎn de. Yàoshi nǐmen yǒu péngyou huòzhě jiārén xiǎng lái kàn bǐsài huòzhě kàn biǎoyǎn, tāmen xūyào zài wǎng shàng dìng piào hé xuǎn wèizi.

　　Zuìhòu, xīwàng nǐmen bú yào tài jǐnzhāng. Bǐsài chéngjì shì hěn zhòngyào, dànshì gèng zhòngyào de shì, nǐmen néng ràng gèng duō rén guānxīn huán bǎo, ràng dàjiā rènshi dào huán bǎo shì měi gè rén dōu kěyǐ zuò de shì!

Shànghǎi Huánjìng Kēxué Dàxué
shíyī yuè wǔ rì

Comprehension Check

		T	F
1	Martin and his friends will be picked up by university volunteers when they arrive in Shanghai.	◯	◯
2	Participants will be responsible for bringing their own food or finding nearby restaurants.	◯	◯
3	On the evening of the competition, university students will perform for the participants.	◯	◯

4 What advice does the writer of the letter give to students who might be nervous about the competition? Do you agree with that advice?

NOTE

1 餐票 is a meal voucher, or a ticket that can be exchanged for food at a place like a cafeteria. 票 can be used by itself to mean "ticket" or it can be combined with some nouns to specify a certain kind of ticket, like 车票, which means "bus or train ticket."

Vocabulary · 生词

Audio

	Word	Pinyin	Meaning
1	封	fēng	(measure word for letters)
2	信	xìn	letter (correspondence)
3	靠	kào	to be next to; to lean on, to lean against
4	老	lǎo	old
5	故事	gùshi	story
6	演	yǎn	to perform, to act
7	订	dìng	to reserve, to book (a ticket, a hotel room, etc.)
8	位子	wèizi	seat

COMMUNICATION

COMMUNITIES
COMPARISONS
CULTURES
CONNECTIONS

The image below shows a typical format for a letter or formal email in Chinese.

1 Chinese letters usually use a colon after the person's name, not a comma. The salutation sometimes includes an adjective in front of the name of the person being written to, like 亲爱的赛吉 (Dear Sanjay), but it isn't required.

2 你好, 您好, and 见信好 are commonly used at the beginning of a letter. 见信好 is similar to saying "hope this letter finds you well."

赛吉：①
　见信好！②
　好久不见！你最近好吗？你还经常跟里奥他们一起玩儿吗？我很想你们。
　　我最近特别忙，又要学习，又要做网店。我很开心我的网店成功了。希望明年暑假可以去北京找你们玩儿！
　祝：③
天天开心！

　　　　　爱林④
　　　　　11月7日

3 To conclude the letter, the writer often wishes (祝) something for the recipient, like 天天开心 (happiness every day), 身体健康 (good health), 比赛成功 (good luck in the competition), or 学习进步 (xuéxí jìnbù, progress in your studies).

4 The date is often written on the right side of the letter, below the writer's name.

What format do you usually use when you are writing a letter or email?

1c Puzzle It Out · 动动脑 PROGRESS CHECK

Complete the exercise below to check your understanding of what you learned in Section 1. If you have questions, consult the Language Reference section.

Choose the best option to complete each dialogue.

1 A: 这些数据分析起来真难啊。
　B: (a) 是很难，我也花了很长时间分析这些数据。
　　 (b) 是不太难，我很快就把这些数据分析完了。

2 A: 我觉得找到一份合适的工作需要有好运气。
　B: (a) 好运气是不太重要。
　　 (b) 找工作是需要好运气。

3 **A:** 那套中号的运动服太好看了！

   B: (a) 那套中号的是不太合适。

      (b) 那套运动服的样子是挺好看的，可是太贵了，我买不起。

Language Reference · 语言注解

1 Using 是 to agree with a statement

The word 是 is sometimes added to a sentence to emphasize that the speaker agrees with something that was just said. When used in this way, 是 is added before a part of the sentence that the speaker agrees with, such as an action, description, or time phrase.

1 **A:** 你弟弟看起来很喜欢踢足球。

    Your brother seems to really like playing soccer.

   B: 他是很喜欢踢足球。他每天都要去公园跟朋友踢。

    He does like to play soccer. He goes to the park to play with his friends every day.

2 **A:** 昨天的作业特别难！

    Yesterday's homework was really difficult!

   B: 是很难，我做到十二点半才睡觉。

    It was difficult. I worked on it and didn't get to sleep until twelve-thirty.

3 **A:** 助听器真贵！

    Hearing aids are so expensive!

   B: 助听器是很贵！所以我是打折的时候买的。

    They are expensive! That's why I got mine when it was on sale.

4 **A:** 你看，她们小组的调查问卷设计得真好看。

    Check this out. Their group's questionnaire was designed very well.

   B: 她们问卷的设计是挺好看的，但是问卷上的问题写得不太好。

    The design is quite good, but the questions aren't very well written.

Note that although 是 is used to indicate agreement, the speaker may only partially agree with the previous person's statement. (See example #4, above.)

Play a guessing game with your partner.

Step 1: Think of a person that you and your partner are both familiar with. The person can be someone in your class, your school, an actor or athlete that you are both familiar with, or a fictional character from books, movies, or TV, but try to think of someone you both know a lot about. Write that person's name down and don't show your partner.

Step 2: Play rock paper scissors (石头剪刀布, shítou jiǎndāo bù) to decide who will ask questions first. When it is your partner's turn, he or she will ask you yes/no questions about the person you wrote down. If the answer is yes, try to use 是 to express your agreement. If you don't know the answer to the question, tell your partner that you don't know.

Example:

A: 他很喜欢讲故事吗?

B: 他是很喜欢讲故事,而且讲得很好。

Step 3: Your partner has to guess whose name you wrote down in twenty questions or less. Then, it is your turn to ask your partner questions about the person he/she wrote down.

Different perspectives and opinions

2a Language Model · 语言范例 TARGET LANGUAGE INPUT

Your teacher will lead a discussion about the images below. Try to participate as much as you can. If there is anything you don't understand, let your teacher know.

Duì wǒ lái shuō, zūnzhòng zìjǐ hěn zhòngyào,
对 我 来 说, 尊重 自己 很 重要,

For me, respecting yourself is very important.

zūnzhòng biérén yě hěn zhòngyào.
尊重 别人 也 很 重要。

It's also important to respect others.

Nǐ juéde ne?
你 觉得 呢?

What do you think?

1

zūnzhòng
尊重别人

to respect other people

2

关心自己

Audio

Listen to the audio and try to understand the online chat between Keke and Miko as much as you can. Then read the dialogue, using the pinyin text and vocabulary list to figure out unfamiliar words.

美子，你在吗？我心情不好。

Měizǐ, nǐ zài ma? Wǒ xīnqíng bù hǎo.

在啊。可可，怎么了？

Zài a. Kěkě, zěnme le?

刚才我告诉我妈妈我得准备比赛。可是她让我先把房间打扫干净，把衣服洗了……

Gāngcái wǒ gàosu wǒ māma wǒ děi zhǔnbèi bǐsài. Kěshì tā ràng wǒ xiān bǎ fángjiān dǎsǎo gānjìng, bǎ yīfu xǐ le. . .

哎，其实我妈妈也会这样。

Āi, qíshí wǒ māma yě huì zhèyàng.

是吗？可是我妈妈还说，女生一定要会做家务。那对男生来说，会做家务不重要吗？

Shì ma? Kěshì wǒ māma hái shuō, nǚshēng yídìng yào huì zuò jiāwù. Nà duì nánshēng lái shuō, huì zuò jiāwù bú zhòngyào ma?

重要啊！我上了大学才知道，学会照顾自己很重要。所以其实我现在觉得我妈妈以前让我学着做家务挺好的。对了，你小时候玩儿过家家[1]吗？我记得那时候女孩子都喜欢演妈妈，在家里做家务。男孩子都喜欢"出去工作"。

Zhòngyào a! Wǒ shàng le dàxué cái zhīdào, xué huì zhàogù zìjǐ hěn zhòngyào. Suǒyǐ qíshí wǒ xiànzài juéde wǒ māma yǐqián ràng wǒ xué zhe zuò jiāwù tǐng hǎo de. Duì le, nǐ xiǎo shíhou wánr guò jiā jiā ma? Wǒ jìde nà shíhou nǚ háizi dōu xǐhuan yǎn māma, zài jiā lǐ zuò jiāwù. Nán háizi dōu xǐhuan "chūqù gōngzuò."

哈哈，是啊！我以前玩儿过家家的时候也是这样的。不过，我发现现在我对很多事的看法[2]开始改变了。我希望我妈妈除了让我做家务以外，也可以问问我有什么样的理想。

Hāha, shì a! Wǒ yǐqián wánr guò jiā jiā de shíhou yě shì zhèyàng de. Búguò, wǒ fāxiàn xiànzài wǒ duì hěn duō shì de kànfǎ kāishǐ gǎibiàn le. Wǒ xīwàng wǒ māma chúle ràng wǒ zuò jiāwù yǐwài, yě kěyǐ wèn wen wǒ yǒu shénme yàng de lǐxiǎng.

我觉得你可以跟你妈妈聊聊你的理想，她一定会尊重你的想法的。

Wǒ juéde nǐ kěyǐ gēn nǐ māma liáo liao nǐ de lǐxiǎng, tā yídìng huì zūnzhòng nǐ de xiǎngfǎ de.

Comprehension Check

		T	F
1	Keke is upset because her mother told her to do her homework.	○	○
2	Miko is glad that her mom used to make her do housework.	○	○
3	If you were Keke, what would you say to your mother after this conversation?		

NOTE

1 过家家 is a game in which Chinese children pretend to be members of a family, like playing "house."

2 "[someone] 对 + [something] 的看法" means "the way [someone] sees [something]" or "what [someone] thinks about [something]." When Keke says 我对很多事的看法开始改变了, it means "the way I see a lot of things has started to change."

Vocabulary · 生词

Audio

	Word	Pinyin	Meaning
9	打扫	dǎsǎo	to clean up (a room, apartment, or house)
10	洗	xǐ	to wash
11	家务	jiāwù	housework, household chores
12	看法	kànfǎ	opinion, point of view, perspective, way of looking at something
13	改变	gǎibiàn	to change, to alter, to transform
14	什么样	shénme yàng	what kind, what sort
15	理想	lǐxiǎng	ideal, dream
16	尊重	zūnzhòng	to respect

The image below contains the saying 尊老爱幼 (zūn lǎo ài yòu), which illustrates a value that is commonly associated with Chinese culture. (Hint: 幼 means "children; young.")

他还常常帮那些有需要的小孩子们。

王明经常去看他的爷爷和奶奶，而且他对别的老人也很尊重。

是啊，他一直是一个尊老爱幼的好同学。

Can you guess what this saying means in English?

2c Puzzle It Out · 动动脑 PROGRESS CHECK

Complete the exercise below to check your understanding of what you learned in Section 2. If you have questions, consult the Language Reference section.

Use the words in the list on the left to complete the passage below. You may use some words more than once.

来说
看法

对我 _____，找到一份能实现自己理想的工作很重要。对我朋友 _____，找到一份能赚很多钱的工作更重要。你对找工作的事有什么 _____ 呢？

2 Explaining a perspective

The word 对 can be used within different patterns to express someone's perspective or opinion. One such pattern is 对 + [someone] + 来说..., which means "as far as [someone] is concerned,..." or "for [someone],...."

1 对我来说，在网上买东西更方便。
For me, buying things online is more convenient.

2 对大学生来说，选什么专业是一个很重要的问题。
For college students, which major to choose is a very important issue.

3 你觉得对高中生来说，看演唱会好玩儿还是去爬山好玩儿？
Do you think going to concerts or hiking in the mountains is more fun for high school students?

4 经济发展对一个国家来说特别重要。
Economic development is very important for a country.

2d Using the Language · 语言应用 INTERPERSONAL/PRESENTATIONAL

Step 1: What are some things that are most important to you? Make a list of 理想 for your future. This list can include things you want to accomplish or anything that is important to you. Pick one or two items on your list that are most important to you.

Step 2: Ask your partner questions about his/her list. Does your partner have any goals that are similar to yours?

Example:

对你来说，毕业以后能去做什么比较重要？

Step 3: Be ready to share some of your and your partners' goals with the class. Use 对 ... 来说 to explain how your and your partner's goals are similar and/or different.

Example:

对你来说，毕业以后直接去上大学很重要。可是对我来说，去别的国家当志愿者比上大学更重要。

No matter

CHAPTER 10

3a Language Model · 语言范例 TARGET LANGUAGE INPUT

Your teacher will lead a discussion about the images below. Try to participate as much as you can. If there is anything you don't understand, let your teacher know.

Wúlùn　nǐ　shì　shéi
无论-你-是-谁，

No matter who you are,

dōu　yǒu　quánlì　qù　shíxiàn　zìjǐ　de　lǐxiǎng.
都-有-权利-去-实现-自己-的-理想。

you have the right to fulfill your dreams.

3b New Words in Context · 语境中学新词 INTERPRETIVE

Martin read the following message on a student website and posted his own response. Listen to the audio and try to understand as much as you can. Then read the passages, using the pinyin text and vocabulary list to figure out unfamiliar words.

上个星期在学校的篮球馆里，我看到一个男生哭了。那个男生平常特别酷、学习很认真、会玩儿很多种乐器，在我们学校里非常受欢迎。我一直以为无论遇到什么事，他都不会哭。我知道男女平等¹，但是我和很多朋友都觉得男生平常不可以哭，哭了就不酷了！如果我说出他的名字，我猜他就不会那么受欢迎了吧。

Shàng gè xīngqī zài xuéxiào de lánqiú guǎn lǐ, wǒ kàn dào yí gè nánshēng kū le. Nàge nánshēng píngcháng tèbié kù, xuéxí hěn rènzhēn, huì wánr hěn duō zhǒng yuèqì, zài wǒmen xuéxiào lǐ fēicháng shòu huānyíng. Wǒ yìzhí yǐwéi wúlùn yù dào shénme shì, tā dōu bú huì kū. Wǒ zhīdào nán nǚ píngděng, dànshì wǒ hé hěn duō péngyou dōu juéde nánshēng píngcháng bù kěyǐ kū, kū le jiù bú kù le! Rúguǒ wǒ shuō chū tā de míngzi, wǒ cāi tā jiù bú huì nàme shòu huānyíng le ba.

认为男人不能哭是一种对男人的刻板印象。无论你的性别是什么，你都可以哭。哭不只是女人的权利，男人哭也没有错。我们每个人每天都在很小心地生活着，生活常常会给我们带来很多压力。我们高中生有的时候也会觉得压力很大。如果哭出来能让你觉得舒服一点儿，那就哭吧。

Rènwéi nánrén bù néng kū shì yì zhǒng duì nánrén de kèbǎn yìnxiàng. Wúlùn nǐ de xìngbié shì shénme, nǐ dōu kěyǐ kū. Kū bù zhǐ shì nǚrén de quánlì, nánrén kū yě méiyǒu cuò. Wǒmen měi gè rén měitiān dōu zài hěn xiǎoxīn de shēnghuó zhe, shēnghuó chángcháng huì gěi wǒmen dài lái hěn duō yālì. Wǒmen gāozhōng shēng yǒu de shíhou yě huì juéde yālì hěn dà. Rúguǒ kū chū lái néng ràng nǐ juéde shūfu yìdiǎnr, nà jiù kū ba.

Comprehension Check

		T	F
1	The person who wrote the post saw a boy crying in the school's basketball gymnasium.	○	○
2	The boy described in the post is not very popular.	○	○
3	The person who wrote the post thinks that boys shouldn't cry.	○	○
4	Martin thinks that girls cry too much.	○	○
5	Martin thinks that people should cry if it helps them feel better.	○	○

6 Explain what you would say if you responded to Martin's post or the original post.

> **NOTE**
>
> 1 The phrase 男女平等 (nán nǚ píngděng) means "equality between men and women" or "gender equality."

Vocabulary · 生词

Audio

	Word	Pinyin	Meaning
17	无论	wúlùn	no matter what, regardless
18	男	nán	male
19	女	nǚ	female
20	平等	píngděng	equality; equal
21	猜	cāi	to guess
22	刻板印象	kèbǎn yìnxiàng	stereotype
23	性别	xìngbié	gender
24	权利	quánlì	right (the right to do something)
25	小心	xiǎoxīn	careful; carefully

Complete the exercise below to check your understanding of what you learned in Section 3. If you have questions, consult the Language Reference section.

Use the words in the list on the left to complete the sentences below. You may use some words more than once.

哪儿
什么
无论

1 那个同学非常聪明。她　　　　都知道。

2 　　　　是靠前的位子还是靠后的位子，都行！

3 我　　　都想去，可是我没那么多钱。

4 　　　　实现自己的理想有多难，我都会努力的。

Language Reference · 语言注解

3 Expressing "no matter..."

The word 无论 (wúlùn) means "it doesn't matter . . . ," "whether. . ." or "no matter. . . ." Sentences with 无论 often follow this pattern: 无论 + [question phrase] + 都. The subject of the sentence can come before or after 无论, or it can come after the question phrase. Note that 都 can sometimes be omitted. In the sentences below, subjects are highlighted in gray and question phrases are highlighted in blue.

wúlùn
1 无论你喜欢不喜欢，都得去上课。
Whether you like it or not, you still have to go to class.

wúlùn
2 无论他在哪儿，都非常受欢迎。
No matter where he is, he is always very popular.

wúlùn
3 无论毕业以后你要去哪儿上大学，都不要忘了俱乐部的朋友们。
No matter where you go to college after you graduate, don't forget your friends from the club.

wúlùn
4 我爷爷很爱喝茶，无论红茶还是绿茶，他都喜欢。
My grandpa really likes drinking tea. It doesn't matter if it's black tea or green tea; he likes them both.

5 无论今天谁表演，我都不想去看。我想在家休息。

wúlùn

It doesn't matter who is performing today; I don't want to go. I want to stay home and rest.

6 这份工作太难做了，我觉得无论我怎么努力，都做得不够好。

wúlùn

This job is too hard. I feel like no matter how hard I try, it won't be good enough.

What a Character!

dāo
刀

The characters 刻, 别, and 利 (lì), all contain the component 刂 (dāo), which comes from the character 刀 (dāo), meaning "knife, blade." This component appears in many characters that relate to cutting or separating things, but it also appears in a wide variety of characters that do not directly relate to cutting or separating.

Can you find all of the "knife" components, including both 刂 and 刀, in the characters below?

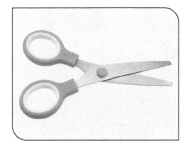

jiǎndāo

1 剪刀

scissors

lìwài

2 例外

exception; to be an exception

jiàzhào

3 驾照

driver's license

lìjiàn

4 利剑

sharp sword

Imagine that many students at your school were discussing equality issues, so you decided to join the discussion and read some posts on an online forum for students, similar to the post Martin responded to on page 274.

Step 1: Read through the posts below. Think about how you might respond to each post. Do you agree or disagree? Why?

Step 2: You and your partner will each pick one post to write a response to. Make sure that you do not pick the same post. Consider how to phrase your response so that it is respectful and helpful.

Example:

我觉得无论一个人穿什么样的衣服，我们都不应该笑他。
因为……

Step 3: Show your partner your response and read the response that your partner wrote. Then, write another response to what your partner wrote. You can agree with your partner, disagree, or express another opinion.

最近有很多同学去看男生的篮球比赛，可是去看女生比赛的人很少。我们女生也打得很好，为什么没有人去看？

上个周末，我朋友都去一个同学家聚会了，可是没有人问我要不要去。后来我听几个朋友说，我穿的衣服和鞋都不太好看。他们担心如果跟我一起玩儿，别人会觉得他们也不酷。我很难过！

有一次上课的时候，老师让我们讨论我们的理想。我说我的理想是在家里做家务、照顾孩子。很多同学都觉得我是一个男生，不应该只在家里，应该出去工作。

上次做小组作业的时候，我有一个非常好的想法。我们在讨论的时候，几个男生让我多听听别人的想法。他们还说，他们男生怎么说，我们怎么做就行了。我们女生都很不高兴！

5Cs
CULTURES
COMMUNITIES
COMMUNICATION
COMPARISONS
CONNECTIONS

For much of China's history, a person's gender has had a tremendous impact on what that individual was able to do in life. However, there have been many historical Chinese figures who performed roles that were not typical for their gender.

The Ballad of Mulan (木兰辞, Mùlán cí, c.386–535 CE) tells the tale of a young woman who joined the military so that her father did not have to go to war. According to the story, she fought in hundreds of battles over twelve years without the other soldiers realizing that she was a woman. Today, many people consider the story fictional, but for centuries people believed that Mulan was a real person.

Wǔ Zétiān (武则天, 624–705 CE) was the only woman to rule China as 皇帝 (huángdì), or "emperor / empress." Before she became ruler, only aristocrats could work as government officials. She created policies that made it easier for men from non-aristocratic backgrounds to become officials. She was also famous as a patron of Buddhism.

A statue of Empress Wu in Guangyuan, Sichuan Province

Wáng Zhēnyí 王贞仪 (1768–1797) was an astronomer and mathematician. Although women from high social classes sometimes did receive an education, Wang's work in math and science was quite rare.

Méi Lánfāng 梅兰芳 (1894–1961) was the most famous Beijing opera artist of the twentieth century and was known for playing female lead roles. He performed in Japan, the U.S., Germany, and Russia. Although men had been acting in female roles onstage for centuries, Mei was famous for his elegant performances and physical beauty.

Can you think of famous historical figures from other cultures who performed roles that didn't fit society's expectations?

This stamp from 1962 features Mei in costume as a female character.

Audio

A · Listening and Reading · 阅读和听力 [INTERPRETIVE]

Passage 1 What's next for Isabella and her friends? Read on. . .

雪儿给春月他们说，她的老师最近让学生们每个人准备一个表演。有一个要求是，他们要在表演里表达出来，想对十年以前的自己说什么。雪儿还没想好要做一个什么样的表演，要讲一个关于什么的故事，所以决定去小时候住的地方看看。春月和大文说，他们来上海以后，还没去看过上海传统的老建筑。海生说他也很久没去那儿了。所以，他们四个人决定一起去雪儿以前住的小区看看……

 雪儿，上海这种样子的老建筑真特别啊！

 嗯，有的老建筑已经有一百多年的历史了。不过，这种建筑现在越来越少了。

 以前雪儿住在这儿的时候，我也经常来这儿玩儿。

 是啊！那你还记得我以前最喜欢玩儿什么吗？

 记得！你那个时候最喜欢玩过家家，演别人的妈妈。

是啊！那个时候女孩子都爱演妈妈，在家做家务，比如，打扫房间、洗衣服、照顾孩子等等。但是长大以后，我发现女人的生活不应该只是这样的。

我们家就是我妈妈不工作，平常在家做家务。我爸爸出去工作赚钱。我认识的很多人家里都是这样的。我觉得这样挺好的。如果不出去上班，压力会小一点儿。

我爸妈平常都要工作，但是我爸爸也经常做家务。

我们家也不是这样的。我妈妈一个人又要工作，又要做家务。不过，我和马丁有的时候会帮妈妈做一些家务。

觉得女人只能在家里做家务是一种对女人的刻板印象。大文，如果你这样想，应该很难找到女朋友了。对吧，春月？

没错！对了，我还发现，在很多广告里，洗衣服的和照顾孩子的都是女人。

是吗？

对，我也发现了。而且很多人觉得不同的性别应该做不同的工作。我大学想学表演，我爸爸开始的时候不同意。他觉得学表演很累，而且很难找工作。他想让我毕业以后当老师，因为他觉得对女生来说，这份工作很合适。

当老师挺好的啊。春月周末也去当老师。

我周末当老师，是因为我喜欢。如果有些男生喜欢当老师，也可以去当啊。

嗯，你说得对，很多人对不同的性别是有一些刻板印象。

没错。我的看法是，我们不应该被刻板印象影响，去做自己不愿意做的事，或者改变自己的想法。我们应该多听听自己的想法。

对，我们应该常常问问自己：我最想过什么样的生活？

 对我来说，我最想做一个成功的厨师。

 大文，那你还觉得做饭是女人的事吗？

 我……我刚才没说做饭是女人的事啊。我想做厨师，是因为我喜欢做饭。但是我没觉得只有女人能做饭……对了，跟你们聊完以后，我在想，我是不是应该鼓励我妈妈出去工作？

 我觉得无论你妈妈想出去工作还是想在家里，都可以。最重要的是，这是她自己选的，她愿意这样。

 嗯，其实每个人都有自己的个性，都是不同的。

 是啊。无论你的性别是什么，都有权利决定自己想过什么样的生活，然后去努力实现它。

 你说得对——男女平等！我知道我要在我的表演里讲什么故事了！我要给十年前的自己写一封信，告诉她：要做自己，还要小心地保护自己的理想。

 说得好！雪儿，你们什么时候表演啊？我也想去看！

 我们也想去看！

 就在下个月！我给你们订几张票吧。

 谢谢，那你能不能帮我们订几张靠前的位子啊？

 没问题！对了，那马丁他们来上海的时候，我们要不要也带他们来看看这些老建筑？

 好主意！

Comprehension Check

                                                                                          T   F

1   The requirement for Xue'er's performance assignment is to express what she would   ◯   ◯
    say to herself ten years ago.

2   Owen's parents both work outside the home.   ◯   ◯

3   Isabella has noticed that a lot of ads she sees show women washing clothes or taking   ◯   ◯
    care of children.

4   In three to five sentences, say some of the things that you think Xue'er will say in her
    performance.

Passage 2 Look at the sign below. What do you think is the purpose of the sign?

Passage 3 Listen to the conversation between two college students and answer the following questions.

1 Why hadn't the girl heard about the show?
  (a) because she missed school for a few days
  (b) because she hasn't been paying attention to the Chinese club's promotion of the show at their school
  (c) because the Chinese club didn't promote the show at school

2 When does the girl say she will be available tomorrow to go to the show?
  (a) only during the evening
  (b) only before 5:30 p.m.
  (c) all day

3 Do you think the girl is really interested in the show? Use details from the conversation to support your
  opinion.

Chapter 10 · Advocating for Yourself and Others

Passage 4 Listen to a student's description of her mom's life and what she thinks about it. Are the statements that follow true (T) or false (F)?

		T	F
1	According to the girl, her dad rarely does housework, although he does take care of her and her younger brother.	○	○
2	The girl felt that she had often been stereotyped by her mother.	○	○
3	The girl thinks that it would be better if her aunt didn't stay at home to take care of her cousin.	○	○
4	The girl's aunt does not want to participate in activities that promote women's rights.	○	○

B Speaking · 口语 INTERPERSONAL

Step 1: Think of situations that you have seen or heard about in which people were being stereotyped. Pick one or two examples to discuss with your partner.

Step 2: With your partner, make a list of reasons why stereotyping can make people sad or upset, or have other negative effects. This list can be based on your and your partner's examples, or general reasons why you think stereotyping can be harmful:

- 刻板印象会给人很多压力
- 有的人很难找到工作，因为别人对他们有不太好的刻板印象

Step 3: Your partner will describe an example that he/she thought of in Step 1. Explain what you think should have happened differently in that situation.

- 我觉得他们那样做是不对的。他们应该……
- 如果我看到了这样的事，我会说……

C Final Project · 结课项目 PRESENTATIONAL

A Letter to My Future Self

Step 1: Write a letter in Chinese to your future self five years from now. You can ask yourself questions about your life, or you can ask yourself questions about how the world has changed. Are you going to college? Do you have a job? Use an appropriate letter format and try to use at least eight words or phrases from the list below:

- 是 (to express agreement)
- 信
- 对 . . . 来说
- 理想
- 什么样
- 看法
- 改变
- 尊重

- 无论
- 平等
- 猜
- 刻板印象
- 性别
- 权利
- 小心

Step 2: Imagine that you are yourself five years in the future, and Future You just received the letter Present You wrote in Step 1. Imagine Future You's responses and write back to yourself. You can answer any questions Present You asked in the letter or provide additional information about how the world has changed. Use an appropriate letter format and try to use at least eight words or phrases from the list above. Be prepared to share some of the details from your letter with the class.

Can-Do Goals · 能力目标

Talk with your teacher if you have questions or if you are not certain you can do the following tasks:

- Explain some ways in which gender equality has changed in China over the last century

- Identify the basic structural elements of a letter or email

- Express your opinion on a familiar subject

- Summarize someone else's perspective on a familiar subject

- Respond to other people's opinions with your own perspective

- Discuss the effects of common stereotypes

Cultural Knowledge · 文化知识

How have women's rights changed in China? Are these changes similar to or different from changes in other countries?

People gather at an event to help protect women's rights in Luannan County, Hebei Province.

Go Far with Chinese 3

Touring Shanghai

时间过得真快！环保比赛的时间
就快到了。今天是 12 月 30 号，
大家正在去上海的路上。学生们
一想到除了参加比赛以外，还可
以在上海玩儿两天，就特别高兴。
马丁的妈妈没有来过上海，而且
她很久没有见到春月了，所以也
跟他们一起来了。大家在路上都
很开心。有的人在跟坐在旁边的
人聊天儿，有的人在看外面的山
和树⋯⋯

Can-Do Goals · 能力目标

In this chapter, you will learn to:

- Name some of Shanghai's attractions
- Use 连 to introduce examples for added emphasis
- Discuss certain societal issues
- Understand basic information when others talk about cultural artifacts

Read the text and try to answer the Chinese questions.

Shànghǎi: yí gè yǒu yǐngxiǎng lì de chéngshì

上海：一个有影响力的城市
Shanghai: An Influential City

Shanghai is the largest and busiest port in China, and it is also a major global financial hub. This coastal, cosmopolitan city attracts (吸引, xīyǐn) people from all over China and the world with its business opportunities, history, culture, architecture, nightlife, and international connections.

哪些东西吸引着人们来到上海？

Modern Development

In 2013, certain areas in Shanghai were designated as part of the Shanghai Free-Trade Zone. This special economic designation boosted global trade and reinforced the area's status as a high-tech hotspot. Even visitors not interested in business might enjoy looking around the area— Pudong district, home to the Free-Trade Zone, also has many modern skyscrapers (摩天大楼, mótiān dà lóu), including the Oriental Pearl Tower and the Shanghai Tower, which is one of the tallest buildings in the world.

现代化的上海是什么样的？

The Shanghai Tower and the Oriental Pearl Tower dominate the Pudong skyline.

By the Numbers

At the end of 2017, nearly 10 million of Shanghai's 24 million Chinese residents were from places outside of Shanghai. Shanghai also has a sizable population of residents from outside Mainland China.

Top 5 Countries of Origin for Foreign Residents in Shanghai (2018)

Country	# of Residents in Shanghai (approx.)
Japan	29,500
United States	22,100
Korea	21,700
France	8,900
Germany	7,700

Top 5 Provinces of Origin for Residents in Shanghai (2010)

Province	# of Residents in Shanghai (approx.)
Anhui	2,600,000
Jiangsu	1,510,000
Henan	780,000
Sichuan	630,000
Jiangxi	450,000

Sources: Shanghai Bureau of Statistics, 2018, 2019, 2011

The China Art Museum: The building that the museum is housed in was originally constructed as an exhibition pavilion for the 2010 Shanghai World Expo.

A City for Everyone

An abundance of festivals represents the diverse identities and interests found in Shanghai. The city hosted a world expo in 2010 — the largest world's fair ever — and is home to the Shanghai International Film Festival (上海国际电影节, Shànghǎi Guójì Diànyǐng Jié), the only competitive film festival in China approved by the International Federation of Film Producers Associations. Beyond festivals, there are also more permanent attractions, including the Shanghai Museum, Shanghai Science and Technology Museum, the China Art Museum, and Shanghai Disneyland! Part of Shanghai's appeal is that, with such a diverse and dynamic population, there always seem to be more things to see and new events to attend.

上海有哪些受欢迎的活动和地方？

Traditional Sights

Although Shanghai is known for its skyscrapers and modern attractions, there are also some scenic places that offer relaxing views of earlier times: Yu Garden and the town of Qibao (七宝镇, Qībǎo zhèn) are two such places. Yu Garden, originally constructed in the late 1500s, is an example of a traditional Chinese garden from the late Ming dynasty. The garden, which includes pavilions, bridges, and carefully arranged water features, is located in downtown Shanghai. Qibao, on the other hand, is located on the outskirts of Shanghai. This ancient town has a history stretching back over a thousand years and is known for its traditional Chinese architecture and for being one example of a 水乡 (shuǐxiāng), or "water town" — a town built along a canal.

七宝镇有多少年的历史？它有哪些特别的地方？

A view of Yu Garden in Shanghai.

REFLECT ON THE ESSENTIAL QUESTION

What makes the identity of people and places unique and complex?

1. What features of a place attract people from around the world?

2. What are some of the possible advantages of globalization in a community?

3. What factors help determine the identity of a place?

Giving examples

1a Language Model · 语言范例　TARGET LANGUAGE INPUT

Your teacher will lead a discussion about the image below. Try to participate as much as you can. If there is anything you don't understand, let your teacher know.

Nǐ　búdàn　Zhōngwén　hé　Yīngwén　shuō　de　hǎo,
你－不但－中文－和－英文－说－得－好，
Not only can you speak Chinese and English well,

lián　Xībānyáyǔ　yě　shuō　de　hěn　hǎo.
连－西班牙语－也－说－得－很－好。
you can even speak Spanish very well.

Wǒ　xiǎng　zhīdào,　nǎ　yí　gè　shì　nǐ　de　mǔyǔ　a?
我－想－知道，哪－一－个－是－你－的－母语－啊？
I want to know, which is your mother tongue?

New Words in Context · 语境中学新词 INTERPRETIVE

Audio

Listen to Ellen video chatting with Isabella and try to understand as much as you can. Then read the dialogue, using the pinyin text and vocabulary list to figure out unfamiliar words.

春月，好久没联系了。最近
怎么样？是不是越来越喜欢
上海了啊？

Chūnyuè, hǎojiǔ méi liánxì le. Zuìjìn
zěnmeyàng? Shì bú shì yuè lái yuè xǐhuan
Shànghǎi le a?

嗯，爱林！我现在不但知道
哪些上海菜好吃，而且连
上海话¹都能听懂一些了。
如果你以后有机会来上海，
我可以给你当导游了。

Ng, Àilín. Wǒ xiànzài búdàn zhīdào
nǎxiē Shànghǎi cài hǎochī, érqiě lián
Shànghǎi huà dōu néng tīng dǒng yìxiē le.
Rúguǒ nǐ yǐhòu yǒu jīhuì lái Shànghǎi,
wǒ kěyǐ gěi nǐ dāng dǎoyóu le.

是吗？那你最推荐什么地方？

Shì ma? Nà nǐ zuì tuījiàn shénme dìfang?

外滩吧！如果你想了解上海
的发展历史，一定要来外滩
看看，尤其要看看外滩的建
筑，很特别。那里有很多跟
中国传统建筑很不一样的
大楼，有的大楼已经有一百
多年的历史了。

Wàitān ba! Rúguǒ nǐ xiǎng liǎojiě Shànghǎi
de fāzhǎn lìshǐ, yídìng yào lái Wàitān
kàn kan, yóuqí yào kàn kan Wàitān de jiànzhù, hěn tèbié. Nàlǐ yǒu hěn duō gēn
Zhōngguó chuántǒng jiànzhù hěn bù yíyàng de
dà lóu, yǒude dà lóu yǐjīng yǒu yì bǎi
duō nián de lìshǐ le.

好！对了，我听说上海特别
国际化。那儿外国人多吗？

Hǎo! Duì le, wǒ tīngshuō Shànghǎi tèbié
guójì huà. Nàr wàiguó rén duō ma?

多啊。我在街上经常听到有
人用英文聊天儿。有一次我
遇到了一个母语是西班牙语²
的人。我们还用西班牙语聊
了一会儿天儿。很多人喜欢
来上海找工作，因为他们
相信在上海有更多的机会。

Duō a. Wǒ zài jiē shàng jīngcháng tīng dào yǒu
rén yòng Yīngwén liáo tiānr. Yǒu yí cì wǒ
yù dào le yí gè mǔyǔ shì Xībānyáyǔ
de rén. Wǒmen hái yòng Xībānyáyǔ liáo
le yí huìr tiānr. Hěn duō rén xǐhuan
lái Shànghǎi zhǎo gōngzuò, yīnwèi tāmen
xiāngxìn zài Shànghǎi yǒu gèng duō de jīhuì.

是吗？那你是不是打算大学
毕业以后也在上海找工作啊？

Shì ma? Nà nǐ shì bú shì dǎsuàn dàxué
bì yè yǐhòu yě zài Shànghǎi zhǎo gōngzuò a?

 这个问题我还没想好。

Zhège wèntí wǒ hái méi xiǎng hǎo.

Comprehension Check

		T	F
1	Isabella has gotten used to life in Shanghai but doesn't understand the Shanghai dialect at all.	○	○
2	The architecture along the Bund is typical of traditional Chinese architecture.	○	○

3 According to Isabella, why do many people come to Shanghai?

> ## NOTE
>
> 1 上海话 refers to the Shanghai dialect, which is very different from Mandarin.
> 2 The character 语 (yǔ) in 西班牙语 (Xībānyáyǔ) is short for 语言 (yǔyán), which means "language." 语 often appears in the names of languages, especially when referring to spoken language as opposed to written language; for example 英语 (Yīngyǔ) refers to (spoken) English.

🔊 Vocabulary · 生词

Audio

	Word	Pinyin	Meaning
1	连	lián	even
2	机会	jīhuì	opportunity
3	外滩	Wàitān	the Bund
4	尤其	yóuqí	especially, particularly
5	母语	mǔyǔ	mother tongue, first language
6	西班牙语	Xībānyáyǔ	Spanish language
7	相信	xiāngxìn	to believe, to trust

5Cs

CULTURES

COMMUNITIES
COMMUNICATION
COMPARISONS
CONNECTIONS

The 外滩 (Wàitān) is known for its historical buildings, featuring a wide variety of different Western architectural styles, from neoclassical to Victorian Romanesque to Art Deco.

The dominance of Western architecture along the Bund is due to Shanghai's history. In the mid-1800s, the British emerged victorious over China in the first Opium War. Consequently, the British were able to make demands that allowed British merchants better trade opportunities. The British also demanded permission to use, and essentially govern, a portion of Shanghai that included the waterfront. Later, other foreign powers (including the United States and France) were also able to demand rights to additional portions of Shanghai. As foreign powers settled into Shanghai, they established buildings to suit their needs, designing them in the Western styles they were accustomed to.

Many of the historical buildings of the 外滩 were built between the late 1800s and the early 1900s. The buildings include many that are British in design, but there are also some American buildings and others that are a fusion of different countries' design styles.

A view along the Bund in Shanghai

Can you think of a place in your country where the prominent style(s) of architecture clearly illustrates the history of that place?

Complete the exercise below to check your understanding of what you learned in Section 1. If you have questions, consult the Language Reference section.

Match the first part of each sentence with the 连 phrase that completes the thought.

1 我太累了,
2 她觉得很奇怪,
3 我想买零食,
4 现在这个结果,

a 连我也没想到。
b 为什么教室里连一个人都没有。
c 连喝水的力气都没有了。
d 可是我包里连一块钱都没有。

Language Reference · 语言注解

1 Giving an example with added emphasis

连 (lián)... 都/也 is a pattern used to emphasize an example as extreme. It is similar to the English "even" or "not even" in sentences such as "I was so tired I couldn't even watch TV." The extreme example can be a thing or a situation, but it can also be the subject of the sentence (highlighted in examples 3–5 below).

lián
1 这家公司的要求不高, 连没有经验的人也可以申请。
This company's requirements are not high; even people without any experience can apply.

lián
2 你太厉害了, 连这么难的问题你都能解决。
You're so impressive; you can even resolve an issue that is this difficult.

lián
3 连我妈妈都忘了祝我生日快乐。
Even my mom forgot to wish me a happy birthday.

lián
4 连中国人都觉得那个字很难写。
Even Chinese people think that that character is difficult to write.

lián
5 连医生都不确定他对什么过敏。
Not even the doctor is certain what he's allergic to.

连 (lián). . . 都/也 can be used to call attention to the lack of something expected or hoped for. In this case, the pattern is 连 (lián) + 一 + [measure word] + [thing] + 都/也 + [negation], with the 连 (lián) being optional.

6 我太忙了，（连）一分钟的休息时间都没有。
<small>lián</small>

I'm too busy; I don't even have a single minute to rest.

7 功课太难了，我（连）一个题也做不出来。
<small>lián</small>

The homework is too difficult; I can't do a single question.

1d Using the Language · 语言应用 INTERPERSONAL/PRESENTATIONAL

Play a game to see who can come up with more extreme examples!

Step 1: You will be divided into three teams. One team will work together to brainstorm an initial statement that can be followed by at least one example using 连 (and ideally, multiple examples using 连).

Example: 他今天考试的时候很紧张。

Step 2: Once they have finished brainstorming, a member of the group will announce the initial statement to the other two teams (the "listening" teams). Each of the two listening teams will then work to come up with as many reasonable follow-up 连 examples as possible within a given time limit.

Example follow-up statements using 连：

1) 连自己的名字都忘了写。

2) 连最简单的题都回答错了。

Step 3: When the time is up, the two competing listening teams will read out their sentences. Whichever team thought of more follow-up examples that make sense wins. Then, one of the two listening teams will take a turn brainstorming a new initial statement, and the game repeats.

Societal issues

2a Language Model · 语言范例 　TARGET LANGUAGE INPUT

Your teacher will lead a discussion about the image below. Try to participate as much as you can. If there is anything you don't understand, let your teacher know.

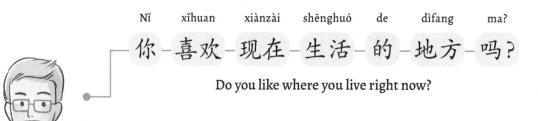

Nǐ	xǐhuan	xiànzài	shēnghuó	de	dìfang	ma?

你 - 喜欢 - 现在 - 生活 - 的 - 地方 - 吗？

Do you like where you live right now?

Nǐ	dǎsuàn	zài	nàr	zhù	xià qù	ma?

你 - 打算 - 在 - 那儿 - 住 - 下去 - 吗？

Do you plan to continue living there?

2b New Words in Context · 语境中学新词 INTERPRETIVE

Audio

Listen to Tianhao's presentation and try to understand as much as you can. Then read the passage, using the pinyin text and vocabulary list to figure out unfamiliar words.

我们小组今天要报告的社会问题是关于从农村来城市打工的人的。城市里有非常多的公司和工厂，工作机会也多，所以在中国很多住在农村的人会到城市里来打工。虽然他们有了比在农村更高的收入，但是也遇到了很多新的问题。比如，有的人没有办法带孩子一起来城市，他们的孩子只能在农村跟爷爷和奶奶一起生活。再比如，有的人遇到过被歧视的问题。有的时候，别人不太尊重他们，对他们不太礼貌。他们想融入城市生活很不容易，所以很多人觉得在城市里没有归属感。我们认为，中国经济的发展离不开每一个人的努力。我们要提高对公平和平等的认识，让每个在城市里打工的人都能更好地生活下去。

Wǒmen xiǎo zǔ jīntiān yào bàogào de shèhuì wèntí shì guānyú cóng nóngcūn lái chéngshì dǎ gōng de rén de. Chéngshì lǐ yǒu fēicháng duō de gōngsī hé gōngchǎng, gōngzuò jīhuì yě duō, suǒyǐ zài Zhōngguó hěn duō zhù zài nóngcūn de rén huì dào chéngshì lǐ lái dǎ gōng. Suīrán tāmen yǒu le bǐ zài nóngcūn gèng gāo de shōurù, dànshì yě yù dào le hěn duō xīn de wèntí. Bǐrú, yǒude rén méiyǒu bànfǎ dài háizi yìqǐ lái chéngshì, tāmen de háizi zhǐ néng zài nóngcūn gēn yéye hé nǎinai yìqǐ shēnghuó. Zài bǐrú, yǒude rén yù dào guò bèi qíshì de wèntí. Yǒude shíhou, bié rén bú tài zūnzhòng tāmen, duì tāmen bú tài lǐmào. Tāmen xiǎng róngrù chéngshì shēnghuó hěn bù róngyì, suǒyǐ hěn duō rén juéde zài chéngshì lǐ méiyǒu guīshǔ gǎn. Wǒmen rènwéi, Zhōngguó jīngjì de fāzhǎn lí bù kāi měi yí gè rén de nǔlì. Wǒmen yào tígāo duì gōngpíng hé píngděng de rènshi, ràng měi gè zài chéngshì lǐ dǎ gōng de rén dōu néng gèng hǎo de shēnghuó xià qù.

Comprehension Check

T   F

1 According to Tianhao, many people from rural China go to cities to find work. ○ ○

2 According to Tianhao, these workers think society is more fair in the city than in the countryside. ○ ○

3 Tianhao mentions several problems that workers encounter. What are they?

Audio

	Word	Pinyin	Meaning
8	社会	shèhuì	society
9	农村	nóngcūn	countryside, village, rural area
10	工厂	gōngchǎng	factory
11	收入	shōurù	income
12	歧视	qíshì	to discriminate against; discrimination
13	礼貌	lǐmào	courteous, polite; courtesy, manners
14	融入	róngrù	to merge into, to meld into, to assimilate
15	归属感	guīshǔ gǎn	sense of belonging
16	公平	gōngpíng	fairness; fair, just, impartial, equitable

LANGUAGE CHALLENGE

Etiquette and manners are important in China. You have already learned several 礼貌用语, or polite phrases, such as: 您好, 请, 谢谢, 不客气, 对不起, 没关系, and 再见. But there are also many sayings related to being polite. One saying is 礼多人不怪. If 怪 here means "blame," can you guess what the full saying means based on the two examples below?

春月第一次到雪儿家吃饭的时候，雪儿的妈妈让春月别客气。春月觉得礼多人不怪，所以她一直很有礼貌地说谢谢。

多用礼貌用语是个非常好的习惯，礼多人不怪。你对别人有礼貌，别人也会对你很客气。

Complete the exercise below to check your understanding of what you learned in Section 2. If you have questions, consult the Language Reference section.

Each sentence below contains the words 下去. In some sentences, 下去 is being used to mean "downwards and away," and in other sentences it means "to continue, to keep [doing something]." Identify the sentences where 下去 means "to continue, to keep [doing something]."

1 你能帮我把古筝从舞台上搬下去吗？

2 你再这样买下去，我们的钱很快就会被花完了。

3 妈妈让我到一楼吃饭。我说："我不想下去了，我可以在二楼吃吗？"

4 这份工作，我们要继续做下去吗？

5 我们不要再讨论下去了，就选这个话题参加比赛吧。

Language Reference · 语言注解

2 Expressing that something will continue into the future

In addition to being used to express a movement down and away, 下去 can be used in a completely different manner: to indicate that an action currently in progress will continue on into the future. Only certain actions, including 买, 生活, 学, 看, 听, 吃, 喝, 住, 说, 工作, and 做, can be used with 下去 this way.

1 你继续说下去啊，后来你们是怎么回家的？
   Keep explaining: how did you get back home afterwards?

2 我喜欢写小说，我会一直写下去的。
   I like writing novels. I will keep on writing novels.

Sometimes, phrases with 下去 are used as a way to comment on a particular topic (highlighted in gray below), as shown in examples 3 and 4.

3 如果经济这样发展下去，大家的生活一定会越来越好。
   If the economy keeps on developing like this, everyone's lives will definitely get better and better.

4 故事这样讲下去就没有意思了。
   If you tell the story like this, it's not interesting.

再 can also be used in sentences with 下去. Sentences with 再 and 下去 together are used to express a negative consequence that will happen if the action continues.

5 你再这样玩儿下去，成绩一定会越来越糟糕。

If you keep playing around like this, your grades will definitely get worse and worse.

6 你不能再这样工作下去了，工作时间太长对身体不好。

You can't continue working like this; working too many hours is bad for your health.

不下去了 can be added after certain actions to indicate that someone cannot bear to continue doing the action.

7 我真的看不下去了。你的房间怎么这么乱？赶快收拾一下。

I really can't stand it anymore. How can your room be so messy? Tidy it up right away.

8 那个音乐太难听了，我听不下去了。

That music is terrible; I can't bear to continue listening to it.

2d Using the Language · 语言应用 INTERPERSONAL

Reflect on where you feel a sense of belonging, and learn about where a classmate feels he/she belongs.

Step 1: By yourself, think of an example of a place, community, or club to which you feel a sense of belonging. What about that example makes you feel comfortable, engaged, or challenged? If it's a club, do you intend to continue with that club activity after you graduate? If it's a place, do you think you will continue living there after you graduate?

Step 2: In pairs, discuss the questions you reflected on in Step 1. As you talk with your classmate, ask questions to make sure you understand the following:

- Why does your partner like this group, place, activity, or community?

- Are your partner's reasons for feeling a sense of belonging towards the place or group he/she chose similar to your reasons? If not, what are the differences?

- Does your partner intend to continue with the activity or stay in the place after graduating?

Examples:

我很喜欢我现在住的小区。这里很安静，也很漂亮。我会在这个小区住下去的。

我很喜欢中文俱乐部。因为我在这里有很多朋友，我们经常一起参加很多有意思的活动。我在中文俱乐部很有归属感。

Reflecting on culture

3a Language Model · 语言范例　

Your teacher will lead a discussion about the images below. Try to participate as much as you can. If there is anything you don't understand, let your teacher know.

Tā　bèi　nàge　diànyǐng　gǎndòng　de　kū　le.

她 - 被 - 那个 - 电影 - 感动 - 得 - 哭 - 了。

She was moved to tears by that movie.

Nǐ　shénme　shíhou　huì　juéde　hěn　gǎndòng?

你 - 什么 - 时候 - 会 - 觉得 - 很 - 感动?

When do you feel very moved?

3b New Words in Context · 语境中学新词 INTERPRETIVE

Listen to the audio and try to understand as much as you can. Then read the dialogue, using the pinyin text and vocabulary list to figure out unfamiliar words.

赵老师，这次能去上海比赛和旅行，我太兴奋了！到上海以后，除了参加比赛以外，我们计划去哪些地方玩儿呢？

Zhào lǎoshī, zhè cì néng qù Shànghǎi bǐsài hé lǚxíng, wǒ tài xīngfèn le! Dào Shànghǎi yǐhòu, chúle cānjiā bǐsài yǐwài, wǒmen jìhuà qù nǎ xiē dìfang wánr ne?

东方明珠和豫园怎么样？一个是现代建筑，一个是中式的传统建筑，都特别有名。上海博物馆也不错，里面有很多文物。我建议大家去的时候认真地听一下博物馆里的人的介绍。他们讲得很棒，你不但能了解到这些文物的历史，还能听到让人感动的中国古代历史故事。

Dōngfāng Míngzhū hé Yùyuán zěnmeyàng? Yí gè shì xiàndài jiànzhù, yí gè shì Zhōngshì de chuántǒng jiànzhù, dōu tèbié yǒumíng. Shànghǎi bówùguǎn yě búcuò, lǐmiàn yǒu hěn duō wénwù. Wǒ jiànyì dàjiā qù de shíhou rènzhēn de tīng yíxià bówùguǎn lǐ de rén de jièshào. Tāmen jiǎng de hěn bàng, nǐ búdàn néng liǎojiě dào zhèxiē wénwù de lìshǐ, hái néng tīng dào ràng rén gǎndòng de Zhōngguó gǔdài lìshǐ gùshi.

赵老师，听了您的介绍以后，我特别想去博物馆看看。

Zhào lǎoshī, tīng le nín de jièshào yǐhòu, wǒ tèbié xiǎng qù bówùguǎn kàn kan.

有兴趣就好。对了，大家把我的手机号码写下来。如果有什么事，能很快地联系到我。我的号码是13912345678¹。

Yǒu xìngqù jiù hǎo. Duì le, dàjiā bǎ wǒ de shǒujī hàomǎ xiě xià lái. Rúguǒ yǒu shénme shì, néng hěn kuài de liánxì dào wǒ. Wǒ de hàomǎ shì 13912345678.

我手机里好像有您的号码。

Wǒ shǒujī lǐ hǎoxiàng yǒu nín de hàomǎ.

最好也在纸上写一下。要是手机没电了，关机²了怎么办？

Zuìhǎo yě zài zhǐ shàng xiě yíxià. Yàoshi shǒujī méi diàn le, guān jī le zěnme bàn?

不用不用，不会的，赵老师。

Bú yòng bú yòng, bú huì de, Zhào lǎoshī.

Comprehension Check

		T	F
1	Keke is excited for their trip to Shanghai.	○	○
2	Mr. Zhao recommends that the students stay with him at the museum so he can explain what they're seeing.	○	○
3	Mr. Zhao tells the students to write down his cell phone number so they can give it to their parents.	○	○
4	Martin says he doesn't need to write down Mr. Zhao's phone number because he already has it memorized.	○	○

5 Which three tourist attractions does Mr. Zhao mention? What does he say is interesting about each of them?

NOTE

1 When listing a string of numbers, such as when giving a phone number or a room number, the digit 1 is pronounced as yāo instead of yī.

2 关机 refers to a machine or electronic device turning off.

Vocabulary · 生词

Audio

	Word	Pinyin	Meaning
17	兴奋	xīngfèn	excited
18	东方明珠	Dōngfāng Míngzhū	Oriental Pearl Tower
19	豫园	Yùyuán	Yu Garden
20	文物	wénwù	cultural artifact
21	感动	gǎndòng	to move (someone), to touch (someone emotionally); moving
22	古代	gǔdài	ancient times, olden times
23	号码	hàomǎ	number

What a Character!

yù 王 ①1 王 ②2 王 ③3 王 ④4 王

The word 明珠 (míngzhū) contains the component 王. Because its appearance is similar to the character 王, this component is often called 王字旁, but actually, the component 王 comes from the character 玉 (yù), which means "jade." The 王 component appears in some words for precious things.

Based on other components you are familiar with, can you match the pinyin to the correct word?

1 dàimào

2 zhēnzhū

3 bōli

4 hǔpò

5 mǎnǎo

6 shānhú

A

珍珠

pearl

B

玛瑙

agate

C

珊瑚

coral

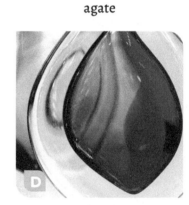

D

玻璃

glass

E

琥珀

amber

F

玳瑁

hawksbill turtle; tortoiseshell

Complete the exercise below to check your understanding of what you learned in Section 3. If you have questions, consult the Language Reference section.

Choose the option from the list on the left that best completes each sentence.

的	1 他在认真 ____ 听老师讲课。
地	2 他练习写字练习 ____ 很认真。
得	3 他是一个做什么事都很认真 ____ 人。

Language Reference · 语言注解

3 Comparing 的, 得, and 地

的, 得, and 地 are each pronounced "de" and are all words that affect the meaning or relation of the words around them. But they function quite differently!

的 is used to indicate possession or to link a description to the thing it is describing. The description can be a single word, or it can be a phrase.

1 那是我的笔。	That's my pen.
2 他穿着一双黄色的鞋。	He's wearing a pair of yellow shoes.
3 这是我昨天拍的我表弟的照片。	This is the photo of my cousin that I took yesterday.

得 is used either to link a descriptive word to a phrase that expresses degree, or to link an action to a phrase that provides important information about how/how well the action was done.

| 4 他开心得跳起舞来了。 | He was so happy, he started dancing. |
| 5 这些家具设计得很漂亮。 | These pieces of furniture are beautifully designed. |

地 links a descriptive word to an action word in order to express in what manner an action was done.

| 6 他开心地跳着舞。 | He dances happily. |
| 7 她正在安静地看小说。 | She is quietly reading a novel. |

What are some cultural artifacts that you've found interesting?

Step 1: Think about some cultural artifacts that you have seen before. They can be artifacts from your own country or a different country. They can be items that you've seen in person, or ones that you've seen online or in videos or books. If you're not sure what you want to talk about, here are some possibilities: 兵马俑, the Mona Lisa, the United States Declaration of Independence, or the mask of Tutankhamun.

Step 2: Choose a cultural artifact that you'd like to tell the class about. Draft a brief report on that item; if necessary, do a little bit of research to learn more about the artifact. Some information you might want to include in your report:

- Where the cultural artifact is from

- When it was made

- Where you saw the artifact

- Why you chose to report on it

Example: 这是中国两千年以前的一件文物。……我是在一本介绍世界古代历史的书上看到这件文物的。我对这件文物有兴趣，是因为我觉得这件文物很漂亮。……

Step 3: Your teacher will assign you a partner. Report on your artifact to your partner. When your partner is presenting, pay close attention to the report and try to think of questions you still have about the artifact or how you think the report could be improved.

Step 4: After your partner has finished, talk to your partner about his/her presentation. Give feedback on what you think he/she did well and try to suggest two to four things that could be changed to improve the report. When your partner is giving you feedback, ask questions if you don't understand what he/she is suggesting.

Example: 你可以说一下这件文物是什么时候被发现的。

Step 5: Based on your partner's comments, make adjustments to your report. Your teacher may ask you to write your report down, so it can be shared with the rest of the class.

A bronze head and mask, from the Sanxingdui culture in China around 3,000 years ago.

A figurine of a horse, made of glazed pottery. Created during the Tang dynasty (618 CE – 907 CE).

Chinese currency from the Qing dynasty (1644 CE – 1912 CE).

A gilt bronze lamp in the shape of a person, from the Han dynasty (206 BCE – 220 CE).

COMMUNITIES
COMMUNICATION
CULTURES
CONNECTIONS

For the majority of Chinese characters, each character has one particular pronunciation. However, there are also quite a few characters that have more than one pronunciation, depending on how they are being used — sometimes only the tone changes, but sometimes the entire syllable sounds different! Characters that have more than one pronunciation are known as 多音字 (duōyīnzì). You may already have noticed examples of this: the character 得 is pronounced "de" in the word 记得, but it is pronounced "děi" when it means "must." The character 地 is pronounced "de" when used to link a descriptive word to an action word, but it is spoken as "dì" in words like 地图. Another example is 还, which is most often pronounced as "hái" but is pronounced "huán" when meaning "to return (something)." Can you think of more 多音字 that you've learned?

de   dì

Does your language have anything similar to 多音字?

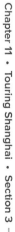

Audio

A Listening and Reading · 阅读和听力 INTERPRETIVE

Passage 1 What's next for Martin, Isabella, and their friends? Read on...

博物馆里的志愿者认真地给马丁他们介绍了很多关于文物的故事。马丁对历史更有兴趣，所以没有跟春月和妈妈一起去东方明珠。早上，他跟赵老师他们去博物馆了。他们在那儿看到了很多文物，还听到了很多关于文物的历史故事。从博物馆出来以后，已经快到午饭时间了。马丁他们一边聊天儿，一边往豫园走。

 这个博物馆真有意思，那个志愿者也讲得很清楚。

 是啊，我了解到了更多中国的文化和历史。

 没错，今天我还了解到了很多关于文物保护的故事。

 虽然我以前来过这儿，但是每次看到这些文物，都会觉得很感动。

 从古代到现在，虽然有些东西改变了，但是在中国的传统文化和习惯里，有些东西一直没有改变。比如，对别人，尤其是对比自己大的人，要有礼貌；要努力地学习，认真地工作。就像马丁刚才说的，关于文物保护啊，我们中国人……哎！马丁呢？他刚才还在这儿呢……糟糕！他的手机关机了。我们赶快找找他吧，我给他妈妈打个电话。

赵老师和学生们在博物馆的时候，春月带着她妈妈和天浩他们来到了东方明珠。

 从这里看上海，好漂亮啊！

 是啊，我从来没有来过这么高的地方！

 我平常不怕高，但是现在有点儿想下去了……

 没事，别紧张，梅雅。

 对，一会儿你就习惯了。大文，你怎么不说话啊？你也怕高吗？

 我当然不怕高了！你们看外面的那些高楼和工厂……我在想上海的机会真的很多，但是，每个生活在这里的人压力也都很大。

 大文，你这么厉害，连你都会觉得有压力啊？

 当然。为了能有更好的生活和更高的收入，每年都有很多人从别的城市或者农村来到上海。所以上海有很多很厉害的人！

 是啊。还有很多人从别的国家来到上海工作和生活。不过，我觉得别人能在这里生活下去，你也一定可以！

 对，刚去北京的时候，我虽然觉得很兴奋，但是也挺紧张的。有的时候，我会觉得在北京挺没有归属感的。不过，现在我觉得我已经融入了那儿的生活。

大文,你比春月他们更早地走进了社会,所以压力可能更大一点儿。不过,我相信你可以实现你的理想。等一下,我接个电话。……什么? 找不到马丁了?

春月的妈妈和学生们赶快从东方明珠出来,然后坐车来到了赵老师那儿。

 怎么办? 我们现在打 110 吧?

 阿姨,现在还不到 24 小时,好像不能打 110……我们再回去找找马丁吧?

 林静,太对不起了。刚才是我太不小心了……

 赵老师,不是您的错,这儿人太多了。

 是啊,这几个地方的人都特别多……要不然我和大文先去那边儿找找吧?

 喂? 请问你是?

 喂? 天浩,是我,马丁!

 马丁? 你是在用别人的手机给我打电话吗?

 是啊! 我的手机没电了,我现在在用路上遇到的一个人的手机给你打电话呢。

 你一个人去哪儿了啊? 我们都非常担心你! 而且你怎么现在才给我打电话啊?

 从博物馆出来以后,我想了一会儿关于环保比赛的事,然后我就找不到赵老师他们了。我想给你们打电话,但是谁的电话号码我都想不起来了……到豫园以后,我看到一家商店的广告上写了一个有很多 6 和 8 的电话号码,我才想起来你的电话号码跟那个很像,后面也有很多 6 和 8!

 啊? 你已经到豫园了?

 是啊！我找不到赵老师他们以后，先等了一会儿，但是没有等到他们。我就想，他们会不会已经去豫园了……我不知道去豫园怎么走，所以我先用中文问了一个中国人。他没听懂我要去哪儿。然后我又用英文问了几个"外国人"，他们也不知道我想去的地方怎么走。最后，我遇到了一个说西班牙语的人，她听懂我要去哪儿了，而且她也要去豫园！所以最后，是她带我来到豫园的。

 那你在那儿等着我们。我们马上就过去！

Comprehension Check

		T	F

1 Xue'er has been to the museum several times, so she no longer feels very moved by the cultural artifacts there.   ○ ○

2 Mr. Zhao is unable to reach Martin because Martin's cell phone is off.   ○ ○

3 Owen feels a lot of pressure because there are many very impressive people in Shanghai.   ○ ○

4 Martin calls Tianhao because he thinks Mr. Zhao might be angry at him for not staying with the group.   ○ ○

5 Why did Martin go to Yu Garden, and how was he able to find his way there?

Passage 2 Look at the poster below. What is it advertising? Based on the context, what do you think 展 (zhǎn) means? Are there any services available to make this event welcoming to a broader audience?

中国古代文物展

9月-10月
中国历史博物馆

有中文、英文、西班牙语志愿者
为您服务

Passage 3 Listen to the conversation between a teacher and her former student. Are the statements that follow true or false?

		T	F
1	Zhao Ming is attending a college in Shanghai.	◯	◯
2	At first, Zhao Ming didn't feel like he belonged in Shanghai because it's a big city and it's very different from his hometown.	◯	◯
3	Zhao Ming does not plan to stay in Shanghai after graduation from college because he is afraid he won't be able to find a job.	◯	◯
4	Ms. Li thinks that Zhao Ming will be able to find a good job in Shanghai.	◯	◯

Passage 4 Listen to a museum guide giving a tour to a group of visitors. Use Chinese to summarize his description of the exhibits in the museum.

The museum guide mentions 如果您想听别的语言的介绍，比如西班牙语、英语、日语等等，您可以找我们的志愿者帮您。What does 语言 (yǔyán) mean? And based on the context, can you guess the meaning of 日语？

B   Speaking · 口语   INTERPERSONAL

Imagine that you plan to move to a new city for college or a new job. What information would you want to know about it?

Your teacher will assign you to a group. In your group, use Chinese to discuss what you would like to know about a place if you were planning to move there. Come up with a list of five to eight things that you would want to know. This could include questions about what there is to do there, what public facilities (e.g. library, tennis courts) the place has, how easy it is to find work there, what the culture there is like, or anything else that comes to mind.

Example:

我想了解一下那个地方有多少人，那儿的经济发展得怎么样，人们的生活水平怎么样，还有那儿附近有什么好玩儿的地方。你们呢？

C   Final Project · 结课项目   PRESENTATIONAL

Newcomers Support Program

Imagine that the place where you live is organizing a newcomers support program to help make things easier for families that have just moved there or are considering moving there.

Step 1: With your group, search online for facts and data about where you live. If people in the group are from different places, just choose one place to focus on. Try to think of things that will help newly arrived families prepare for life in your hometown, using some of the ideas you came up with in the Speaking exercise. Try to also include the following information:
- Is your hometown a city or a rural area?
- Are there any useful organizations or programs available? How might those organizations or programs be helpful?
- What are the best ways to find job opportunities in your community?
- What are some facilities in the community?

Step 2: Prepare a short presentation that you could give to Chinese-speaking families who have just moved to your town. If possible, use slides or display boards to showcase your information.

Step 3: Give your presentation to the class and talk about why you think the information in the presentation will be helpful to the families. As an alternative, you could film a video presentation with the newly-arrived families as your intended audience.

Example video script:

欢迎大家来到我们这个小城市。为了帮大家更好地了解这个城市、融入社会生活、找到工作机会，我们做了这个视频。希望你们可以很快地融入这里的生活，找到归属感，在这里快乐地生活下去。……

Can-Do Goals · 能力目标

Talk with your teacher if you have questions or if you are not certain you can do the following tasks:

- Name some of Shanghai's attractions
- Use 连 to introduce examples for added emphasis
- Discuss certain societal issues
- Understand basic information when others talk about cultural artifacts

Cultural Knowledge · 文化知识

What have you learned about Shanghai?

Looking Back, Looking Ahead

春月：马丁，你觉得上海好玩儿吗？

马丁：好玩儿啊！我也有点儿想来上海上大学了。

春月：那你这次参加完环保比赛以后，回去努力学习吧！

马丁：知道了。对了，明天是1月1号。赵老师今天晚上想带我们去外滩玩儿。你们去吗？

春月：去啊。我再问问海生去不去。

马丁：好！

Can-Do Goals · 能力目标

In this chapter, you will learn to:

- Talk about some plans for development that the Chinese government has initiated
- Understand and talk about travel preparations
- Express that an action has been completed successfully
- Discuss challenges and responsibilities
- Share your wishes for the new year and understand the wishes of others

Zhōngguó de wèilái guīhuà
中国的未来规划
China Plans for the Future

Goal-setting is an effective way for people, communities, companies, and even countries to grow and move forward. Since 1953, China has used a program of Five-Year Plans (五年计划) to chart a course for the country's development. These plans reflect the monumental transformations that have taken place in China during this time.

你的国家、你的学校，或者你自己有这样的五年计划吗？

The First Five-Year Plan

In the 1950s, the Chinese Communist Party (CCP) hoped to transform the Chinese economy. Over 80 percent of China's population lived in rural areas, and the country's economy was largely (主要, zhǔyào) agricultural (农业, nóngyè). The first Five-Year Plan set ambitious targets for industrial (工业, gōngyè) growth and funneled resources toward the creation of factories. At the same time, the CCP increased government control over the economy, setting production targets for exactly how much of certain goods needed to be created — a system similar to the Soviet Union's economy at the time.

中国的第一个五年计划主要是关于什么的？

Mao Zedong's portrait hangs above the gate of the Forbidden City. He was the leader of the CCP when the first Five-Year Plan was created.

New Economy, New Goals

China has continued to develop Five-Year Plans, but as it has moved away from a government-planned economy to a more market-based economy, the plans have become more general. They are now referred to as 五年规划 (wǔ nián guīhuà), literally, Five-Year Guidelines. The plans of the 21st Century also reflect new national priorities and have put an emphasis (重点, zhòngdiǎn) on promoting innovation and addressing social issues. The Chinese government set targets to increase spending on scientific research and to increase the average number of years of education per person. In addition, the plans promote controlled urbanization — moving people from the countryside to small- and medium-sized cities while limiting the growth of megacities (特大城市).

除了发展经济以外，中国最新的五年规划还把重点放在了哪些问题上？

A girl in Shanghai plays with a robot assistant

Preserving and Promoting Chinese Culture

Recent plans recognize the need to encourage the arts and to protect (保护, bǎohù) China's unique cultural heritage (文化遗产, wénhuà yíchǎn). Measures to achieve this goal include digitizing important historical documents, increasing the protection of ancient artifacts and buildings, and supporting performance art projects, including film and local operas.

This temple in Qufu, Confucius' hometown, is protected as part of a national archeological park.

为了保护传统文化，中国政府做了哪些计划？

By the Numbers

Environmental protection is a prominent aspect of recent plans. Goals have been set to cover a range of issues from saving energy (能源, néngyuán) to decreasing pollution. The protection of important habitats is also a priority.

在最近的五年计划里，中国有哪些重要的环保目标？

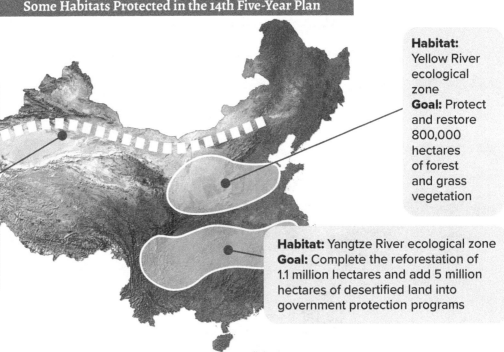

Some Habitats Protected in the 14th Five-Year Plan

Habitat: Northern sand control belt
Goal: Complete the forestation of 2.2 million hectares, and bring an additional 7.5 million hectares of desertified land and 2.7 million hectares of degraded grassland into government protection programs

Habitat: Yellow River ecological zone
Goal: Protect and restore 800,000 hectares of forest and grass vegetation

Habitat: Yangtze River ecological zone
Goal: Complete the reforestation of 1.1 million hectares and add 5 million hectares of desertified land into government protection programs

Source: 中华人民共和国国民经济和社会发展第十四个五年规划和2035年远景目标纲要, 2021

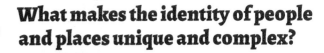

REFLECT ON THE ESSENTIAL QUESTION

What makes the identity of people and places unique and complex?

1 How do the changes in the Five-Year Plans show the changes in Chinese society through the decades?

2 How do the goals of the Five-Year Plans help China to protect its unique culture and places?

3 Why is it important to reflect on your identity when planning for the future?

Preparing for a trip

1a Language Model · 语言范例 TARGET LANGUAGE INPUT

Your teacher will lead a discussion about the images below. Try to participate as much as you can. If there is anything you don't understand, let your teacher know.

Wǒ　zài　wǎng　shàng　chá　bú　dào　wǒ　xiǎng　yào　de　xìnxī,
我 — 在 — 网 — 上 — 查 — 不 — 到 — 我 — 想 — 要 — 的 — 信息,

I could not find the information I wanted online.

zài　nǎr　chá　de　dào　ne?
在 — 哪儿 — 查 — 得 — 到 — 呢?

Where can I find it?

1

地图

2

书

3

网上

1b New Words in Context · 语境中学新词 INTERPRETIVE

Audio

Listen to the audio and try to understand as much as you can. Then read the dialogue, using the pinyin text and vocabulary list to figure out unfamiliar words.

春月，你们能到中国来上学真好！如果有机会的话[1]，我也想去别的国家学习或者旅行。你能跟我分享一下你的经验吗？讲讲去别的国家需要做哪些准备呢？

Chūnyuè, nǐmen néng dào Zhōngguó lái shàng xué zhēn hǎo! Rúguǒ yǒu jīhuì de huà, wǒ yě xiǎng qù biéde guójiā xuéxí huòzhě lǚxíng. Nǐ néng gēn wǒ fēnxiǎng yíxià nǐ de jīngyàn ma? Jiǎng jiang qù biéde guójiā xūyào zuò nǎxiē zhǔnbèi ne?

可以啊！首先，你要办护照。然后，如果你想去的国家需要签证的话，你还得办签证。这个过程比较麻烦，你得先认真地查一下签证怎么办，然后把需要的东西准备好。比如：关于你的信息、你的学习或者旅行计划、最近的照片，等等。

Kěyǐ a! Shǒuxiān, nǐ yào bàn hùzhào. Ránhòu, rúguǒ nǐ xiǎng qù de guójiā xūyào qiānzhèng de huà, nǐ hái děi bàn qiānzhèng. Zhège guòchéng bǐjiào máfan, nǐ děi xiān rènzhēn de chá yíxià qiānzhèng zěnme bàn, ránhòu bǎ xūyào de dōngxi zhǔnbèi hǎo. Bǐrú: guānyú nǐ de xìnxī, nǐ de xuéxí huòzhě lǚxíng jìhuà, zuìjìn de zhàopiàn, děng děng.

好，首先要准备好办护照或者签证需要的东西，明白了。

Hǎo, shǒuxiān yào zhǔnbèi hǎo bàn hùzhào huòzhě qiānzhèng xūyào de dōngxi, míngbai le.

其次，去办签证以前，你可能得先把去那个国家的和回国的飞机票买好。在网上就买得到，也可以打电话买。有的人很快就能在网上买到便宜的飞机票，有的人半天都买不到。这要看你的运气。

Qícì, qù bàn qiānzhèng yǐqián, nǐ kěnéng děi xiān bǎ qù nàge guójiā de hé huí guó de fēijī piào mǎi hǎo. Zài wǎng shàng jiù mǎi de dào, yě kěyǐ dǎ diànhuà mǎi. Yǒude rén hěn kuài jiù néng zài wǎng shàng mǎi dào piányi de fēijī piào, yǒude rén bàn tiān dōu mǎi bú dào. Zhè yào kàn nǐ de yùnqi.

是啊！那如果我早点儿去买飞机票，就能买到更便宜的吧？

Shì a! Nà rúguǒ wǒ zǎo diǎnr qù mǎi fēijī piào, jiù néng mǎi dào gèng piányi de ba?

 对，要是你计划好了就早点儿去买飞机票，别等得太晚了。对了，别忘了早点儿把行李收拾好。你要好好地查一下，去那个国家学习或者旅行要带哪些东西，然后把东西都准备好。

Duì, yàoshi nǐ jìhuà hǎo le jiù zǎo diǎnr qù mǎi fēijī piào, bié děng de tài wǎn le. Duì le, bié wàng le zǎo diǎnr bǎ xíngli shōushi hǎo. Nǐ yào hǎohāo de chá yíxià, qù nàge guójiā xuéxí huòzhě lǚxíng yào dài nǎxiē dōngxi, ránhòu bǎ dōngxi dōu zhǔnbèi hǎo.

 嗯，好！这些信息都很有用，谢谢！哎，春月，你在这个过程中² 遇到过什么糟糕的事吗？

Ǹg, hǎo! Zhèxiē xìnxī dōu hěn yǒuyòng, xièxie! Āi, Chūnyuè, nǐ zài zhège guòchéng zhōng yùdào guò shénme zāogāo de shì ma?

 有，多得很。比如：我第一次去办签证的时候就没办成，因为我带的照片大小不合适。

Yǒu, duō de hěn. Bǐrú: wǒ dì yī cì qù bàn qiānzhèng de shíhou jiù méi bàn chén yīnwèi wǒ dài de zhàopiàn dàxiǎo bù héshì.

 那是很糟糕，还要再办一次。

Nà shì hěn zāogāo, hái yào zài bàn yí cì.

 嗯！还有一次在机场，我的行李找不到了，后来我才知道是别人把我的行李拿走了。

Ǹg, hái yǒu yí cì zài jīchǎng, wǒ de xíngli zhǎo bú dào le, hòulái wǒ cái zhīdào shì biérén bǎ wǒ de xíngli ná zǒu le.

 啊，还有这样的事啊！

À, hái yǒu zhèyàng de shì a!

Comprehension Check

		T	F
1	Keke asks Isabella about the pros and cons of studying abroad.	○	○
2	Isabella says that the process of getting a visa can be a hassle.	○	○
3	Isabella says that it's always quick and easy to purchase plane tickets online.	○	○

4 What unfortunate thing once happened to Isabella at an airport?

NOTE

1. The phrase 如果...的话 has the same meaning as 如果 but is more casual and mostly used in spoken Chinese.

2. The phrase 在...中 means "in" or "during..." Thus, 在这个过程中 means "during this process." Other common uses are 在我的生活中 (in my life) and 在这个故事中 (in this story).

Vocabulary · 生词

Audio

	Word	Pinyin	Meaning
1	办	bàn	to do, to handle, to deal with, to arrange for
2	护照	hùzhào	passport
3	签证	qiānzhèng	visa
4	过程	guòchéng	process, course of events
5	查	chá	to check, to look into, to look up
6	飞机	fēijī	airplane
7	行李	xíngli	luggage, baggage
8	成	chéng	to become, to turn into, to achieve
9	机场	jīchǎng	airport

1c Puzzle It Out · 动动脑 PROGRESS CHECK

Complete the exercise below to check your understanding of what you learned in Section 1. If you have questions, consult the Language Reference section.

Use the words in the list on the left to complete each sentence. You will use each word at least once.

到
成
来
去

1. 你的签证今天办_____了吗？
2. 别玩儿手机了，老师已经走过_____了。
3. 我们离那个地方太远了，得走过_____才看得_____。
4. 我这个周末买_____了一把又舒服又好看的椅子。

Language Reference · 语言注解

1 Using the word 成 (chéng)

The word 成 (chéng) has several uses. When used by itself, it often means "to become."

1 我很开心我们成了朋友。

I'm very happy that we've become friends.

2 这件事我们得快点儿解决，要不然可能会成一个大问题。

We ought to resolve this matter quickly, otherwise it might turn into a big problem.

When used together with other verbs, it often carries the meaning of "to achieve," "to complete," or "to finish."

3 那套武术雪儿已经练成了。

Xue'er has already mastered that wushu routine.

4 这件大事我们今天办成了！

We (successfully) completed this major task today!

An additional example of how 成 (chéng) can add information to another verb is provided below in Language Reference 2.

2 Reviewing how to add detailed information to a verb

In Chinese, words can be added after a verb to describe the result or direction of an action. Words describing the result include 完, 好, 到, 错, 对, 懂, 成 (chéng), and 清楚. Words describing the direction include 进, 出, 上, 下, 来, and 起来. In the examples below, these words have been highlighted in gray.

1 你好像写错了一个字。

It seems that you wrote one character wrong.

2 你刚才说的话我没听懂。

I didn't understand what you just said.

3 我把刚买的零食拿到客厅来了。

I brought the snacks that we just bought into the living room.

4 他小心地从图书馆的书架上拿下来一本书。

He carefully took a book from the library's bookshelf.

In addition, some words, such as 到, 完, 懂, 成 (chéng), and 清楚 can paired with 得 or 不 to indicate that the speaker can or cannot complete the action.

5 你看得懂这个小说吗?

Can you understand this novel?

6 我听不清楚老师在说什么。

I can't hear what the teacher is saying very clearly.

                                         chéng

7 明天好像要下雨。我们可能去不成豫园了……

It seems like it's going to rain tomorrow. We probably can't go to Yu Garden…

1d Using the Language • 语言应用 INTERPERSONAL/PRESENTATIONAL

Take your classmates on a mystery trip using only the written word.

Step 1: Brainstorm the steps needed to prepare for a trip. Write out the process of completing those preparations as a list of steps. Your list should be at least five and no more than ten sentences long and must contain at least three items from the word bank below. Try to be creative with how you use the word bank items!

Step 2: Your teacher will pair you with another student. Use a piece of notebook paper, a mini whiteboard, or your school's online communication tool to exchange information with your partner. Take turns asking for the next step in each other's process. Make sure to write in complete sentences and to give all the steps in the correct order.

Example:

A: 你得先把签证办成。

B: 然后呢? 签证办成了以后要做什么?

C: 签证办成了以后, 你还得订旅馆。

Step 3: Once you have learned all the steps to your partner's process, take a guess at what sort of trip he or she has told you how to prepare for. Switch partners and play again.

Step 4: Your teacher will call time after a few minutes. If you are willing, raise your hand and read your process aloud one step at a time. Will the rest of your classmates be able to guess what kind of trip you are preparing them for?

Word Bank

去机场	订旅馆	申请宿舍	办护照
go to the airport	book a hotel	apply for a dorm	get a passport

买礼物	办签证	查资料	准备行李
buy gifts	get a visa	look up information	pack luggage

What a Character!

yáng

昜

1. **昜**   2. **昜**   3. **昜**

The word 场 (chǎng) contains the component 昜 (yáng), which means "sunlight," although not all words with this component have this meaning. This component often appears on the right side of a character. Characters that include this component are often pronounced as "yang" or "chang."

Each of the Chinese words below contains the 昜 component. Keeping in mind other components you have learned previously, can you match the Chinese word to its meaning in English?

a to fly up, to rise

yáng

1 杨树

yáng

2 飞扬

chàng

3 舒畅

b comfortable, worry-free

c poplar tree

Meeting challenges

2a Language Model · 语言范例　TARGET LANGUAGE INPUT

Your teacher will lead a discussion about the image below. Try to participate as much as you can. If there is anything you don't understand, let your teacher know.

Rúguǒ	yǒu	hěn	duō	rén	guānzhù	wǒ,	wǒ	jiù	huì	juéde
如果	有	很	多	人	关注	我,	我	就	会	觉得

If a lot of people paid attention to me, I would feel

hěn	bù	shūfu.	Nǐ	xǐhuān	bèi	biérén	guānzhù	ma?
很	不	舒服。	你	喜欢	被	别人	关注	吗?

really uncomfortable. Do you like it when others pay attention to you?

2b New Words in Context · 语境中学新词 INTERPRETIVE

Listen to the audio and try to understand as much as you can. Then read the passage, using the pinyin text and vocabulary list to figure out unfamiliar words.

世界上有很多个国家，有的是发达国家，有的是发展中国家[1]。每个国家都有自己关注的问题。发达国家和发展中国家关注的问题可能不太一样，但是有一些问题是很多国家的政府都非常关注的。比如：环保问题、节约资源问题、性别平等问题、教育公平问题，等等。这些问题不但是挑战，而且也是机会。我认为每个国家的政府都应该迎接这些挑战，把这些挑战变成机会，一起合作来更好地解决这些问题。其实除了不同国家的政府以外，有一些国际组织也一直在努力解决这些问题。我认为我们要认识到，关注和解决这些问题不但是政府和一些国际组织的责任，也是我们每个人的责任！你听过那句话吗？"保护环境，人人有责[2]！"就像对环境问题一样，如果我们对一些社会问题都能更有责任感[3]，那我们的社会一定会越来越好。大家同意我的看法吗？

Shìjiè shàng yǒu hěn duō gè guójiā, yǒu de shì fādá guójiā, yǒude shì fāzhǎn zhōng guójiā. Měi gè guójiā dōu yǒu zìjǐ guānzhù de wèntí. Fādá guójiā hé fāzhǎn zhōng guójiā guānzhù de wèntí kěnéng bú tài yíyàng, dànshì yǒu yìxiē wèntí shì hěn duō guójiā de zhèngfǔ dōu fēicháng guānzhù de. Bǐrú: huán bǎo wèntí, jiéyuē zīyuán wèntí, xìngbié píngděng wèntí, jiàoyù gōngpíng wèntí, děng děng. Zhèxiē wèntí búdàn shì tiǎo zhàn, érqiě yě shì jīhuì. Wǒ rènwéi měi gè guójiā de zhèngfǔ dōu yīnggāi yíngjiē zhèxiē tiǎo zhàn, bǎ zhèxiē tiǎo zhàn biàn chéng jīhuì, yìqǐ hézuò lái gèng hǎo de jiějué zhèxiē wèntí. Qíshí chúle bùtóng guójiā de zhèngfǔ yǐwài, yǒu yìxiē guójì zǔzhī yě yìzhí zài nǔlì jiějué zhèxiē wèntí, wǒ rènwéi wǒmen yào rènshi dào, guānzhù hé jiějué zhèxiē wèntí búdàn shì zhèngfǔ hé yìxiē guójì zǔzhī de zérèn, yě shì wǒmen měi gè rén de zérèn! Nǐ tīng guò nà jù huà ma? "Bǎohù huánjìng, rén rén yǒu zé!" Jiù xiàng duì huánjìng wèntí yíyàng, rúguǒ wǒmen duì yìxiē shèhuì wèntí dōu néng gèng yǒu zérèngǎn, nà wǒmen de shèhuì yídìng huì yuèláiyuè hǎo. Dàjiā tóngyì wǒ de kànfǎ ma?

Comprehension Check

                                                           T   F

1   In her opinion statement, Isabella talks about both developed and developing countries. ○ ○

2   Isabella thinks that only developed nations need to pay attention to the problem of equal education opportunities. ○ ○

3   Isabella seems to think that some problems are too big for individuals to help with. ○ ○

4   Use at least two complete sentences to respond to Isabella's final question.

NOTE

1   The phrase 发展中国家 means "developing country" or "developing nation."

2   The phrase 人人有责 (rén rén yǒu zé) translates to ". . . is everyone's responsibility."

3   Just as 归属感 means "a sense of belonging," the phrase 责任感 (zérèngǎn) means a "sense of responsibility."

Vocabulary · 生词

Audio

	Word	Pinyin	Meaning
10	发达	fādá	developed, flourishing
11	关注	guānzhù	to pay close attention to, to follow with interest, to follow (on social media)
12	政府	zhèngfǔ	government
13	挑战	tiǎo zhàn	challenge; to challenge
14	迎接	yíngjiē	to go and welcome, to greet, to meet (a challenge)
15	变	biàn	to become different, to change, to transform
16	组织	zǔzhī	organization; to organize
17	责任	zérèn	responsibility

LANGUAGE CHALLENGE

The character 变 (biàn) means "to become different, to change, to transform." It appears in many 成语 (chéngyǔ), or proverbs, alongside either 化 or 不 to express that something is ever-changing or that it never changes. Based on the context, can you guess what these expressions mean?

1 这个表演千变万化，太有意思了！
2 这儿的天气变化无常，刚才还好好的，现在就下雨了！
3 世界上没有一成不变的东西，很多人和事都一直在变化。

2c Puzzle It Out · 动动脑 PROGRESS CHECK

Complete the exercise below to check your understanding of what you learned in Section 2. If you have questions, consult the Language Reference section.

Use the words on the left to complete the following conversation. You will use each word more than once.

把

被

A: 是你 _____ 我的海报拿走了吗？

B: 你说什么？我听不清楚！我 _____ 你的什么东西拿走了？

A: 我说，我最喜欢的海报 _____ 别人拿走了，是你 _____ 它拿走了吗？

B: 你最喜欢的海报 _____ 别人拿走了啊？不是我拿的。是谁 _____ 它拿走了呢？

A: 不是你 _____ 它拿走的啊？那我再问问别人吧。

3 Review of 把 and 被

The character 把 is used to indicate that an action is done to something. It can be thought of as meaning "taking something and doing something to it." 把 is used before the thing that is being acted upon. The 把 phrase comes between the subject and the verb.

1 谁把我的包放到这儿了？
    Who put my bag here?

2 我已经把这本书看完了。
    I have already finished reading this book.

3 我姐姐把时间都花在看电视上了，我把时间都花在踢足球上了。
    My sister spends all her time watching TV; I spend all my time playing soccer.

The word 被 can be used in sentences where the focus is on the person or thing that is acted upon — and not on who is doing the action. The verb is always followed by something else, such as a word showing the result or direction of the action.

4 那个蛋糕已经被吃完了。
    That cake was already eaten.

5 糟糕！我们的调查报告被小明带回家了！
    Oh no! Our survey report was taken home by Xiaoming!

6 这件文物是在 1982 年被发现的。
    This cultural artifact was discovered in 1982.

While 被 is the most commonly used word in this structure, you might also hear 让 and 叫 used this way.

7 您的包让谁拿走了？
    By whom was your bag taken?

8 我的汉堡叫狗吃了！
    My hamburger was eaten by the dog!

Activity 1 What challenges do you see at your school or in your community that you think could be turned into opportunities (把挑战变成机会)? Work together with your groupmates to come up with a strategy for overcoming a challenging situation.

Step 1: Brainstorm some challenges or issues you see around you. If you don't know how to talk about a particular challenge in Chinese, consult a dictionary or ask your teacher for help.

Step 2: Your teacher will put you in groups. Share your list of challenges with your group and listen as they share their lists. Take a vote to choose the one challenge your group most wants to turn into an opportunity for the school or community.

Step 3: What needs to happen to turn your chosen challenge into an opportunity for improvement? Work with your groupmates to think of what needs to be done and by whom.

Step 4: Share your strategy with the class. Can you work with your school, local organizations, or even local government to put any of your class's strategies into action?

Activity 2 Who ate all the cake? Play a guessing game with your classmates to find out.

Step 1: As a class, brainstorm a list of questions that use the word 把, for example 谁把蛋糕吃完了? Your teacher will compile a final list to use in the game.

Step 2: Your teacher will assign each student an action from the list. This means that the action assigned to you was done by you! Your task is to figure out who did the other actions on the list.

Step 3: Move around the classroom asking your classmates questions about what they've done lately. You may not directly ask if they have done one of the actions on the list! Once you think you know who did one of the actions, jot it down.

Step 4: Once you have a guess for each action, or when your teacher calls time, share your guesses with the class. How many did you guess correctly?

Example:

A: 你最近吃甜的东西了吗?

B: 嗯，我最近吃甜的东西了。你最近要去旅行吗?

A: 对。

Later...

A: 我觉得 B 把蛋糕吃完了! or 我觉得蛋糕被 B 吃了。

B: 我被发现了! A，是不是你的行李已经准备好了?

A: 不是!

New Year's wishes

3a Language Model · 语言范例 TARGET LANGUAGE INPUT

Your teacher will lead a discussion about the image below. Try to participate as much as you can. If there is anything you don't understand, let your teacher know.

Wǒ　de　xīnnián　yuànwàng　yǐjīng　shíxiàn　le　liǎng　gè　le.
我 — 的 — 新年 — 愿望 — 已经 — 实现 — 了 — 两 — 个 — 了。

Two of my New Year's wishes have already come true.

Zuìhòu　yí　gè　yuànwàng　yě　huì　shíxiàn　ma?
最后 — 一 — 个 — 愿望 — 也 — 会 — 实现 — 吗?

Will the last one also come true?

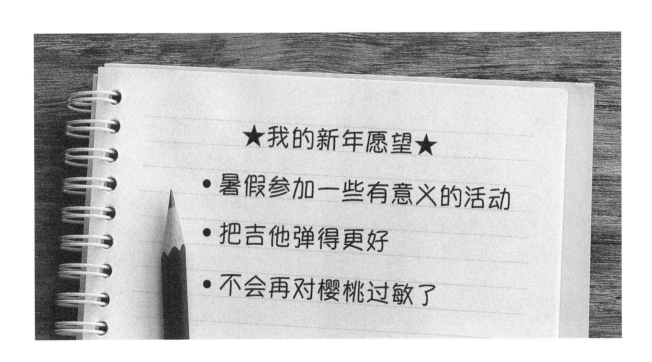

★我的新年愿望★

• 暑假参加一些有意义的活动

• 把吉他弹得更好

• 不会再对樱桃过敏了

Listen to the audio and try to understand as much as you can. Then read the dialogue, using the pinyin text and vocabulary list to figure out unfamiliar words.

时间过得真快啊！大学的第一个学期马上就要结束了。

Shíjiān guò de zhēn kuài a! Dàxué de dì yī gè xuéqī mǎshàng jiù yào jiéshù le.

是啊！而且寒假就要开始了，新年也快要到了！对了，哥，春月跟你说了吗？大家想请你明天晚上一起去外滩玩儿。

Shì a! Érqiě hánjià jiù yào kāishǐ le, xīnnián yě kuài yào dào le! Duì le, gē, Chūnyuè gēn nǐ shuō le ma? Dàjiā xiǎng qǐng nǐ míngtiān wǎnshàng yìqǐ qù wàitān wánr.

嗯，我已经跟春月约好了。明天晚上我跟你们一起倒数。元旦那天我跟我朋友一起过。

Ng̀, wǒ yǐjīng gēn Chūnyuè yuē hǎo le. Míngtiān wǎnshàng wǒ gēn nǐmen yìqǐ dàoshǔ. Yuándàn nà tiān wǒ gēn wǒ péngyou yìqǐ guò.

好！对了，你的新年愿望想好了吗？我今天得赶快把我的新年愿望想好。我去年的三个新年愿望已经实现了两个了：回上海上大学，还有举办一场有意义的表演。

Hǎo! Duì le, nǐ de xīnnián yuànwàng xiǎng hǎo le ma? Wǒ jīntiān děi gǎnkuài bǎ wǒ de xīnnián yuànwàng xiǎng hǎo. Wǒ qùnián de sān gè xīnnián yuànwàng yǐjīng shíxiàn le liǎng gè le: huí Shànghǎi shàng dàxué, hái yǒu jǔbàn yì chǎng yǒu yìyì de biǎoyǎn.

我的新年愿望已经想好了！我想做志愿者，让社会上更多的人了解手语，然后让更多的人学会用手语交流。哎，那你还没实现的第三个愿望是什么？

Wǒ de xīnnián yuànwàng yǐjīng xiǎng hǎo le! Wǒ xiǎng zuò zhìyuànzhě, ràng shèhuì shàng gèng duō de rén liǎojiě shǒuyǔ, ránhòu ràng gèng duō de rén xué huì yòng shǒuyǔ jiāoliú. Āi, nà nǐ hái méi shíxiàn de dì sān gè yuànwàng shì shénme?

是在大学里找一个……啊，你的愿望好像比我的有意义多了！我还是不告诉你了吧。

Shì zài dàxué lǐ zhǎo yí gè... À, nǐ de yuànwàng hǎoxiàng bǐ wǒ de yǒu yìyì duō le! Wǒ háishì bú gàosù nǐ le ba.

Comprehension Check

		T	F
1	The first semester is ending and winter break is about to start.	○	○
2	Haisheng plans to spend New Year's Eve alone this year.	○	○
3	Xue'er wishes she could have put on a meaningful performance this year.	○	○
4	What might Xue'er's third wish be? Use your imagination!		

Vocabulary · 生词

Audio

	Word	Pinyin	Meaning
18	结束	jiéshù	end; to end
19	寒假	hánjià	winter break
20	新年	xīnnián	the new year
21	倒数	dàoshǔ	to count down, to count back
22	元旦	Yuándàn	New Year's Day
23	愿望	yuànwàng	wish, aspiration, desire
24	有意义	yǒu yìyì	to have meaning or significance; meaningful
25	交流	jiāoliú	to interact, to exchange (ideas, experiences, etc.), to communicate

5Cs CONNECTIONS

COMMUNITIES
COMMUNICATION
COMPARISONS
CULTURES

张海迪 (Zhāng Hǎidí) is an author, translator, and inspirational speaker from China. Born in Shandong Province (山东省) in 1955, she became paraplegic at the age of five. Despite her challenges, she committed herself to academics and eventually was awarded a Master of Philosophy from Jilin University and an honorary Doctorate from York University. She has advocated for people with disabilities in China, including improving their access to public facilities. She is seen as an inspirational figure by many in China. Who inspires you?

Complete the exercise below to check your understanding of what you learned in Section 3. If you have questions, consult the Language Reference section.

Read the Chinese sentences, then choose the best English translation.

1 他已经走了，你也要走了吗？

(a) He has left already. Will you be leaving, too?
(b) He has left already. Have you left, too?

2 我吃了午饭就开始做作业。

(a) After I eat lunch, I'll do my homework.
(b) I ate lunch and then did my homework.

3 这本书你看了几遍了？

(a) You have read this book before, haven't you?
(b) How many times have you read this book already?

Language Reference · 语言注解

4 Reviewing the uses of 了

The character 了 can change the meaning of a sentence in several different ways.

了 can demonstrate completion of an action.

1 你吃晚饭了吗？

Did you eat dinner?

2 我下午下了课就去找你。

(After) I get out of class in the afternoon, I will go look for you.

了 can show a change of situation or that something is about to change or happen.

3 我肚子饿了。

I'm hungry (but I wasn't before).

4 我们要走了，你准备好了吗？

We're about to leave; are you ready?

了 can convey the idea of "until now" or "so far" in sentences that include a length of time or a number of times or things. Take note of the second 了 in the following sentences.

5 西安我已经去了好几次了。

I have already been to Xi'an several times (and will probably go again).

6 我已经做完了两门课的作业了。

I have finished the homework for two classes so far.

In addition, 了 appears in a number of set phrases, such as 为了, 对了, and 算了.

7 算了，我不跟你讨论这个问题了。

Forget it; I'm done discussing this issue with you.

8 为了解决这个问题，我们需要大家一起合作。

In order to solve this problem, we need everyone to work together.

9 对了，你打算去参加迎接新同学的活动吗？

By the way, do you plan to attend the event to welcome the new students?

3d Using the Language • 语言应用 INTERPERSONAL/PRESENTATIONAL

For this activity, you will write a passage about your Chinese language learning journey. Imagine that you will be sharing this passage with students at your school who are taking Chinese classes that you have already completed. Your passage should encourage them in their study of Chinese while also demonstrating the different ways that 了 can be used.

Step 1: Write a short passage that uses 了 in at least three different ways. Use the checklist below to help you.

Step 2: Trade your passage with a partner and check each other's work. Help your partner by correcting any errors you find or by offering ideas for adding another meaning of 了 to the passage. (Check the Language Reference section if you need reminders.) When you are finished, return the passage to the original author and get your own passage back.

Step 3: Make edits to your passage based on what your partner suggested. Finally, write one or two questions to help younger students check their understanding of your passage. Then turn in your passage to your teacher so it can be reviewed and used to help younger students.

- 了 to indicate completion of action
- 了 to indicate a change of situation
- 了 to indicate something is about to happen
- Double 了 to indicate "until now, so far"
- 了 in a set phrase, such as 对了, 为了, or 算了

5Cs

COMMUNICATION

COMMUNITIES
COMMUNICATION
COMPARISONS
CONNECTIONS

In Chinese, there are many phrases you can use when parting from friends or family for an extended period of time.

If someone is leaving on a trip, you might say 旅途愉快！(Lǚ tú yúkuài!), which means "Have a nice trip!" You might also say 一路平安！(Yí lù píng'ān!) or 一路顺风！(Yí lù shùn fēng!), which both translate to something like "Bon voyage!" or "Have a safe trip!" It is important to note, though, that 一路顺风 is not used when speaking to people who are about to board a flight. The phrase literally means "May your road be with the wind." Since an airplane moves against the wind at takeoff and landing, wishing someone 一路顺风 before a flight could bring them bad luck!

In other circumstances, you might just want to tell someone to take care. If so, you might say 保重！(Bǎozhòng!) or 珍重！(Zhēnzhòng!). To tell a person specifically to take good care of themselves, you could say 照顾好自己！(Zhàogù hǎo zìjǐ!).

Finally, if you are parting ways and don't know when you'll see each other gain, make sure to say 保持联系！(Bǎochí liánxì!), or "Keep in touch!"

Put the Pieces Together! · 融会贯通

Audio

A   Listening and Reading · 阅读和听力   INTERPRETIVE

Passage 1 What's next for Martin, Isabella, and their friends? Read on...

晚上，大家看着漂亮的外滩，准备一起迎接新年。

 晚上的外滩和东方明珠真漂亮啊。

 是啊！对了，比赛你们准备得怎么样了？

 上次虽然我们赢了比赛，不过老师们都希望我们可以多讲讲关于水污染的问题。现在我们觉得防止水污染不但是每个人的责任，也是每个公司和工厂的责任，还有政府的责任。所以，我们又做了一些调查。

 我们现在还打算和一些国际环保组织合作，建议更多的公司、工厂和政府可以更关注这个问题。

 让发达国家和发展中国家可以有更多的讨论和合作，一起迎接环境问题的挑战。

 你们这个宣传计划越来越有意思了。

谢谢，海生！对了，离新年还有一个多小时。我们这样等好像没有意思啊……我们做点儿什么吧？

 那我们每个人在纸上写一个自己的新年愿望吧？

 好啊！那我们都别写自己的名字，然后大家猜一下每个愿望是谁写的？

 好主意！我写的时候你不要看啊。

大家写完以后，都把写着愿望的纸给了赵老师。

 好，第一个愿望是，"我希望明年可以把菜做得更好吃。"

 这个一定是大文的愿望！

 对，大文你怎么写了一个这么好猜的愿望？

 好猜是好猜，但是你们不想我能实现我的愿望吗？

 想，想，想！

 那我们来看一下第二个愿望吧，"我希望明年可以跟老师做一些研究，调查一下小孩子经常上网对健康和学习的影响。"

 做研究和调查得分析数据，我猜这是梅雅写的吧？

Go Far with Chinese 3

你猜错了，马丁！

 那是不是天浩写的？我知道他现在也挺喜欢分析数据的。

 你又猜错了，马丁！

 春月，这个是你写的吗？我记得你说你下个学期想换专业，去学教育学？

 春月，大文说的是真的吗？

 没错！我现在已经实习了快一个学期了，我发现我对教育越来越有兴趣了。这次帮马丁他们做完调查以后，我对学生的上网习惯给他们带来的影响也很有兴趣。

 好，为了实现你的目标，努力吧！

 加油，春月！然后下一个愿望是，"我希望明年暑假可以去 一个国际环保组织实习。"

 这个一定是梅雅写的愿望。马丁，你看，我比你更了解梅雅吧？

 哎，这个应该是梅雅写的……

 不对，你们都猜错了。

 我知道了！这个愿望是关于环保的，但是不是梅雅写的，也一定不是里奥和马丁写的。我也没写这个愿望，所以这是可可写的！

 但是可可以前对环保没那么有兴趣吧？

 天浩说对了！开始的时候，我是对环保没有那么大的兴趣。现在我觉得"保护环境，人人有责"！比赛虽然快结束了，但是环境保护还要继续。

 可可说得对！我看看，下一个愿望也是关于环保比赛的，"无论这次比赛的结果怎么样，我希望我们都能过一个开心的新年。"

啊？开心还不够，我们得赢啊！如果我们能赢，就可以去别的国家参加下场比赛了。对了，可可，你们要不要先开始准备办签证？

 签证啊，我再等等吧……

 里奥，我觉得这次比赛的结果不是最重要的，我们一起努力解决问题的过程更重要。

 我同意！

 对，这次能和你们一起参加这么有意义的比赛，我真的很开心。

 我们帮你们做问卷调查，也挺开心的！

 哈哈，这个愿望不是里奥的！是马丁的吧？

 啊……被你们发现了……

 哈哈，下个愿望是……

 你们听，倒数开始了！

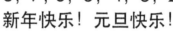 8, 7, 6, 5, 4, 3, 2, 1……
新年快乐！元旦快乐！

Comprehension Check ✓

		T	F
1	Martin thinks that the issue of water pollution is mostly the government's responsibility.	○	○
2	It's Isabella's idea to guess who wrote which New Year's wish.	○	○
3	Maya wants to study the effect of internet use on children's health and academic performance.	○	○
4	Martin guesses the author of two wishes and is correct once.	○	○
5	What are Leo and Martin's opinions about the most important aspect of the environmental protection competition? Who do you agree with?		

Passage 2 Chinese people often paste poetic couplets on their doors during holidays. Based on the characters you recognize, what holiday has the couplet below been prepared for? Bonus: Use a dictionary to look up words you don't know and try to summarize the meaning of the couplet.

Passage 3 Listen to a student summarizing two points of view on the topic of different countries' level of responsibility when it comes to protecting the environment. Which point of view do you agree with? Use two to three complete Chinese sentences to supply a conclusion to his summary based on your own opinion.

Passage 4 Listen to the conversation between two students. Are the statements that follow true or false?

		T	F
1	Winter break started three days ago.	○	○
2	The boy has a Chinese passport, so he doesn't need a visa to go to China.	○	○
3	Based on the context of the conversation and the poster below, 奖学金 (jiǎngxuéjīn) most likely means "scholarship."	○	○
4	The boy doesn't know anything about New Year's celebrations in New York, so he asks the girl.	○	○

明年暑假想去中国旅行和学习的同学们……

我们会给申请到奖学金的同学买机票，一起去北京、上海和西安，一边玩儿，一边学中文！

快来申请奖学金吧！

中国国际交流组织
电话：81234567

B Speaking · 口语 INTERPERSONAL

Play a New Year's wish guessing game with your classmates.

Step 1: Your teacher will put you in groups. Discuss with your groupmates some of the things you wish for in the next year. It could be something you hope for yourself, for your school, for your community, or even for the world.

Step 2: Based on the discussion with your groupmates, choose one New Year's wish and write it down on a small piece of paper. Then fold the paper up as small as you can and give it to your teacher.

Example:

我的愿望是明年会有更多的学生选中文课。

Step 3: Your teacher will choose one wish at a time from the pile and read it aloud. Try to guess who wrote each wish.

Wishes Come True

Write a story about someone's New Year's wish coming true.

Step 1: Re-read Passage 1, taking special note of everyone's wishes for the new year. Choose one character from the story to write about. If you prefer, you can invent your own character or write about one of your classmates if that classmate agrees to appear in your story.

Step 2: Imagine how that person's New Year's wish might come true. Make a step-by-step list of what would have to happen or what that person could do to realize their wish.

Example:

马丁的愿望是……。为了实现这个愿望，我认为马丁应该这样做。首先……，其次……，然后……，最后……。

Step 3: Based on your list, write a first draft of a story about how that person's wish comes true. Your story should be at least 150 characters long and written in complete Chinese sentences.

Step 4: Exchange first drafts with a partner. Read your partner's first draft carefully and offer feedback about how he or she could improve the story. (Hints: Ask clarification questions if there are any parts of the story that you don't understand. Suggest ways to make the story more engaging or action-packed to keep the reader's interest. Point out places where your partner could add more detail or give more vivid descriptions.)

Step 5: Once you get your story back from your partner, edit it based on his or her comments. Finally, turn in your finished story to your teacher, who will add it to the class library for future Chinese students to read!

Can-Do Goals · 能力目标

Talk with your teacher if you have questions or if you are not certain you can do the following tasks:

- Talk about some plans for development that the Chinese government has initiated
- Understand and talk about travel preparations
- Express that an action has been completed successfully
- Discuss challenges and responsibilities
- Share your wishes for the new year and understand the wishes of others

Cultural Knowledge · 文化知识

What are some goals from China's Five-Year Plans?

This woman's work at a laboratory that restores historic texts contributes to China's efforts to preserve its rich culture.

Photo Credits

Every effort has been made to accurately credit the copyright owners of materials reproduced in this publication. Omissions brought to our attention will be corrected in subsequent editions.

Unit 1 Opener

p.1, Africa Studio/Shutterstock.com; **p.2,** SeventyFour/Shutterstock.com

Chapter 1

p.4, Lynxs Photography/Shutterstock.com; NASA; **p.5,** August_0802/Shutterstock.com; chuyuss/Shutterstock.com; **p.6,** Ronald Sumners/Shutterstock.com; Wanwalit Tongted/Shutterstock.com; wavebreakmedia/Shutterstock.com; Gorodenkoff/Shutterstock.com; **p.11,** Wangkun Jia/Shutterstock.com; **p.12,** vsl/Shutterstock.com; Aedka Studio/Shutterstock.com; Humannet/Shutterstock.com; **p.14,** Maggiezhu/Shutterstock.com; **p.15,** Farknot Architect/Shutterstock.com; Oksana Buday/Shutterstock.com; Africa Studio/Shutterstock.com; Pormezz/Shutterstock.com; **p.16,** Yontsen/Shutterstock.com; Taiga/Shutterstock.com; Kginger/Shutterstock.com; travelershin/Shutterstock.com; **p.17,** TK Kurikawa/Shutterstock.com; **p.22,** Said Marroun/Shutterstock.com; **p.23,** coasehsieh/Shutterstock.com; **p.28,** Air Elegant/Shutterstock.com; vsl/Shutterstock.com; DD Images/Shutterstock.com; Chiristsumo/Shutterstock.com; Aedka Studio/Shutterstock.com; yuda chen/Shutterstock.com; Humannet/Shutterstock.com; **p.30,** ABCDstock/Shutterstock.com

Chapter 2

p.33, Pixeljoy/Shutterstock.com; ShutterStockStudio/Shutterstock.com; **p.34,** Vlada Art/Shutterstock.com; **p.37,** AlenD/Shutterstock.com; Dragon Images/Shutterstock.com;Quorthon1/Shutterstock.com; YAKOBCHUK VIACHESLAV/Shutterstock.com; **p.39,** testing/Shutterstock.com; **p.40,** ESB Professional/Shutterstock.com; **p.42,** Rawpixel.com/Shutterstock.com; **p.44,** bbernard/Shutterstock.com; Tracy ben/Shutterstock.com; HelloRF Zcool/Shutterstock.com; **p. 45,** Freer/Shutterstock.com; **p.46,** wavebreakmedia/Shutterstock.com; **p.48,** Jinward/Shutterstock.com; **p.55,** humphery/Shutterstock.com; **p.56,** Deliris/Shutterstock.com; Sergey Nivens/Shutterstock.com; Chinnapong/Shutterstock.com; ssuaphotos/Shutterstock.com; **p.57,** photos for composite image by SQS/Shutterstock.com and Susurrus/Shutterstock.com; **p.58,** Shan_shan/Shutterstock.com

Chapter 3

p.60, NASA; **p.61,** Zhang BinSir/Shutterstock.com; humphery/Shutterstock.com; **p.62,** Iryna Inshyna/Shutterstock.com; **p.64,** humphery/Shutterstock.com; **p.67,** PR Image Factory/Shutterstock.com; **p.68,** Aleksey Boyko/Shutterstock.com; Harsanyi Andras/Shutterstock.com; Naypong Studio/Shutterstock.com; **p.71,** Krakenimages.com/Shutterstock.com; **p.72,** Andrii Bezvershenko/Shutterstock.com; **p.73,** oneinchpunch/Shutterstock.com; Maridav/Shutterstock.com; McLittle Stock/Shutterstock.com; **p.77,** Marie Maerz/Shutterstock.com; Ko Backpacko/Shutterstock.com; **p.81,** United Nations; **p.82,** Cienpies Design/Shutterstock.com; **p.83,** photos for composite image by wavebreakmedia/Shutterstock.com, lovelyday12/Shutterstock.com, KenSoftTH/Shutterstock.com, and Surachart Saehur/Shutterstock.com; **p.84,** bonandbon/Shutterstock.com

Unit 2 Opener

p.85, becauz gao/Shutterstock.com; **p.86,** Tero Vesalainen/Shutterstock.com

Chapter 4

p.89, noophoto/Shutterstock.com; **p.90,** Standret/Shutterstock.com; **p.93,** sirtravelalot/Shutterstock.com; imtmphoto/Shutterstock.com; michaeljung/Shutterstock.com; **p.95,** pzRomashka/Shutterstock.com; LightField Studios/Shutterstock.com; Toa55/Shutterstock.com; Elnur/Shutterstock.com; **p.99,** XiXinXing/Shutterstock.com; toonman/Shutterstock.com; szefei/Shutterstock.com; **p.100,** ImageFlow/Shutterstock.com; BearFotos/Shutterstock.com; Daniel M Ernst/Shutterstock.com; **p.105,** Ermin13/Shutterstock.com; **p.110,** G-Stock Studio/Shutterstock.com; wee dezign/Shutterstock.com; Pepsco Studio/Shutterstock.com; fizkes/Shutterstock.com; **p.111,** photo and illustration for composite image by ESB Basic/Shutterstock.com and jesadaphorn/Shutterstock.com; **p.112,** vectorfusionart/Shutterstock.com

Chapter 5

p.114, HelloRF Zcool/Shutterstock.com; Peter Hermes Furian/Shutterstock.com; **p.115,** Kunertus/Shutterstock.com; **p.116,** anek.soowannaphoom/Shutterstock.com; **p.121,** Sumeth anu/Shutterstock.com; **p.122,** NataLima/Shutterstock.com; **p.123,** Chatchai.wa/Shutterstock.com; **p.128,** fizkes/Shutterstock.com; **p.129,** Prostock-studio/Shutterstock.com; one photo/Shutterstock.com; **p.132,** Poring Studio/Shutterstock.com; Oleg Shakirov/Shutterstock.com; JUN YANG/Shutterstock.com; **p.133,** Monkey Business Images/Shutterstock.com; photos for composite image by Andrey_Popov/Shutterstock.com and Pavlo S/Shutterstock.com; Monkey Business Images/Shutterstock.com; **p.134,** fizkes/Shutterstock.com; **p.138,** Kostsov/Shutterstock.com; **p.140,** Alexey Lesik/Shutterstock.com

Chapter 6

p.142, yutthana-landscape/Shutterstock.com; Emily Petit/Cheng & Tsui; Daniel Y. Chen/Shutterstock.com; **p.143,** Charlesimage/Shutterstock.com; Images By Kenny/Shutterstock.com; Shi Yali/Shutterstock.com; **p.144,** Sanga Park/Shutterstock.com; **p.149,** 54613/Shutterstock.com; **p.150,** Richie Chan/Shutterstock.com; Ravi Ghelani/Shutterstock.com; **p.153,** smpoly/Shutterstock.com; romakoma/Shutterstock.com; 06photo/Shutterstock.com; **p.154,** photos for composite image by mutee meesa/Shutterstock.com and moloko_vector/Shutterstock.com; **p.155,** brize99/Shutterstock.com; Uskarp/Shutterstock.com; Dan Eady/Shutterstock.com; elwynn/Shutterstock.com; **p. 156,** clkraus/Shutterstock.com; Saga Photo and Video/Shutterstock.com; **p.159,** Geir Olav Lyngfjell/Shutterstock.com; beau_berry/Shutterstock.com; **p.161,** Rawpixel.com/Shutterstock.com; **p.165,** hain.tarmann/Shutterstock.com; **p.166,** KabirK/Shutterstock.com; By topimages/Shutterstock.com; **p.167,** Byron Li/Shutterstock.com; aksenovden/Shutterstock.com; **p.168,** NH/Shutterstock.com

Unit 3 Opener

p.169, B.Zhou/Shutterstock.com; **p.170,** Pressmaster/Shutterstock.com

Chapter 7

p. 171, illustrations for composite image by On Lollipops/Shutterstock.com and yayasya/Shutterstock.com; **p.172,** StreetVJ/Shutterstock.com; YueStock/Shutterstock.com; **p.173,** B.Zhou/Shutterstock.com; **p.174,** hxdbzxy/Shutterstock.com; **p.180,** Natali Snailcat/Shutterstock.com; Voinau Pavel/Shutterstock.com; Di Qin/Shutterstock.com; **p. 181,** Sanit Ratsameephot/Shutterstock.com; Arra Vais/Shutterstock.com; lynnette/Shutterstock.com; **p.184,** John Lock/Shutterstock.com; **p.186,** Dima Moroz/Shutterstock.com; 134lnstudio/Shutterstock.com; Paul Rich Studio/Shutterstock.com; James Marvin Phelps/Shutterstock.com; Svetlana MKM/Shutterstock.com; Baloncici/Shutterstock.com; Maxx-Studio/Shutterstock.com; donatas1205/Shutterstock.com; Rozhnovskaya Tanya/Shutterstock.com; KsanderDN/Shutterstock.com; Aleksandr Kurganov/Shutterstock.com; kibri_ho/Shutterstock.com; **p.187,** Brandon Fike/Shutterstock.com; **p.190,** Aniko Gerendi Enderle/Shutterstock.com; alexandre zveiger/Shutterstock.com; Zonda/Shutterstock.com; **p.192,** Dariusz Jarzabek/Shutterstock.com; Greg Zimmermann/Shutterstock.com; Berg Dmitry/Shutterstock.com; romakoma/Shutterstock.com; **p.197,** zhangjin_net/Shutterstock.com; **p.198,** Aleksandr Kurganov/Shutterstock.com; VoytPix/Shutterstock.com; maxstockphoto/Shutterstock.com; Sofiaworld/Shutterstock.com; **p.199,** f11photo/Shutterstock.com; **p.200,** StreetVJ/Shutterstock.com

Chapter 8

p.202, Yaping/Shutterstock.com; supermodel/Shutterstock.com; **p.203,** dadao/Shutterstock.com; **p.204,** HelloRF Zcool/Shutterstock.com; leungchopan/Shutterstock.com; Krakenimages.com/Shutterstock.com; wavebreakmedia/Shutterstock.com; **p.208,** Eric007/Shutterstock.com; **p. 209,** Antonio Guillem/Shutterstock.com; Rawpixel.com/Shutterstock.com; This Is Me/Shutterstock.com; Krakenimages.com/Shutterstock.com; **p.212,** Pongsak2021/Shutterstock.com; Master1305/Shutterstock.com; **p.213,** Monkey Business Images/Shutterstock.com; **p.215,** Sakdawut Smanbut/Shutterstock.com; Galyna Andrushko/Shutterstock.com; **p.218,** Monkey Business Images/Shutterstock.com; Daniel Jedzura/Shutterstock.com; Xato/Shutterstock.com; **p.220,** martinho Smart/Shutterstock.com; HelloRF Zcool/Shutterstock.com; Mo Wu/Shutterstock.com; Lixiang/Shutterstock.com; **p.225,** Rawpixel.com/Shutterstock.com; **p.227,** RIE SAKAE/Shutterstock.com; **p.228,** Joseph GTK/Shutterstock.com

Chapter 9

p.230, NG-Spacetime/Shutterstock.com; Katoosha/Shutterstock.com; **p.231,** i viewfinder/Shutterstock.com; ArtisticPhoto/Shutterstock.com; **p.232,** Stokkete/Shutterstock.com; XiXinXing/Shutterstock.com; Qilin's prance Filmmaker/Shutterstock.com; Dmytrenko Vlad/Shutterstock.com; **p.236,** articular/Shutterstock.com; KENG

MERRY paper art/Shutterstock.com; The Creative Guy/Shutterstock.com; Taawon Graphics/Shutterstock.com; **p.237,** KOBE611/Shutterstock.com; **p.240,** mavo/Shutterstock.com; Syda Productions/Shutterstock.com; Ladanifer/Shutterstock.com; **p.242,** illustrations for composite image by SiuWing/Shutterstock.com and Anatolir/Shutterstock.com; **p.243,** trairut noppakaew/Shutterstock.com; **p.244,** Monkey Business Images/Shutterstock.com; **p.247,** bane.m/Shutterstock.com; Rawpixel.com/Shutterstock.com; bonchan/Shutterstock.com; **p.249,** illustrations for composite image by MicroOne/Shutterstock.com, olly_ta/Shutterstock.com, Radha Design/Shutterstock.com, anigoweb/Shutterstock.com; **p.253,** photos for composite image by Chayjitti Hongmanee/Shutterstock.com, VN STOCK/Shutterstock.com, bemyself780/Shutterstock.com, leolintang/Shutterstock.com, wuzefe/Shutterstock.com, Tao Jiang/Shutterstock.com, and ittipon/Shutterstock.com; **p.255,** Evellean/Shutterstock.com; **p.256,** katunes pcnok/Shutterstock.com

Unit 4 Opener
p.257, Bystrov/Shutterstock.com; **p.258,** Prostock-studio/Shutterstock.com

Chapter 10
p.260, wantanddo/Shutterstock.com; The Stefan R. Landsberger collection/chineseposters.net; **p.261,** Michael Gross/Public Domain; photos for composite image by Pro Symbols/Shutterstock.com, davooda/Shutterstock.com, and IhorZigor/Shutterstock.com; **p.262,** Chanintorn.v/Shutterstock.com; Dudarev Mikhail/Shutterstock.com; Rawpixel.com/Shutterstock.com; Frame Stock Footage/Shutterstock.com; **p.265,** 4zevar/Shutterstock.com; **p.267,** Andrey_Popov/Shutterstock.com; **p.268,** Africa Studio/Shutterstock.com; WAYHOME studio/Shutterstock.com; **p.271,** illustrations for composite image by Qualit Design/Shutterstock.com and GoodStudio/Shutterstock.com; **p.272,** Billion Photos/Shutterstock.com; **p.273,** LightField Studios; **p.274,** Ermin13/Shutterstock.com; **p.277,** Kozak Sergii/Shutterstock.com; welcomeinside/Shutterstock.com; michaeljung/Shutterstock.com; Nattawit Khomsanit/Shutterstock.com; **p.278,** GoodStudio/Shutterstock.com; **p.279,** beibaoke/Shutterstock.com; Sean Xu/Shutterstock.com; **p.283,** KingTa/Shutterstock.com; **p.284,** Andrii Yalanskyi/Shutterstock.com; **p.285,** GoodStudio/Shutterstock.com; **p.286,** chinahbzyg/Shutterstock.com

Chapter 11
p.288, zhao dongfang/Shutterstock.com; **p.289,** ABCDstock/Shutterstock.com; Amehime/Shutterstock.com; **p.290,** Pensee Sauvage/Shutterstock.com; **p.293,** Luciano Mortula - LGM/Shutterstock.com; **p.295,** Tatiana Ivleva/Shutterstock.com; **p.296,** photos for composite image by Ronald E Grafe/Shutterstock.com, Asier Romero/Shutterstock.com, Ebtikar/Shutterstock.com, and Asier Romero/Shutterstock.com; **p.301,** mpohodzhay/Shutterstock.com; Anatoliy Karlyuk/Shutterstock.com; Dmytro Zinkevych/Shutterstock.com; CGN089/Shutterstock.com; **p.304,** silvae/Shutterstock.com; Albert Russ/Shutterstock.com; iarecottonstudio/Shutterstock.com; Art of Life/Shutterstock.com; Igor Stramyk/Shutterstock.com; Isabelle Kuehn/Shutterstock.com; **p.306,** fenghui/Shutterstock.com; Shan_shan/Shutterstock.com; **p.307,** Baiploo/Shutterstock.com; Shan_shan/Shutterstock.com; **p.312,** Shan_shan/Shutterstock.com; **p.314,** Inspired Vision Studio/Shutterstock.com

Chapter 12
p.316, Meeh/Shutterstock.com; Zapp2Photo/Shutterstock.com; **p.317,** 4045/Shutterstock.com; JCElv/Shutterstock.com; **p.318,** GaudiLab/Shutterstock.com; Stockbakery/Shutterstock.com; insta_photos/Shutterstock.com; **p.324,** Igor Podgorny/Shutterstock.com; BlurryMe/Shutterstock.com; lorenzobovi/Shutterstock.com; **p.325,** Mix and Match Studio/Shutterstock.com; **p.331,** pada smith/Shutterstock.com; **p.336,** Dusan Petkovic/Shutterstock.com; **p.341,** Emi UFO/Shutterstock.com; **p.342,** Maridav/Shutterstock.com; **p.343,** Farknot Architect/Shutterstock.com; **p.344,** Unique Vision/Shutterstock.com

The Chinese–English Vocabulary Index is alphabetized according to pinyin. Words containing the same first Chinese character are grouped together. Words with the same pinyin spelling are organized according to their tone (that is, first tones first, second tones second, third tones third, fourth tones fourth, and neutral tones last).

Chinese	Pinyin	English	Page
A			
阿姨	āyí	respectful way to address a female adult; aunt (rarely used)	19
哎	āi	(word used to express surprise or dissatisfaction)	97
安静	ānjìng	quiet, peaceful	118
B			
百分之	bǎi fēn zhī	percent	42
班	bān	class	125
搬	bān	to move (furniture, large items); to move (from one living space to another)	183
办	bàn	to do, to handle, to deal with, to arrange for	321
办公室	bàngōngshì	office	118
饱	bǎo	full, stuffed (after a meal)	14
保护	bǎohù	to protect, to safeguard	42
报告	bàogào	to report; report, speech, presentation	75
被	bèi	(word that indicates that an action was done to someone or something)	246
笔	bǐ	pen	206
遍	biàn	(measure word for a completed action, indicates how many times in succession the action has been done)	131
变	biàn	to become different, to change, to transform	327
变化	biànhuà	change; to change	36

Chinese	Pinyin	English	Page
表达	biǎodá	to express (feelings, thoughts); expression (of a thought or feeling)	240
表妹	biǎomèi	younger female cousin (on the mother's side or the daughter of the father's sister)	19
冰箱	bīngxiāng	refrigerator	189
不下	búxià	(added to a verb to indicate there is not enough space to hold something)	14
不好意思	bù hǎoyìsi	sorry; to feel embarrassed, to feel shy; embarrassing	125
		C	
猜	cāi	to guess	275
参加	cānjiā	to participate in, to take part in, to join	48
查	chá	to check, to look into, to look up	321
尝	cháng	to try (a food), to taste	8
成	chéng	to become, to turn into, to achieve	321
厨房	chúfáng	kitchen	189
厨师	chúshī	chef, professional cook	158
传统	chuántǒng	tradition; traditional	152
窗户	chuānghu	window	189
		D	
打工	dǎgōng	to work at a temporary or part-time job	92
打扫	dǎsǎo	to clean up (a room, apartment, or house)	270
当	dāng	to be, to work as, to serve as	92
导游	dǎoyóu	tour guide	152
倒数	dàoshǔ	to count down, to count back	333
得分	dé fēn; défēn	to earn points; score	234
地	de	(word that connects a descriptive word to a verb)	234
灯	dēng	light, lamp	70

Chinese	Pinyin	English	Page
电	diàn	electricity, battery power	70
电脑	diànnǎo	computer	70
电视剧	diànshìjù	TV drama, TV series	211
电子邮件	diànzǐ yóujiàn	email	206
调查	diàochá	to investigate, to survey; investigation, survey	131
订	dìng	to reserve, to book (a ticket, a hotel room, etc.)	264
东方明珠	Dōngfāng Míngzhū	Oriental Pearl Tower	303
豆腐	dòufu	tofu, bean curd	8
E			
儿子	érzi	son	19
耳机	ěrjī	headphones, earbuds	19
F			
发达	fādá	developed, flourishing	327
发现	fāxiàn	to realize, to discover, to find out	246
发展	fāzhǎn	to develop, to advance, to grow	158
防止	fángzhǐ	to prevent, to guard against	42
房子	fángzi	house, apartment, building	183
房租	fángzū	rent (for an apartment, house, etc.)	183
放学	fàng xué	to be finished with the school day	217
飞机	fēijī	airplane	321
分析	fēnxī	to analyze; analysis	48
分享	fēnxiǎng	to share; (the action of) sharing	240
封	fēng	(measure word for letters)	264
父母	fùmǔ	parents, father and mother (formal)	19

Chinese	Pinyin	English	Page
		G	
改变	gǎibiàn	to change, to alter, to transform	270
干净	gānjìng	clean	36
感动	gǎndòng	to move (someone), to touch (someone emotionally); moving	303
赶快	gǎnkuài	at once, immediately, hurriedly	70
工厂	gōngchǎng	factory	298
公交车	gōngjiāo chē	bus	97
功课	gōngkè	assignment, homework, classwork	75
公平	gōngpíng	fairness; fair, just, impartial, equitable	298
公司	gōngsī	company, corporation	97
恭喜	gōngxǐ	congratulations; to congratulate	183
古代	gǔdài	ancient times, olden times	303
故事	gùshi	story	264
关	guān	to close, to turn off	70
关心	guānxīn	to care about; concern	217
关于	guānyú	about, in regard to	48
关注	guānzhù	to pay close attention to, to follow with interest, to follow (on social media)	327
广告	guǎnggào	advertisement	189
归属感	guīshǔ gǎn	sense of belonging	298
国际	guójì	international	118
国家	guójiā	nation, country	240
过程	guòchéng	process, course of events	321
		H	
哈哈	hāha	ha ha	48
孩子	háizi	child	92

Chinese	Pinyin	English	Page
海报	hǎibào	poster	64
寒假	hánjià	winter break	333
好处	hǎochù	advantage, benefit, good point, pro	246
好久	hǎojiǔ	for a long time, quite a while	146
号	hào	size, number	176
号码	hàomǎ	number	303
合作	hézuò	to cooperate, to work together; cooperation	118
护照	hùzhào	passport	321
花	huā	to spend	189
化	huà	(added after a word to indicate that something has become more [word], similar to -ize or -ization in English)	118
话题	huàtí	topic	217
坏	huài	bad, harmful; broken	246
还	huán	to return (something), to give (something) back, to repay (a loan)	125
环境	huánjìng	environment, surroundings	42
换	huàn	to change (one thing for another), to exchange	70
黄	huáng	yellow	146
回答	huídá	to answer; answers to a question	97
回收	huíshōu	to recycle	36
J			
机场	jīchǎng	airport	321
机会	jīhuì	opportunity	292
记录	jìlù	to take notes, to keep records; notes, records	234
家	jiā	(measure word for businesses)	146
家常	jiācháng	home-style	8

Chinese	Pinyin	English	Page
家具	jiājù	furniture	183
家务	jiāwù	housework, household chores	270
建筑	jiànzhù	building; architecture; to build, to construct	158
讲	jiǎng	to speak, to say, to tell; to explain	64
交流	jiāoliú	to interact, to exchange (ideas, experiences, etc.), to communicate	333
教育	jiàoyù	education	152
节	jié	(measure word for class periods)	125
结果	jiéguǒ	result; as a result	217
结束	jiéshù	end; to end	333
节约	jiéyuē	to save (money, electricity, water), to cut down (one's use of something)	70
解决	jiějué	to resolve, to solve	75
经济	jīngjì	economy; economic	158
经验	jīngyàn	experience; to go through, to experience	102
句	jù	sentence; (measure word for speech)	64
决定	juédìng	to decide; decision	132

K

Chinese	Pinyin	English	Page
开	kāi	to open, to turn on	70
开车	kāi chē	to drive a car	152
看法	kànfǎ	opinion, point of view, perspective, way of looking at something	270
靠	kào	to be next to; to lean on, to lean against	264
刻板印象	kèbǎn yìnxiàng	stereotype	275
客人	kèrén	guest, customer	92
客厅	kètīng	living room	189

Chinese	Pinyin	English	Page
孔子	Kǒngzǐ	Confucius, a Chinese philosopher who lived from 551 to 479 BC, also known as 孔夫子 (Kǒngfūzǐ)	152
筷子	kuàizi	chopsticks	14

<table>
<tr><td colspan="4" align="center">L</td></tr>
</table>

Chinese	Pinyin	English	Page
垃圾	lājī	trash, garbage	36
浪费	làngfèi	to waste	240
老	lǎo	old	264
礼貌	lǐmào	courteous, polite; courtesy, manners	298
里面	lǐmiàn	inside, interior	146
理想	lǐxiǎng	ideal, dream	270
连	lián	even	292
联系	liánxì	to contact, to get in touch; connection, relation	206
脸	liǎn	face	211
了解	liǎojiě	to understand, to know someone well, to find out; understanding	64
邻居	línjū	neighbor(s)	70
林璎	Lín Yīng	Maya Lin, a Chinese American architectural designer	159
另外	lìngwài	in addition, besides	240
刘海生	Liú Hǎishēng	Liu Haisheng (a person's name)	14
楼	lóu	multi-storied building, a floor (of a multi-level building)	118
录音	lùyīn	audio recording; to record	125
乱	luàn	messy, random, arbitrary; messily, randomly, arbitrarily	211

<table>
<tr><td colspan="4" align="center">M</td></tr>
</table>

Chinese	Pinyin	English	Page
马马虎虎	mǎmǎ-hūhū	not very good, just so-so	8
慢	màn	slow	8

Chinese	Pinyin	English	Page
毛	máo	(measure word for one tenth of a unit of currency)	176
米饭	mǐfàn	cooked rice	8
面试	miànshì	to interview (for a position); interview	92
庙	miào	temple, shrine	152
母语	mǔyǔ	mother tongue, first language	292
目标	mùbiāo	goal, objective, target	75
N			
男	nán	male	275
嗯	ǹg	(word used to express agreement)	125
农村	nóngcūn	countryside, village, rural area	298
女	nǚ	female	275
女儿	nǚ'ér	daughter	19
女士	nǚshì	Miss, lady	92
P			
爬山	pá shān	to hike (in the mountains), to climb a mountain; hiking	217
盘	pán	(plate, dish, measure word for food)	14
瓶	píng	(measure word for bottles)	234
平等	píngděng	equality; equal	275
评价	píngjià	evaluation, appraisal; to evaluate, to appraise	189
Q			
其次	qícì	next, secondly; secondary	246
歧视	qíshì	to discriminate against; discrimination	298
起来	qǐ lái	(word added after an action or state of being to indicate that it began suddenly or unexpectedly)	211
气候	qìhòu	climate	42

Chinese	Pinyin	English	Page
签证	qiānzhèng	visa	321
青菜	qīngcài	bok choy, any leafy green vegetable	14
庆祝	qìngzhù	to celebrate	97
权利	quánlì	right (the right to do something)	275
		R	
认为	rènwéi	to think, to consider, to have an opinion	246
认真	rènzhēn	conscientiously, earnest; to take seriously	102
扔	rēng	to throw	36
融入	róngrù	to merge into, to meld into, to assimilate	298
		S	
商场	shāngchǎng	shopping mall, shopping center, department store	176
上车	shàng chē	to get on (a car, bus, train, etc.)	97
上网	shàng wǎng	to go online, to use the internet	206
社会	shèhuì	society	298
设计	shèjì	design; to design	159
申请	shēnqǐng	to apply; application	102
什么样	shénme yàng	what kind, what sort	270
师傅	shīfu	master, master worker; term of address for a skilled worker	97
实习	shíxí	an internship; to do an internship	102
实现	shíxiàn	to achieve (a goal), to realize (an objective), to carry out (a plan)	75
世界	shìjiè	world	234
收	shōu	to receive, to accept	217
收入	shōurù	income	298
手	shǒu	hand	206

Chinese	Pinyin	English	Page
首先	shǒuxiān	first (of all), above all	246
手语	shǒuyǔ	sign language	102
书架	shūjià	bookcase, bookshelf	183
叔叔	shūshu	uncle (father's younger brother); respectful way to address a male adult	19
数据	shùjù	data	48
双	shuāng	(measure word for a pair)	176
水平	shuǐpíng	skill level, level, standard	102
死	sǐ	to die; (word sometimes used in an exaggeration)	36
宿舍	sùshè	dormitory, hostel	159
酸辣汤	suānlàtāng	hot and sour soup	14
T			
台北	Táiběi	Taipei (capital of Taiwan)	152
讨论	tǎolùn	to discuss	48
套	tào	(measure word for things that come in sets)	176
提高	tígāo	to raise, to improve, to increase	75
提醒	tí xǐng	to remind, to warn; reminder	234
挑战	tiǎo zhàn	challenge; to challenge	327
同	tóng	same, alike	125
投票	tóu piào	to vote, to take a vote	75
图书馆	túshūguǎn	library	64
推荐	tuījiàn	to recommend	146
W			
外国	wàiguó	foreign country	118
外面	wàimiàn	outside, exterior	146
外滩	Wàitān	the Bund	292

Chinese	Pinyin	English	Page
晚饭	wǎnfàn	dinner	146
万	wàn	ten thousand	48
网络	wǎngluò	internet, network	206
位	wèi	(polite measure word for people)	92
为了	wèile	for, for the sake of, in order to	75
位子	wèizi	seat	264
文物	wénwù	cultural artifact	303
问卷	wènjuàn	questionnaire	132
污染	wūrǎn	pollution, contamination; to pollute, to contaminate	42
无论	wúlùn	no matter what, regardless	275
午饭	wǔfàn	lunch	14

		X	
西班牙语	Xībānyáyǔ	Spanish language	292
洗	xǐ	to wash	270
先生	xiānsheng	Mr., sir, gentleman	92
现代	xiàndài	modern, contemporary	159
相信	xiāngxìn	to believe, to trust	292
想法	xiǎngfǎ	idea, opinion, way of thinking	132
想起来	xiǎng qǐlái	to suddenly remember, to recall	240
像	xiàng	to resemble, to be like	131
消息	xiāoxi	news, information	234
小说	xiǎoshuō	novel, fiction book	211
小心	xiǎoxīn	careful; carefully	275
小组	xiǎo zǔ	small group	75
笑	xiào	to laugh, to laugh at, to smile	211

Chinese	Pinyin	English	Page
效果	xiàoguǒ	result, effect, efficacy	234
鞋	xié	shoes	176
新年	xīnnián	the new year	333
新闻	xīnwén	news	217
信	xìn	letter (correspondence)	264
信息	xìnxī	information	206
兴奋	xīngfèn	excited	303
行	xíng	all right, OK	125
行李	xíngli	luggage, baggage	321
性别	xìngbié	gender	275
需要	xūyào	to need, to require; requirement, needs	42
Y			
呀	ya	(word added at the end of a sentence to add emphasis, excitement, or surprise)	36
压力	yālì	pressure	36
盐	yán	salt	8
演	yǎn	to perform, to act	264
眼睛	yǎnjing	eyes	211
养	yǎng	to raise, to care for (plants or animals)	211
样子	yàngzi	style, appearance	176
要求	yāoqiú	requirements; to require	97
夜市	yèshì	night market	146
医院	yīyuàn	hospital	102
一共	yígòng	altogether	125
一刻	yí kè	fifteen minutes, a quarter of an hour	48
姨妈	yímā	aunt (mother's sister)	19

Chinese	Pinyin	English	Page
椅子	yǐzi	chair	183
亿	yì	hundred million	240
意思	yìsi	meaning	64
一直	yìzhí	always, continuously; straight	8
迎接	yíngjiē	to go and welcome, to greet, to meet (a challenge)	327
影响	yǐngxiǎng	influence, effect; to influence, to affect, to have an impact	36
尤其	yóuqí	especially, particularly	292
游泳	yóu yǒng	to swim; swimming	217
有意义	yǒu yìyì	to have meaning or significance; meaningful	333
有用	yǒuyòng	useful	234
鱼	yú	fish	14
遇到	yù dào	to run into, to encounter	131
豫园	Yùyuán	Yu Garden	303
元	yuán	(measure word for Chinese currency, most often used in written communication)	176
元旦	Yuándàn	New Year's Day	333
愿望	yuànwàng	wish, aspiration, desire	333
愿意	yuànyì	to be willing, to want, to wish	64
约	yuē	to make an appointment	125
运气	yùnqi	fortune, luck (good or bad)	152
Z			
责任	zérèn	responsibility	327
赵	Zhào	Zhao (a surname)	132
这么	zhème	so, such, like this	64
政府	zhèngfǔ	government	327

Chinese	Pinyin	English	Page
正在	zhèngzài	(word that shows an action is ongoing or in process)	64
值得	zhí dé	to be worth, to deserve	132
直接	zhíjiē	direct, immediate	189
纸	zhǐ	paper	206
志愿者	zhìyuànzhě	volunteer	246
中	zhōng	medium; middle	176
中间	zhōngjiān	between, middle, center	146
中式	zhōngshì	Chinese style	159
重	zhòng	heavy, severe	183
助听器	zhùtīngqì	hearing aid	19
专业	zhuānyè	major (in college), speciality	102
资源	zīyuán	natural resource	42
字	zì	character	206
自信	zìxìn	confident	102
租	zū	to rent	183
组织	zǔzhī	organization; to organize	327
尊重	zūnzhòng	to respect	270

The English – Chinese Vocabulary Index is organized based on the alphabetical order of the English definitions.

English	Chinese	Pinyin	Page
A			
about, in regard to	关于	guānyú	48
to achieve (a goal), to realize (an objective), to carry out (a plan)	实现	shíxiàn	75
(added after a word to indicate that something has become more [word], similar to -ize or -ization in English)	化	huà	118
(added to a verb to indicate there is not enough space to hold something)	不下	búxià	14
advantage, benefit, good point, pro	好处	hǎochù	246
advertisement	广告	guǎnggào	189
airplane	飞机	fēijī	321
airport	机场	jīchǎng	321
all right, OK	行	xíng	125
altogether	一共	yígòng	125
always, continuously; straight	一直	yìzhí	8
to analyze; analysis	分析	fēnxī	48
ancient times, olden times	古代	gǔdài	303
to answer; answers to a question	回答	huídá	97
to apply; application	申请	shēnqǐng	102
assignment, homework, classwork	功课	gōngkè	75
at once, immediately, hurriedly	赶快	gǎnkuài	70
audio recording; to record	录音	lùyīn	125
aunt (mother's sister)	姨妈	yímā	19

English	Chinese	Pinyin	Page
B			
bad, harmful; broken	坏	huài	246
to be, to work as, to serve as	当	dāng	92
to be finished with the school day	放学	fàng xué	217
to be next to; to lean on, to lean against	靠	kào	264
to be willing, to want, to wish	愿意	yuànyì	64
to be worth, to deserve	值得	zhí dé	132
to become different, to change, to transform	变	biàn	327
to become, to turn into, to achieve	成	chéng	321
to believe, to trust	相信	xiāngxìn	292
between, middle, center	中间	zhōngjiān	146
bok choy, any leafy green vegetable	青菜	qīngcài	14
bookcase, bookshelf	书架	shūjià	183
building; architecture; to build, to construct	建筑	jiànzhù	158
the Bund	外滩	Wàitān	292
bus	公交车	gōngjiāo chē	97
C			
to care about; concern	关心	guānxīn	217
careful; carefully	小心	xiǎoxīn	275
to celebrate	庆祝	qìngzhù	97
chair	椅子	yǐzi	183
challenge; to challenge	挑战	tiǎo zhàn	327
change; to change	变化	biànhuà	36
to change, to alter, to transform	改变	gǎibiàn	270
to change (one thing for another), to exchange	换	huàn	70

Go Far with Chinese 3

English	Chinese	Pinyin	Page
character	字	zì	206
to check, to look into, to look up	查	chá	321
chef, professional cook	厨师	chúshī	158
child	孩子	háizi	92
Chinese style	中式	zhōngshì	159
chopsticks	筷子	kuàizi	14
class	班	bān	125
clean	干净	gānjìng	36
to clean up (a room, apartment, or house)	打扫	dǎsǎo	270
climate	气候	qìhòu	42
to close, to turn off	关	guān	70
company, corporation	公司	gōngsī	97
computer	电脑	diànnǎo	70
confident	自信	zìxìn	102
Confucius, a Chinese philosopher who lived from 551 to 479 BC, also known as 孔夫子 (Kǒngfūzǐ)	孔子	Kǒngzǐ	152
congratulations; to congratulate	恭喜	gōngxǐ	183
conscientiously, earnest; to take seriously	认真	rènzhēn	102
to contact, to get in touch; connection, relation	联系	liánxì	206
cooked rice	米饭	mǐfàn	8
to cooperate, to work together; cooperation	合作	hézuò	118
to count down, to count back	倒数	dàoshǔ	333
countryside, village, rural area	农村	nóngcūn	298
courteous, polite; courtesy, manners	礼貌	lǐmào	298
cultural artifact	文物	wénwù	303

English	Chinese	Pinyin	Page
D			
data	数据	shùjù	48
daughter	女儿	nǚ'ér	19
to decide; decision	决定	juédìng	132
design; to design	设计	shèjì	159
to develop, to advance, to grow	发展	fāzhǎn	158
developed, flourishing	发达	fādá	327
to die; (word sometimes used in an exaggeration)	死	sǐ	36
dinner	晚饭	wǎnfàn	146
direct, immediate	直接	zhíjiē	189
to discriminate against; discrimination	歧视	qíshì	298
to discuss	讨论	tǎolùn	48
to do, to handle, to deal with, to arrange for	办	bàn	321
dormitory, hostel	宿舍	sùshè	159
to drive a car	开车	kāi chē	152
E			
to earn points; score	得分	dé fēn; défēn	234
economy; economic	经济	jīngjì	158
education	教育	jiàoyù	152
electricity, battery power	电	diàn	70
email	电子邮件	diànzǐ yóujiàn	206
end; to end	结束	jiéshù	333
environment, surroundings	环境	huánjìng	42
equality; equal	平等	píngděng	275
especially, particularly	尤其	yóuqí	292

English	Chinese	Pinyin	Page
evaluation, appraisal; to evaluate, to appraise	评价	píngjià	189
even	连	lián	292
excited	兴奋	xīngfèn	303
experience; to go through, to experience	经验	jīngyàn	102
to express (feelings, thoughts); expression (of a thought or feeling)	表达	biǎodá	240
eyes	眼睛	yǎnjing	211

F

English	Chinese	Pinyin	Page
face	脸	liǎn	211
factory	工厂	gōngchǎng	298
fairness; fair, just, impartial, equitable	公平	gōngpíng	298
female	女	nǚ	275
fifteen minutes, a quarter of an hour	一刻	yí kè	48
first (of all), above all	首先	shǒuxiān	246
fish	鱼	yú	14
for a long time, quite a while	好久	hǎojiǔ	146
for, for the sake of, in order to	为了	wèile	75
foreign country	外国	wàiguó	118
fortune, luck (good or bad)	运气	yùnqi	152
full, stuffed (after a meal)	饱	bǎo	14
furniture	家具	jiājù	183

G

English	Chinese	Pinyin	Page
gender	性别	xìngbié	275
to get on (a car, bus, train, etc.)	上车	shàng chē	97
to go and welcome, to greet, to meet (a challenge)	迎接	yíngjiē	327

English	Chinese	Pinyin	Page
to go online, to use the internet	上网	shàng wǎng	206
goal, objective, target	目标	mùbiāo	75
government	政府	zhèngfǔ	327
to guess	猜	cāi	275
guest, customer	客人	kèrén	92
H			
ha ha	哈哈	hāha	48
hand	手	shǒu	206
to have meaning or significance; meaningful	有意义	yǒu yìyì	333
headphones, earbuds	耳机	ěrjī	19
hearing aid	助听器	zhùtīngqì	19
heavy, severe	重	zhòng	183
to hike (in the mountains), to climb a mountain; hiking	爬山	pá shān	217
home-style	家常	jiācháng	8
hospital	医院	yīyuàn	102
hot and sour soup	酸辣汤	suānlàtāng	14
house, apartment, building	房子	fángzi	183
housework, household chores	家务	jiāwù	270
hundred million	亿	yì	240
I			
idea, opinion, way of thinking	想法	xiǎngfǎ	132
ideal, dream	理想	lǐxiǎng	270
in addition, besides	另外	lìngwài	240
income	收入	shōurù	298

English	Chinese	Pinyin	Page
influence, effect; to influence, to affect, to have an impact	影响	yǐngxiǎng	36
information	信息	xìnxī	206
inside, interior	里面	lǐmiàn	146
to interact, to exchange (ideas, experiences, etc.), to communicate	交流	jiāoliú	333
international	国际	guójì	118
internet, network	网络	wǎngluò	206
an internship; to do an internship	实习	shíxí	102
to interview (for a position); interview	面试	miànshì	92
to investigate, to survey; investigation, survey	调查	diàochá	131
K			
kitchen	厨房	chúfáng	189
L			
to laugh, to laugh at, to smile	笑	xiào	211
letter (correspondence)	信	xìn	264
library	图书馆	túshūguǎn	64
light, lamp	灯	dēng	70
Liu Haisheng (a person's name)	刘海生	Liú Hǎishēng	14
living room	客厅	kètīng	189
luggage, baggage	行李	xíngli	321
lunch	午饭	wǔfàn	14
M			
major (in college), speciality	专业	zhuānyè	102
male	男	nán	275
to make an appointment	约	yuē	125

English	Chinese	Pinyin	Page
master, master worker; term of address for a skilled worker	师傅	shīfu	97
Maya Lin, a Chinese American architectural designer	林璎	Lín Yīng	159
meaning	意思	yìsi	64
(measure word for a completed action, indicates how many times in succession the action has been done)	遍	biàn	131
(measure word for a pair)	双	shuāng	176
(measure word for bottles)	瓶	píng	234
(measure word for businesses)	家	jiā	146
(measure word for Chinese currency, most often used in written communication)	元	yuán	176
(measure word for class periods)	节	jié	125
(measure word for letters)	封	fēng	264
(measure word for one tenth of a unit of currency)	毛	máo	176
(measure word for things that come in sets)	套	tào	176
medium; middle	中	zhōng	176
to merge into, to meld into, to assimilate	融入	róngrù	298
messy, random, arbitrary; messily, randomly, arbitrarily	乱	luàn	211
Miss, lady	女士	nǚshì	92
modern, contemporary	现代	xiàndài	159
mother tongue, first language	母语	mǔyǔ	292
to move (furniture, large items); to move (from one living space to another)	搬	bān	183
to move (someone), to touch (someone emotionally); moving	感动	gǎndòng	303
Mr., sir, gentleman	先生	xiānsheng	92
multi-storied building, a floor (of a multi-level building)	楼	lóu	118

English	Chinese	Pinyin	Page
N			
nation, country	国家	guójiā	240
natural resource	资源	zīyuán	42
to need, to require; requirement, needs	需要	xūyào	42
neighbor(s)	邻居	línjū	70
the new year	新年	xīnnián	333
New Year's Day	元旦	Yuándàn	333
news	新闻	xīnwén	217
news, information	消息	xiāoxi	234
next, secondly; secondary	其次	qícì	246
night market	夜市	yèshì	146
no matter what, regardless	无论	wúlùn	275
not very good, just so-so	马马虎虎	mǎmǎ-hūhū	8
novel, fiction book	小说	xiǎoshuō	211
number	号码	hàomǎ	303
O			
office	办公室	bàngōngshì	118
old	老	lǎo	264
to open, to turn on	开	kāi	70
opinion, point of view, perspective, way of looking at something	看法	kànfǎ	270
opportunity	机会	jīhuì	292
organization; to organize	组织	zǔzhī	327
Oriental Pearl Tower	东方明珠	Dōngfāng Míngzhū	303
outside, exterior	外面	wàimiàn	146

English	Chinese	Pinyin	Page
P			
paper	纸	zhǐ	206
parents, father and mother (formal)	父母	fùmǔ	19
to participate in, to take part in, to join	参加	cānjiā	48
passport	护照	hùzhào	321
to pay close attention to, to follow with interest, to follow (on social media)	关注	guānzhù	327
pen	笔	bǐ	206
percent	百分之	bǎi fēn zhī	42
to perform, to act	演	yǎn	264
(plate, dish, measure word for food)	盘	pán	14
(polite measure word for people)	位	wèi	92
pollution, contamination; to pollute, to contaminate	污染	wūrǎn	42
poster	海报	hǎibào	64
pressure	压力	yālì	36
to prevent, to guard against	防止	fángzhǐ	42
process, course of events	过程	guòchéng	321
to protect, to safeguard	保护	bǎohù	42
Q			
questionnaire	问卷	wènjuàn	132
quiet, peaceful	安静	ānjìng	118
R			
to raise, to care for (plants or animals)	养	yǎng	211
to raise, to improve, to increase	提高	tígāo	75
to realize, to discover, to find out	发现	fāxiàn	246
to receive, to accept	收	shōu	217

English	Chinese	Pinyin	Page
to recommend	推荐	tuījiàn	146
to recycle	回收	huíshōu	36
refrigerator	冰箱	bīngxiāng	189
to remind, to warn; reminder	提醒	tí xǐng	234
to rent	租	zū	183
rent (for an apartment, house, etc.)	房租	fángzū	183
to report; report, speech, presentation	报告	bàogào	75
requirements; to require	要求	yāoqiú	97
to resemble, to be like	像	xiàng	131
to reserve, to book (a ticket, a hotel room, etc.)	订	dìng	264
to resolve, to solve	解决	jiějué	75
to respect	尊重	zūnzhòng	270
respectful way to address a female adult; aunt (rarely used)	阿姨	āyí	19
responsibility	责任	zérèn	327
result, effect, efficacy	效果	xiàoguǒ	234
result; as a result	结果	jiéguǒ	217
to return (something), to give (something) back, to repay (a loan)	还	huán	125
right (the right to do something)	权利	quánlì	275
to run into, to encounter	遇到	yù dào	131
S			
salt	盐	yán	8
same, alike	同	tóng	125
to save (money, electricity, water), to cut down (one's use of something)	节约	jiéyuē	70
seat	位子	wèizi	264

English	Chinese	Pinyin	Page
sense of belonging	归属感	guīshǔ gǎn	298
sentence; (measure word for speech)	句	jù	64
to share; (the action of) sharing	分享	fēnxiǎng	240
shoes	鞋	xié	176
shopping mall, shopping center, department store	商场	shāngchǎng	176
sign language	手语	shǒuyǔ	102
size, number	号	hào	176
skill level, level, standard	水平	shuǐpíng	102
slow	慢	màn	8
small group	小组	xiǎo zǔ	75
so, such, like this	这么	zhème	64
society	社会	shèhuì	298
son	儿子	érzi	19
sorry; to feel embarrassed, to feel shy; embarrassing	不好意思	bù hǎoyìsi	125
Spanish language	西班牙语	Xībānyáyǔ	292
to speak, to say, to tell; to explain	讲	jiǎng	64
to spend	花	huā	189
stereotype	刻板印象	kèbǎn yìnxiàng	275
story	故事	gùshi	264
style, appearance	样子	yàngzi	176
to suddenly remember, to recall	想起来	xiǎng qǐlái	240
to swim; swimming	游泳	yóu yǒng	217

T

English	Chinese	Pinyin	Page
Taipei (capital of Taiwan)	台北	Táiběi	152
to take notes, to keep records; notes, records	记录	jìlù	234

English	Chinese	Pinyin	Page
temple, shrine	庙	miào	152
ten thousand	万	wàn	48
to think, to consider, to have an opinion	认为	rènwéi	246
to throw	扔	rēng	36
to try (a food), to taste	尝	cháng	8
tofu, bean curd	豆腐	dòufu	8
topic	话题	huàtí	217
tour guide	导游	dǎoyóu	152
tradition; traditional	传统	chuántǒng	152
trash, garbage	垃圾	lājī	36
TV drama, TV series	电视剧	diànshìjù	211

U			
uncle (father's younger brother); respectful way to address a male adult	叔叔	shūshu	19
to understand, to know someone well, to find out; understanding	了解	liǎojiě	64
useful	有用	yǒuyòng	234

V			
visa	签证	qiānzhèng	321
volunteer	志愿者	zhìyuànzhě	246
to vote, to take a vote	投票	tóu piào	75

W			
to wash	洗	xǐ	270
to waste	浪费	làngfèi	240
what kind, what sort	什么样	shénme yàng	270
window	窗户	chuānghu	189

English	Chinese	Pinyin	Page
winter break	寒假	hánjià	333
wish, aspiration, desire	愿望	yuànwàng	333
(word used to express surprise or dissatisfaction)	哎	āi	97
(word added after an action or state of being to indicate that it began suddenly or unexpectedly)	起来	qǐ lái	211
(word added at the end of a sentence to add emphasis, excitement, or surprise)	呀	ya	36
(word that connects a descriptive word to a verb)	地	de	234
(word that indicates that an action was done to someone or something)	被	bèi	246
(word that shows an action is ongoing or in process)	正在	zhèngzài	64
(word used to express agreement)	嗯	ńg	125
to work at a temporary or part-time job	打工	dǎgōng	92
world	世界	shìjiè	234

Y			
yellow	黄	huáng	146
younger female cousin (on the mother's side or the daughter of the father's sister)	表妹	biǎomèi	19
Yu Garden	豫园	Yùyuán	303

Z			
Zhao (a surname)	赵	Zhào	132